Exploring the Roots
of Digital and Media Literacy
through Personal Narrative

Exploring the Roots of Digital and Media Literacy through Personal Narrative

Edited by **Renee Hobbs**

TEMPLE UNIVERSITY PRESS
Philadelphia • *Rome* • *Tokyo*

TEMPLE UNIVERSITY PRESS
Philadelphia, Pennsylvania 19122
www.temple.edu/tempress

Library of Congress Cataloging-in-Publication Data

Names: Hobbs, Renee, editor.
Title: Exploring the roots of digital and media literacy through personal narrative
/ edited by Renee Hobbs.
Description: Philadelphia, Pennsylvania : Temple University Press, 2016. |
Includes bibliographical references and index.
Identifiers: LCCN 2015039689| ISBN 9781439911570 (hardback : alk. paper) |
ISBN 9781439911587 (paperback : alk. paper) | ISBN 9781439911594 (e-book)
Subjects: LCSH: Media literacy. | Digital media. | Mass media—Philosophy.
| Digital media—Philosophy. | Mass media and culture. | Mass media in
education. | Scholars—Biography. | Intellectuals—Biography. | BISAC:
SOCIAL SCIENCE / Media Studies. | EDUCATION / Computers &
Technology.
Classification: LCC P96.M4 E87 2016 | DDC 302.23—dc23 LC record available at
http://lccn.loc.gov/2015039689

Printed in the United States of America

9 8 7 6 5 4 3 2

Contents

Exploring the Roots
of Digital and Media Literacy
through Personal Narrative

Introduction

RENEE HOBBS

I f you're lucky enough to have known your genetic grandparents, you may have heard stories about their life experiences, which may be entertaining, amusing, or just strange. If you're really lucky, your grandparents may shed insight on your culture and your values, reflecting the recent past as experienced in ordinary life. Once in a while, our grandparents may help us understand our own parents and even our own lives. I am lucky to have known three of my four grandparents, who were hard-working children of immigrants living in Minersville, Pennsylvania, raising families and working in the coal fields and dress factories of the region. Although I remember some marvelous stories about their struggles and adventures in the Roaring Twenties, I wish I had been able to know my grandparents better. But they lived far away, and our family had only limited contact with them while I was growing up.

My intellectual grandparents, on the other hand, are people I feel that I know quite well. Even though I have only encountered them in books, their ideas resonate deeply with my own experiences, dreams, and ideas. Because I'm an inveterate reader, of course, many authors and creative people have influenced my thinking—not just when I was young but throughout my life. I feel like I have spent the better part of a lifetime reflecting on the ideas of scholars such as John Dewey, Lev Vygotsky, Rudolf Arnheim, Marshall McLuhan, George Gerbner, Paulo Freire, Jerome Bruner, and many others. However, like many people, I'm often not even fully aware of how the ideas of others become woven into mine. I may read, view, or listen to something; embed those ideas in my own thinking; and then forget all about the original source material. The new ideas get intertwined with my own.

Personal Narratives as History

Because media literacy encompasses a constellation of competencies, different people with interests in media literacy may claim any of a number of influences. When asked about their symbolic or metaphorical grandparents, people may look to the work of humanists, philosophers, media theorists, education scholars, social psychologists, activists, filmmakers, and literary and cultural critics, just to name a few.

The identification and selection of one's intellectual grandparents is highly personal; they are those authors or creative people whose work inspires our own creative thinking, research, and ideas. Their ideas, arguments, evidence, and passions fit with the particular challenges we face, or their work speaks to larger cultural and social issues that capture our interest at a certain time; they may provide core themes, values, and ideas that bind members of a discourse community together, connecting people across time and space. Their work may even offer an articulation of foundational concepts on which both new knowledge and practical field-based programs have been built.

This book introduces readers to some of the historical roots of digital and media literacy through sixteen personal narratives written by influential scholars and practitioners who each focus on a fascinating man or woman who has served as an intellectual grandparent. In the pages that follow, you will encounter contemporary writers describing their own life histories as they describe how they encountered the writings of people from an earlier generation. The authors in this volume come from a variety of fields—including writing and composition, media psychology, literacy education, technology in society, sociology, cultural studies, media studies, and communication arts. They all share an interest in digital and media literacy. Each has selected an author who aligns with his or her own passions, interests, and scholarly DNA. Because the essays mix personal storytelling with an introduction to complex theoretical concepts, readers may sense both the conceptual and the emotional connectedness that bind the authors to their metaphorical grandparents and gain a big-picture understanding of the many diverse, scholarly voices contributing to media literacy as a subdisciplinary field of inquiry and as a social movement. By weaving together two sets of personal stories—those of the contributing author and the historical figure under scrutiny—this book examines the origins of some of the key concepts, theories, and ideas of media literacy.

It's obvious that the power of narrative helps connect people across time and space. But, of course, ideas cannot be separated from their historical contexts or tagged narrowly to specific individuals. Historians of science have long recognized that ideas are in the air, "out there for anyone with the wit and the will to find them" (Gladwell 2008, 59). To understand the historical roots of digital and media literacy, an examination of the crosscurrents of thought at different points in time and from many different vantage points can be valuable.

Defining Digital and Media Literacy

As this book reveals, there is no singular history of digital and media literacy, because perspectives on this topic are shaped by our own personal and intellectual histories. Some scholars rely on the definition established at the Aspen Institute—"the ability to access, analyze, evaluate and communicate messages in a wide variety of forms"—which was collaboratively hammered out by participants who attended the 1992 Aspen Media Literacy Leadership Institute (Aufderheide and Firestone 1993, 7). The Center for Media Literacy offers a definition of media literacy that emphasizes citizenship and democracy, noting, "Media literacy builds an understanding of the role of media in society as well as essential skills of inquiry and self-expression necessary for citizens of a democracy" (Thoman and Jolls 2005, 190). In *Digital and Media Literacy: A Plan of Action*, I emphasize that media literacy includes specific competencies, including the ability to (1) make responsible choices and access information by locating and sharing materials and comprehending ideas; (2) analyze messages by identifying the author, purpose, and point of view and evaluating the quality and credibility of the content; (3) create content in a variety of forms, making use of language, images, and sounds and using digital tools and technologies; (4) reflect on one's own conduct and communication behavior by applying social responsibility and ethical principles; and (5) take social action by working individually and collaboratively to share knowledge and solve problems in the family, workplace, and community (Hobbs 2010, vii–viii).

Like members of any community, digital and media literacy stakeholders offer diverse, contradictory, and even conflicting perspectives and views. Some embrace and celebrate Internet culture and popular media and appreciate the artistry of remix creativity, while others see mass media as replete with racist, sexist, and homophobic messages and distorted representations of aggressive behavior, sexuality, and human relationships. Some frame the practice of critical analysis in terms of the economics of capitalism; others value the complex process of assessing message authority, credibility, and trustworthiness; and still others see critical analysis as a socially constructed practice of interpretation and meaning-making. Some deeply situate media literacy in relation to expanding the concept of literacy—including the practices of speaking, listening, reading, and writing—while others see the connection as more or less metaphorical. If you are looking for a simple, singular, or stable definition of media literacy, you will not find it in this book. That's because as changes in digital media and technology reshape culture, media literacy educators continue to debate what it means to be media literate. In articulating seven of the great debates in media literacy, I have noted that the media literacy community had the possibility of becoming a "big tent" of sorts, with a few overarching core values and plenty of room for diverse stakeholders with divergent perspectives (Hobbs 1998, 2011). Such coalitions are necessary for activist movements to thrive. In exploring the historical legacy that has shaped digital and media literacy and in thinking about the relationship between the past, present, and future, perhaps we can also see it as a strong old tree with deep roots and many branches.

This book does not present an authoritative, decontextualized theory of the origins of the field. Instead, it situates the history of media literacy in relation to the lived experience of those who are now helping advance it through scholarship, teaching, advocacy, and outreach. The sharing of personal narratives that connect the present and future with the past may help people understand the entrepreneurial and often tenacious spirit that drives people's passion for this work. Historical research inquiry may help recover key ideas from across several disciplines and fields to continue to shape the practice of media literacy education in the twenty-first century and beyond.

Media Literacy History Matters

The book you are reading now was inspired by previous work looking at the early history of media literacy from the point of view of those who helped develop it. When James A. Brown (1991) identified the most significant work of practitioners, organizations, and scholars who were teaching about television during the 1970s and 1980s, he catalogued various projects of the time period but did not offer analysis of the development of the concepts, discourses, and practices of the field. Michael RobbGrieco's (2014) analysis of the complete corpus of *Media & Values* magazine, edited by Elizabeth Thoman from 1977 to 1993 at the Center for Media Literacy in Los Angeles, uses document analysis and critical discourse analysis to identify key themes in the development of media literacy in the United States. In outlining some of the current arguments inspired by the MacArthur Foundation's significant investment in digital media and learning, Henry Jenkins, Mizuko Ito, and danah boyd (2015) explain that it is important to understand the predigital roots of the practices of participatory culture in a networked era even as we examine the wide array of new competencies increasingly recognized as required or desirable in digital media culture.

When it comes to the broader intersections of the study of language, images, media, technology, culture, and education, researchers have attempted to chronicle key historical moments that have shaped contemporary practices in media education. For example, Dana Polan's *Scenes of Instruction* (2007) looks at the rich tradition of teaching about film at Harvard, Columbia, New York University, and the University of Southern California during the first thirty years of the twentieth century. Larry Cuban, a leading education historian, describes and analyzes the ways in which the use of and resistance to educational technology developed in American schools in his book *Teachers and Machines: The Use of Classroom Technology since 1920* (1986). Examining the field of writing, rhetoric, and composition, Jason Palmieri (2012) traces the history of multimodal composition, looking at the early practices of writing teachers who were inviting students to compose visual texts like photographs, film, and video. These works offer much depth to our understanding of media literacy's past.

In her online project, *Voices of Media Literacy: International Pioneers Speak*, Tessa Jolls of the Center for Media Literacy in Los Angeles conducted twenty in-depth interviews with scholars and practitioners in media literacy education from the United States, Canada, the United Kingdom, Australia, and Switzerland who have been in practice since 1990 or earlier. Interview subjects included Marieli Rowe, Len Masterman, Cary Bazalgette, David Buckingham, Barry Duncan, Elizabeth Thoman, and Kathleen Tyner. But in relation to the family tree of media literacy, I consider these individuals not as grandparents but as my American, British, and Canadian cousins. Scholars, writers, and educators such as Sut Jhally, Henry Giroux, Erica Scharrer, Art Silverblatt, Joyce Valenza, Cyndy Scheibe, Erica Austin, Brian Primack, Faith Rogow, Howard Rheingold, Doug Rushkoff, Joshua Meyrowitz, Bill Christ, Mindy Faber, Dan Gillmor, John McManus, Tony Streit, Bill Kist, Bill Costanzo, Stanley and Susan Baran, Chris Sperry, Sherri Hope Culver, and W. James Potter; activists such as Jean Kilbourne and Tessa Jolls; and media and education professionals such as Howard Schneider and Jordi Torrent have made contributions to advance the theory and practice of media literacy in the United States. Further afield, international cousins include Gerhard Tulodziecki, Keval Kumar, Divina Frau-Meigs, José Manuel Pérez Tornero, Manuel Pinto, Asli Telli Aydemir, Susanne Krucsay, Ulla Carlsson, Reijo Kupiainen, Silke Grafe, Sirkku

Kotilainen, Sally Reynolds, Thierry deSmedt, and Alex Fedorov. And a new generation of brilliant and passionate young leaders are in full flower now—too many to name here. They are initiating media literacy programs and exploring new pedagogies, conducting research, and strengthening the community, which includes diverse stakeholders such as parents, educators, scholars, media makers, public health professionals, librarians, technologists, activists, and community development specialists. We're connected by a shared passion for digital and media literacy. We've fumbled along, doing what we can do, fueled by curiosity, imagination, collaboration, and good ideas. These individuals—among the many hundreds of others not named here—helped shepherd the media literacy community through an important period of regional, national, and global growth beginning in the 1970s and continuing today. In my interview with Tessa Jolls, I shared a bit of my own life narrative as a journey of discovery stretching over nearly thirty years, describing various delights and tribulations as a media literacy teacher, researcher, and practitioner creating organizational networks, professional development programs, state-level initiatives, curricula, videos, multimedia materials, and other programs to reach K–12 students and educators (Jolls 2011). Jolls's interviews tell the story of the struggle to bring media literacy forward in the late twentieth century.

Rereading these interviews, I wondered, could we discover the even deeper theoretical origins of media literacy's history? Could the foundational humanistic and social scientific concepts that underpin digital and media literacy be explored in an approachable volume designed to help the newest generation of scholars, teachers, researchers, and media professionals? Could a book introduce readers to the many influential figures of the early twentieth century, those who were writing about mass media, technology, culture, and education even before the field of communication developed into a discipline, and well before people first began to use the term media literacy? Could it help people reflect on their own life narratives and promote metacognitive thinking about how to take action in response to those ideas that capture our imagination? Could a deep-dive look at the historical origins of media literacy inspire new and as yet unimagined possibilities for its future? In the pages ahead, a group of distinguished authors generously offer their insights on these important questions, taking you on a journey that is both personal and political, time-bound and timeless.

REFERENCES

Aufderheide, P., and C. Firestone. 1993. *Media Literacy: A Report of the National Leadership Conference on Media Literacy.* Queenstown, MD: Aspen Institute.

Brown, J. A. 1991. *Television "Critical Viewing Skills" Education: Major Media Literacy Projects in the United States and Selected Countries.* Mahwah, NJ: Lawrence Erlbaum.

Cuban, L. 1986. *Teachers and Machines: The Use of Classroom Technology since 1920.* New York: Teachers College Press.

Gladwell, M. 2008. "In the Air." *New Yorker* 84 (13): 50–60.

Hobbs, R. 1998. "The Seven Great Debates in the Media Literacy Movement." *Journal of Communication* 48 (2): 9–29.

———. 2010. *Digital and Media Literacy: A Plan of Action.* Washington, DC: Aspen Institute.

———. 2011. "The State of Media Literacy: A Response to Potter." *Journal of Broadcasting and Electronic Media* 55 (3): 419–430.

Jenkins, H., M. Ito, and d. boyd. 2015. *Participatory Culture in a Networked Era.* Malden, MA: Polity Press.

Jolls, T. 2011. "Voices of Media Literacy: International Pioneers Speak; Renee Hobbs Interview Transcript." March 10. Available at http://www.medialit .org/reading-room/voices-media-literacy-international-pioneers-speak -renee-hobbs-interview-transcript.

Palmieri, J. 2012. *Remixing Composition: A History of Multimodal Writing Pedagogy.* Carbondale: Southern Illinois University Press.

Polan, D. 2007. *Scenes of Instruction: The Beginnings of the U.S. Study of Film.* Berkeley: University of California Press.

RobbGrieco, M. 2014. "Media and Media Literacy: Discourses of the Media Literacy Education Movement in *Media & Values* Magazine, 1977–1993." Ph.D. diss., Temple University.

Thoman, E., and T. Jolls. 2005. "Media Literacy Education: Lessons from the Center for Media Literacy." *Yearbook of the National Society for the Study of Education* 104:180–205.

1 /

Historical Roots
of Media Literacy

RENEE HOBBS

> The opportunistic teacher who embraces the leisure interests
> of his pupils in the hope of leading them to higher things is
> as frequently unsympathetic to the really valuable qualities of
> popular culture as his colleague who remains resolutely hostile.
> A true training in discrimination is concerned with pleasure.
>
> —STUART HALL AND PADDY WHANNEL,
> *THE POPULAR ARTS*

What are the historical roots of media literacy, and why do they matter to the future of the field? This book is an effort to recover some ideas about media, technology, culture, and education using personal memoir as a vehicle for inquiry. When the term *media literacy* is used, it's generally in reference to the knowledge, competencies, and social practices involved in using, analyzing, evaluating, and creating mass media, popular culture, and digital media. But media literacy also invites a deeper exploration of important issues concerning how to heighten critical consciousness of message form, content, and context; the social nature of representation and interpretation; the dialectic of protection and empowerment; the role of art in the practice of civic activism; the changing nature of literacy; and learning as a means to engage the head, heart, hands, and spirit. In this chapter, I provide an overview of the roots of media literacy as conceptualized by the sixteen remarkable authors who contributed to this volume, in relation to my own lived experience. As we will see in the pages that follow, although the historical roots of media literacy are unique to the lived experiences of those who value it, insights of the previous generation have supplied both the nutrients and the stability needed for media literacy's future growth and development.

Awareness of Form, Content, and Context

> All illusions are potential ways of ordering reality. The goal of criticism should therefore be not to destroy illusions but to make us more sensitive to their workings and their complexity.
>
> —LEO BRAUDY, *THE WORLD IN A FRAME*

Because language is the first and most important symbol system for conveying personal and social identity, media literacy educators have long come from the ranks of those in language arts and literacy education who emphasize the importance of developing a heightened awareness of language and its power to shape lived experience. When British media literacy educator Len Masterman articulated the importance of what he called "media awareness education," he offered up eighteen principles that reflected what he had learned over the course of two decades of teaching students about the media. Among them is the importance of illuminating the life situations of learners in relation to wider historic and ideological issues (Masterman 1989).

Wrestling with the big ideas of philosophy, in Chapter 2, David Weinberger shares his own experience exploring the power of language to shape how we view the world and our role in it. A fellow at the Berkman Center for Internet and Society, Weinberger is a philosopher who writes about the epistemology of the Internet. He is famous for his book *The Cluetrain Manifesto*, which explores how the Internet shifted power dynamics in the business community and reshaped marketing communication strategies. In his chapter in this book, Weinberger recalls his life as a young undergraduate facing an existential crisis. Weinberger discovered the work of Martin Heidegger, the German philosopher, who disrupted his thinking about the transmission model of communication and helped him discover the simple majesty in our connected relationships. As beings in time, Weinberger finds, we participate in "a language-soaked, shared world," are embedded in social networks, and live with others who, although they may care about different things than we do, give us great gifts: they use language and other symbol systems to show us how the world looks to them. Through our use of symbols to share meaning, we embody Heidegger's idea of the "quiet power of the possible," offering our understandings of life to each other through ordinary talk in ways that have the potential to open us up to new realms of thought and feeling as lifelong learners (Flint and Needham 2007, 90).

When people live through a cultural shift during which one form of communication rises to dominate contemporary culture, it forces them to notice how media shape consciousness. When writing was first introduced, Plato feared the loss of human memory and imagination. Thousands of years later, when printing came to dominate European culture, the concept of a fact emerged as superior to the proverbs and wisdom of oral and manuscript cultures. Print encouraged hierarchical structures of authority and contributed to romantic ideas about individual originality and creativity as emerging from the author's unique point of view. When Walter Ong (1982) compared verbal expression in an oral culture to forms of expression in literate cultures, he noted how patterns of thinking and social relationships were restructured to valorize some cultural ideas and restrict or limit others. Of course, changes in media inevitably reshape education. Looking critically at Italian universities during the Gutenberg revolution, a Latin scholar in 1477 observed that "an abundance of books makes men less studious" (quoted in Ong 1982, 78).

Hundreds of years later, the rise of film and television created similar challenges for educators who wanted to find ways to make education more relevant to the students in their classes. In Chapter 3, after describing his own (largely negative) experience with the first generation of communication arts classes offered in New York City high schools in the 1970s, Lance Strate remembers how he discovered the work of Marshall McLuhan, vividly capturing the sense of awe he experienced. Strate is a professor of communication at Fordham University and one of the leaders in the media ecology community, which is a subdiscipline of media studies. By showing how media-symbol systems reflect and shape the apparatus of perception, Strate writes, McLuhan helps us recognize how film and television contributed to changes in society and culture. In his chapter, Strate reminds us that the first goal of media education is to "restore the sense of novelty, that experience of strangeness, that we so easily lose regarding our modes of communication." By defamiliarizing media, we treat them as objects of study, using the practice of critical distance to "look at them rather than through them." Therefore, media literacy education emphasizes the use of instructional strategies to help heighten conscious awareness of the constructedness of media form and content, always in relation to context and culture. Now we examine how cell phones, tablets, and the always-on broadband environment of work, home, and leisure spaces may be reshaping consciousness in ways that promote intellectual curiosity and lifelong learning, as well as contributing to the mental state of perpetual distractedness or fertilizing an ever-growing thirst for the novel, the profane, and the shocking.

To reflect on how media shapes consciousness, defamiliarization is an important process that can take many forms. Because all the phenomena of everyday life—not just linguistic communication— can carry symbolic and expressive meaning, even ordinary forms of consumerism and popular culture, including shopping, sporting matches, games, advertising, and fashion must be analyzed. In Chapter 4, film scholar Dana Polan, a cinema-studies professor at New York University and author of *Scenes of Instruction* (2007), a book about the history of higher-education film studies in the United States, introduces us to the work of Roland Barthes, who looked at how mass culture signifies various ideological positions to maintain (or challenge) the social status quo. Barthes showed that ideological values are grafted onto the ordinary objects and practices of the world. Representations are never neutral or natural. Close reading of texts of popular culture, through semiotics, enables us to engage in critical analysis that can demystify symbol systems. Barthes explains that "our conversation, our remarks about the weather, a murder trial, a touching wedding, the cooking we dream of, the garments we wear, everything, in everyday life, is dependent on representations . . . between the man and the world" (Barthes [1957] 2012, 252). Therefore, careful, active interpretation of the representations we create and the ones that circulate among our peers, families, and communities is essential for living an informed and reflective life.

The Social Nature of Representation and Interpretation

When media literacy education was first being promulgated in the 1970s, it was common to talk about the many stereotypes that pervaded entertainment and informational media. Stereotypes reproduced traditional hierarchies associated with gender, race, class, sexuality, and occupation. Debates raged about whether particular depictions were accurate or inaccurate because media texts are not simply external ways of representing reality; they constitute the meaning of reality (Hall 1980). When the term *media representation* began to circulate among media scholars, cultural critics, and media literacy educators in the 1980s, it captured a broader, more nuanced practice of recognizing how media constructs versions of reality that shape our lives and identities. Media representations do not merely document experience; they actually create cultural practices and ways of thinking. For example, reality TV and Facebook have helped create a new, mediated form of reality whereby ordinary people may think of themselves as always performing their identities in competition with each other. By critiquing representations and creating their own alternative representations through media productions, people may explore alternative, transformative ways of perceiving and acting in the world.

Media representations can't be oversimplified: they are not merely true or false, accurate or inaccurate. Consciously or unconsciously, authors shape representations to maintain the social status quo or to construct and convey a particular ideological agenda. As Daniel Chandler (2002) explains, representations are made to seem "natural." Because media cultures offer up ways of making sense of the world, Rick Beach (2007) explains, "they provide us with frameworks for classifying the world according to some hierarchical value system—what is most versus least valued; who has power and who does not; what practices are or are not condoned or sanctioned."

But since both readers and writers live within particular temporal and spatial contexts, meanings and interpretation are inherently unstable. In Chapter 5, Cynthia Lewis, a literacy and education researcher at the University of Minnesota, introduces us to the work of Mikhail Bakhtin, a Russian literary critic and philosopher working in the 1920s whose works first became available to European and American scholars in the 1960s. Lewis explains that we can't make much sense of media representations if they are not contextualized within the lives and identities of both writers and readers. In describing the contribution of Bakhtin to her scholarship and teaching, Lewis explains that "both readers and texts are situated within social, cultural, and institutional frameworks that both constrain (close) and destabilize (open) meanings." Any particular media message can contain within it competing discourses and meaning potentials to be activated differentially by particular interpreters in specific contexts or situations. Issues of representation and interpretation are deeply embedded in the ideological values of the historical contexts in which they are situated. The implication? Meaning can't be controlled—not by authors, producers, teachers, or assessments. Meanings are in people. That makes media literacy a potentially powerful device for inspiring social and political change.

Today we take for granted the idea that scholars use a variety of research methodologies to examine contemporary political and social issues. The social and political issues we are concerned about in 2016 may include the growing polarization and stagnation of our political system, global migration, the rise of big data, privacy and surveillance, the continuing scourge of terrorism, and the growing inequity between rich and poor. But as Srividya Ramasubramanian shows, the idea that scholarship should be directly relevant to contemporary social issues was once a path-breaking and novel idea. In Chapter 6, Ramasubramanian, a professor of communication at Texas A&M University, explores the work of Gordon Allport, who was one of the founders of the field of social psychology. His work explored the role of media in diminishing prejudice and promoting intergroup relations, showing how scholarship can connect to the wider social arena, contribute to political activism, and advance democratic values. Since then, we have learned that under the right circumstances, simply talking about media can contribute to political tolerance, cooperation, and respect for cultural differences (Paluck 2009).

It's also noteworthy that Allport didn't become trapped by his own theory or his methodology: he was an expansive and inclusive scholar who fought against dogmatic or extreme stances. Ramasubramanian herself explains how she developed an openness to various methodological approaches and multidisciplinary perspectives, which played an important role in her journey into media literacy.

Our own personal narratives, as learners, teachers, researchers, and creative people, shape our approach to digital and media literacy. Ramasubramanian's interest in media stereotyping was shaped by her own life experience, as we see in her chapter, just as Allport's socially relevant, solution-driven, theoretically grounded empirical approach allowed him to explore the role of media and communication in relation to real-world social problems. People who affiliate with the concept of media literacy often seek to create engaged scholarship that links theory to practice in ways that accelerate real-world social, institutional, and cultural change.

In Chapter 7, Michael RobbGrieco introduces us to his metaphorical grandfather, Michel Foucault, the preeminent intellectual historian of the twentieth century, who offers a poststructural perspective on representation and interpretation, asserting that knowledge is constructed and we need to understand the systems that produce it. We must understand subjectivity, or how it is we come to know ourselves in particular ways. As a musician, media artist, teacher, and scholar, RobbGrieco explores the constructedness of media in relation to knowledge, truth, and reality. In his chapter, he writes that although media literacy "is often positioned as a way to interrupt the processes of media influence through awareness and active reasoning, the critical function of interrupting taken-for-granted meanings can also be seen as productive—a way of opening up space to think and communicate differently." By interrupting the flow of automatic meaning-making, we can "ask questions about whom these meanings benefit and harm, where they come from, how they might be understood differently, what purposes and political projects they serve, and how they relate to reality; in short, interruption allows us to ask questions about power." When it comes to teaching and learning, RobbGrieco balances three interrelated aims: supporting students' sense of agency, offering access to academic discourses that increase social power, and helping students challenge and transform power relations through critical analysis and creative production.

Reflecting Noddings's (1984) ideas about the ethic of care, media literacy education also embodies elements of relational ethics with a focus on multiple ways of knowing and interpretation through an examination of everyday uses of representation and interpretation. This is not a new idea. In ancient times, the Greeks and Romans recognized that to behave properly, in order to practice freedom properly, it is necessary to care for the self, both in order to know oneself (*gnothi seauton*) and to improve oneself—to surpass oneself, "to master the appetites that risk engulfing you" (Fornet-Betancourt et al. 1987, 116). Deconstructing messages to probe their indeterminacy is a prime way to know and care for the self.

The Dialectic of Protection and Empowerment

> Understanding the new media and using them constructively and creatively actually require[] developing a new form of literacy . . . [to] enable students to deal constructively with complex new modes of delivering information, new multisensory tactics for persuasion, and new technology-based art forms.
>
> —NATIONAL COUNCIL OF TEACHERS OF ENGLISH, "RESOLUTION ON PROMOTING MEDIA LITERACY"

For some people, there is nothing really problematic about media, aside from minor personal annoyances when favorite shows are canceled or when bandwidth limitations contribute to technology snafus. Such individuals are more or less oblivious to media. They absorb the entertainment and informational content but are media indifferent, in a sense. But many people experience a mix of both "mediaphobia" and "media euphoria" (Hediger 2013). Today, many people have developed new routines for using the ubiquitous mobile phones in their lives. When using the mobile phone to maintain our social relationships, we may coordinate our actions with friends and family in a finely grained way, enabling social connections. Yet the very same expectation of inclusion and connectedness can become a burden and create overdependence along with feelings of entrapment (Hall and Baym 2012).

The rise of digital networks has expanded the communication capacities of many, increasing the potential for revitalizing the values of diversity and democracy. Even when celebrating the rise of participatory culture, which offers low barriers to creative and civic engagement, informal peer-to-peer mentoring, and increased access to technologies for sharing ideas and information, Henry Jenkins, Mizuko Ito, and danah boyd recognize that it is not inherently democratizing, since "misinformation can go unchecked and be widely disseminated to mislead, manipulate, or induce fear . . . [because] participatory culture enables—if not empowers—disturbing practices alongside positive ones" (2015, 24). Thus, it is natural for people to respond with deep swings of the emotional pendulum in response to the ambivalence generated by changing patterns of communication, expression, knowledge, information, entertainment, and advocacy that result from historical, technological, and cultural change.

In the United States, discourses of protection and empowerment have been woven into the historical fabric of media literacy since the beginning of the twentieth century, as the proliferation of new immigrants and the rise of film and radio offered new forms of leisure to people. Even when leisure time was scarce, before laws limited the workweek to forty hours, middle-class people worried about the behavior of the poor and working-class and their interest in popular entertainment, which the middle class considered inferior to more elite forms (Levine 1990). The Payne Fund studies, the first large-scale studies of media influence, were inspired by these concerns. Scholars aimed to discover how the content and form of films were affecting children's knowledge acquisition, their attitudes toward racial and ethnic groups, and even their sleep patterns (DeFleur and DeFleur 2010). The results showed a fascinating mix of positive and negative impacts.

Today, I remain ambivalent about the ever-expanding rise of celebrity culture, the always-on nature of my own habits of social media communication, and the fragmentation of family life made possible by wireless broadband, gaming, and social media. I worry about the rise of an Internet culture obsessed with manipulating human attention and emotional response for commercial ends. In discussing these topics, I gain clarity about my ideas. By asking people to think deeply about what they love and what they hate about their own use of mass media, popular culture, social media, journalism, or the Internet, media literacy insists on being multivocal about both the empowering and the limiting aspects of life with contemporary media and technology.

Of course, the deep pleasure we experience in encountering media texts and creating and sharing media messages is profound. As Todd Gitlin said, "Collectively, we are in thrall to media—because they deliver to us many of the psychic goods we crave, and we know no other way to live" (quoted in Thompson 2003). But while the pleasure is profound, so also is the resentment and anxiety we may experience when we reflect on the many variations of depravity, triviality, and inhumanity that masquerade as entertainment or the humility we feel when we encounter the full scope of our dependence on media and technology. Digital media makes everyone a producer and gives everyone a voice, but now we live our lives in front of screens. Parents may feel a need to protect themselves (and their children) from uses of media and technology that diminish or trivialize family relationships. And yet at the same time we want to be able to engage with the best, most beautiful, and most powerful texts, tools, and technology for personal and social empowerment. There is so much to love!

Throughout history, whenever media has been new, there have been tensions between "classes, families, and professional communities [who] struggled to come to terms with the novel acoustic and visual devices" (Marvin 1988, 5). To address these contradictions, the discourse of empowerment and protection emerged as among the most distinctive features of media literacy. In the early twentieth century, in response to the rise of film and radio, social critics recognized the changing power relations made possible by mass communication. Concerns about the rise of mass culture created the birth of critical theory, which uses social critique for enlightenment and social change. Because it aims to explore the paradoxes, inconsistencies, ironies, and contradictions in the dominant worldview, critical theory also must apply the critical process to itself by examining the relationship between theory and practice. Originally located in Germany in the early part of the twentieth century, these scholars moved to Columbia University in New York City to escape Nazi Germany. Known as the Frankfurt School and led by Max Horkheimer, a sociologist, this group included Erich Fromm, Herbert Marcuse, and Theodor Adorno, among others. In Chapter 8, Gianna Cappello, a professor of sociology and education at the University of Palermo in Italy, introduces us to the work of Adorno, who believed that hope and redemption were achievable through critical inquiry, knowledge seeking, and social commitment.

Why? Art is one of the major tools for renewing the human spirit. Adorno worried that mass media was replacing art, giving people clichéd and oversimplified representations of reality; he believed that mass-produced forms of art do not genuinely enlighten and inspire. According to Adorno, they merely maintain the social status quo by pandering to people's preconceived, stereotypical ideas. In her chapter, Cappello explains why media literacy educators value self-reflection as the most important form of professional development. She wants us to embrace the inherent paradoxes of this work and ponder these compelling questions: Are people truly "free" in creating art? Are people really "active" in making sense of media messages? Or are we more like sheep, merely following the crowd and reproducing or accepting dominant ideologies of the culture? When teachers teach media literacy, are they imposing their own ideological meanings on students? Or are they promoting independent, critical engagement with texts and culture? By rediscovering the contributions of Adorno, Cappello invites us to retheorize and repoliticize media literacy so that media literacy educators can resist the "technologist drift dominating their field." She imagines a future that explores more fully the nexus between critical analysis and creative production.

The dialectic of empowerment and protection continues in Chapter 9, as UCLA professor of education Douglas Kellner introduces us to the work of Herbert Marcuse, a distinguished philosopher and Marxist sociologist (and in his youth, a postdoctoral student of Martin Heidegger). Marcuse extends the work of Adorno and Horkheimer to show how capitalism is invested in the production and transmission of media spectacles, which transmit the ideology of consumerism through popular entertainment and displace the primal role of the family as agent of socialization. Kellner's own important work in sociology and philosophy examines how film addresses contemporary social and political struggles and passions of the day; he shows how active interpretation of film sheds insights on the fantasies, fears, hopes, and dreams of people living in a particular time and place. Because of corporations' quest to control the government and the media, Kellner argues, we have lost the separation and division of power between the executive, legislative, and judiciary; the media are co-opted by corporate interests and politicians are co-opted by their need for fundraising. But technology's continual push for creative destruction continually constructs "new forms of economy, politics, culture, and everyday life, as well as new forms of domination and resistance." As an activist and a public intellectual who has used the power of cable access and alternative media to share ideas in the public forum, Kellner sees critical media literacy as helping people recognize that new media and technologies are forms of power that impact all aspects of contemporary life.

During the early part of the twentieth century, in England, the rise of popular culture led literary critics F. R. Leavis and Denys Thompson to argue that educators needed to provide training in critical awareness as a means to address the paradoxes of empowerment and protection. In their book *Culture and Environment* ([1933] 1973), education is described as both "a weapon and a tool-kit—a weapon to resist the whims of rampant consumerism; and a tool-kit to discriminate between, on the one hand, the quick-fix sensationalism of mass media and advertising, and on the other, the best of what has been written, shown or performed" (Laughey 2011). In articulating the power of art to transform society, nineteenth-century scholar Matthew Arnold offered an optimistic perspective, hoping that culture could renew contemporary society and help counter our blind faith in technological machinery. Coming from this tradition, media literacy educators have been part of the classic modernist English-education legacy of wanting to help learners discover how to discriminate—to consider the key distinctions between credible and incredible, quality and junk, superficial and trite, beautiful and ugly, professional and amateur.

Here, the dialectic of empowerment and protection is rooted in the concept of discrimination, which is a culturally learned practice. Educators preserve cultural traditions and cultural identity through making such distinctions, but this perspective was seriously challenged when Raymond Williams resisted the inherent elitism of such training in taste. By reframing the concept of culture to focus not on works of classic literature, music, and art but on the lived experiences of ordinary people, Williams rejected the high-low binaries of class hierarchy and celebrated the rich variety of cultural practices among working-class people through folk, common, and popular culture. The creative practices involved in fan fiction and remix culture, in particular, offer opportunities for readers of media texts to identify and reflect on kernels of rich insight, including also the contradictions, silences, and potentials (Jenkins and Kelley 2013).

In Chapter 10, Henry Jenkins, a professor of communication, journalism, and cinematic arts at the University of Southern California, introduces us to the work of his mentor, John Fiske, who was a student of Raymond Williams, illustrating how ideas from Williams and Fiske are embedded in the Core Principles of Media Literacy Education (NAMLE 2007). Williams offered a powerful counterpoint to Adorno by rejecting the idea that media entrap audiences into an ideological system that works against their own interests. And although Fiske was critical of inequalities of opportunity and the imposition of cultural hierarchies, he was respectful of diverse forms of popular culture and cultural experience. By democratizing the concept of culture, these scholars helped media literacy education make room for the serious study of popular culture, however variously the term is defined.

For me, as a young undergraduate literature major at the University of Michigan in the late 1970s, the idea that film and television were as multilayered as poetry and thus worthy of equally serious attention was truly the animating discovery of my life. It was profoundly empowering for me. At the same time, I appreciated that the corporate structure of media industries and the ordinary economics of commercial mass media were structuring my experiences and encounters with messages and meanings. But in my work with students, I did not find, as Fiske did, that students had little need of academics like me. Because critical understanding of a media text is aided by understanding the political, economic, and cultural context in which it is produced, my students genuinely appreciated my efforts to create an inquiry-based learning environment that intensified learners' intellectual curiosity about media institutions and systems. As a co-learner along with my students, I modeled the empowering process of inquiry.

For Jenkins, the "aha!" of media literacy came from his discovery of how ordinary people use mass-media content "as raw materials for constructing their own stories, songs, artworks, or videos" and how fans create out of a need to satisfy their "fascination and frustration" with favored texts, rewriting them to speak to both their deep pleasures and their unmet needs. His conceptualization of participatory culture is rooted in the explosion of media and technologies that make it possible for average consumers to "archive, annotate, appropriate, and recirculate media content in powerful new ways."

A belief in the transformative power of art is of central value to many media literacy educators. In *Reading in a Participatory Culture*, Jenkins and Kelley urge teachers to connect reading and writing together with "media-diverse modes of expression" and new literary forms, with the goal to "embrace those changes that deepen and enrich human consciousness and push back on those that trivialize and distract" (2013, 17). By using, sharing, and creating, media, groups, organizations, and networks can exert influence on political, economic, and social issues. Art and communication must help activate the civic imagination, because "before we can change the world, we need to be able to imagine what another, better world might look like" (Jenkins, Ito, and boyd 2015, 152).

The Arts and Social Activism

Man with a Movie Camera is a film that literally changed my life. When I was an undergraduate at the University of Michigan, I took an art history class with Rudolf Arnheim, the author of *Film as Art* ([1932] 1957) and *Art and Visual Perception* ([1957] 1974) and a class in Soviet film with Professor Herbert Eagle. At the time, I was studying English literature. I was captivated by film theory, of course, but *Man with a Movie Camera*, created by Dziga Vertov in 1929 as an experimental silent film, became my obsession. At that point in my life, I had seen no experimental films, so such work was beyond strange to me. The film was fast-paced and evocative: it seemed to be a mind-blowing type of visual poetry about the precious lyricism of everyday life. Eagle not only helped me deeply understand the technical elements of a film (i.e., lighting, set design, use of color, shot composition, and editing); he introduced me to the theories of the Russian formalists, led by Roman Jakobson, who were writing about film as language. I also learned that the Russian avant-garde artists of the 1920s truly believed in their ability to change the world. After repeated viewings of *Man with a Movie Camera* and other Soviet films and reading deeply the work of Arnheim, Sergei Eisenstein, Béla Belázs, and other scholars, the following question captured my imagination, and it has continued to obsess me for my entire professional career: How do people learn with and about visual images?

Of course, the Russian formalists' ideas about montage as a reconstruction of thought processes were later to become important in my empirical work in exploring the way people who had never before seen film or television could interpret videos that used a variety of editing conventions (Hobbs et al. 1988). But at the time, I was intrigued by the idea of dialectical montage, which suggests that a new idea can emerge from the presentation of two conflicting shots. I had experienced for myself the deep pleasure of "filling in the gaps" by making inferences as a reader of literature. It seemed to me that such inference making in responding to literature, film, and television could open up people's minds in powerful, life-affirming ways.

In Chapter 11, Amy Peterson Jensen identifies Bertolt Brecht as an intellectual grandfather who reimagined the role of the spectator by creating politically motivated theater in which audiences needed to critically engage with ideas. He wanted to help audiences see themselves in new ways through theater. What does it mean for artists to not just explain or react to the world but also aim to change it? When people go to a sporting event, they participate and help create the event; when they go the to theater, they may sit passively, waiting for a spell to be cast. This was a problem for Brecht. He believed that theater artists shouldn't aim to hypnotize audiences or put them into an emotional trance. Rather, he believed that there must be a shock of some sort to wake up people's awareness. *Man with a Movie Camera* was that shock for me, igniting a powerful intellectual curiosity that wrested me from complacency. Jensen considers the connection between artists who use theater to awaken people by heightening their consciousness of social injustice and the work of Brazilian educator Paulo Freire, noting that educational revolutions cannot happen "without love" (McLaren and Leonard 1993, 82). Brecht channeled his anger about the injustices of the world into love, and this brought passion to his work; he was able to gather people together for the collaborative art of theater. As a scholar of theater arts and media at

Brigham Young University, Jensen also wants art and education to engage in the complex problems of the contemporary social world. This inevitably entails a focus on the work that individual artists do, using their time, talent, and treasure to express lived experience though material form.

When it comes to personal and social identity, I have never been much for labels. As a young teenager, in the process of discovering myself, I experienced the stresses of adolescence as a time of profound angst and disorientation. The expectations that my parents, friends, and family placed on me were oppressive. The absurdities of the world overwhelmed me, and this sense of confusion led me to discover the philosophy of existentialism. I remember that I truly loved the idea that I alone was responsible for my self-definition; through my actions and their consequences on others, I create my own identity. I wanted very much to be an existentialist, even as I felt intense social pressure and the limits placed on me because of my gender, social class, and appearance.

Donna Alvermann explores these issues in Chapter 12 through the work of Simone de Beauvoir, a French feminist and existentialist who challenged the limits of socially imposed gender roles in her writings about freedom, interpersonal relationships, and the experience of living as a human body. As a distinguished scholar of literacy at the University of Georgia, Alvermann's own work is voluminous and resists easy labeling, but one thing is certain: she has led literacy researchers into recognizing and appreciating the power and relevance of mass media, popular culture, and digital media. In researching and teaching about adolescent literacy practices, she has been dedicated to helping youth who self-identify as nonreaders in school by discovering the complex literacy practices they use while engaging autonomously with digital media in informal learning contexts. For example, when such students are allowed to select their own online resources to read, they often demonstrate high levels of literacy competence.

But as Alvermann sees it, de Beauvoir's ideas about gender and power come with a warning: educators who aim to liberate students but ignore the individual's free will and free choice are likely to intentionally or unintentionally impose new tyrannies of oppression. She reminds us of the existentialist's paradox: in valuing the primacy of my own individual freedom and responsibility, I must respect the fact that other people possess the same desires. When de Beauvoir wrote, "Each of us is responsible for everything and to every human being" (1948, 1), she captured something that is simultaneously daring, disquieting, profound, and optimistic about humanity: we must mind the gap between our selfishness and our social responsibility. As Alvermann reveals, the rich variability inherent in the meaning-making process cannot be controlled. When it comes to meaning, the work of speakers and listeners, writers and readers, filmmakers and film viewers, and producers and consumers is fundamentally unstable. That's why media literacy educators aim to increase people's tolerance for—and appreciation of—ambiguity and uncertainty. Fortunately, we are aided by artists who use creative expression to address the many paradoxes of living and by educators who inspire and challenge us to ask critical questions about what we read, watch, listen to, see, play, and use.

Learning and Literacy

> If students are not trained to ask basic questions about the images which confront them, if they are not asked to examine the knowledge and assumptions which they already possess, they are being denied the opportunity to develop the most simple and essential critical tools.
>
> —CARY BAZALGETTE, "THE MYTH OF TRANSPARENCY"

Although Raymond Williams described the word culture as one of the most challenging to define with precision, the words learning and literacy are pretty slippery, as well. Scholars and educators continue to struggle to define the full range of knowledge, skills, competencies, and habits of mind embodied in the concept of literacy. For most of human history, to be well educated meant to be able to master the practices of daily living. More specialized societies led to the emergence of apprenticeship systems, in which one worked side-by-side with a master to gain the specialized knowledge and skills of a craft or trade. After the Gutenberg revolution, things changed. The rise of civil society brought about by the Enlightenment meant that high levels of literacy, specifically the practices of reading and writing, became essential for the middle and upper-middle classes. To be learned was to be able to understand and appreciate great authors and the great works that represented our literary, historical, and cultural heritage.

Today we are seeing a return to apprenticeship. Outside of any formal education context, I can harvest ideas from experts by reading an online discussion group or bulletin board, listening to a podcast featuring insightful commentators and experts, or watching a how-to video on YouTube. Because we deeply recognize the medium-specific competencies involved in sense-making, media literacy educators have always resisted the implication that film, television, and digital technologies are the cause of declining interest in reading. Good reading comprehension skills are more important than ever as a result of the rise of the Internet and the sharing of information through social media. Today, while everyone rattles on about the crisis of nonreaders, "books aren't as imperiled as some critics believe, and in some ways they might even be thriving" (Striphas 2009, 2). Electronic books, online bookselling, and online reading communities like Goodreads signal that, even apart from the economics of the industry, printed books, images, film, and digital media all complement each other with a remarkable array of synergies.

Print literacy is one of the most amazing social practices of all time. One of the pioneers of literacy education was Lev Vygotsky, a Russian psychologist who examined the acquisition of language and written symbol systems by considering meaning in relation to the cultural practices of daily life. As a historical materialist, Vygotsky recognized how reading and writing were differentially imbued with social power. He saw reading and writing as extensions of speaking and listening that always reflect and embody cultural values. Vygotsky recognized that as children use oral language to participate in family life, they "bring their meanings into line with meanings in the adult world" (Mahn and John-Steiner 2005, 81).

After World War II, reading researchers began to discover that reading is a multidimensional set of cognitive, social, and cultural practices that involve perception, attention, decoding, literal comprehension, inference making, critical analysis, aesthetic appreciation, interpretation, and study skills (Bormuth 1973). We began recognizing that people's reading patterns varied from genre to genre, as people read nonfiction works differently than they read textbooks, novels, or poetry. In exploring appropriate ways to define, teach, and measure print literacy, educators and researchers also began to appreciate the importance of oral literacy, as it was discovered that some kinds of classroom discussion practices support reading comprehension, critical analysis, and interpretation (Alvermann and Hayes 1989).

The fascinating topic of how reading, writing, learning, and media were separated into distinct academic disciplines is beyond the scope of this book. But writing teachers are deeply engaged in multimodal literacy practices and have contributed many key figures in the media literacy movement. Today, many in English education are enacting fundamental practices of media literacy whether they use the term or not. A growing movement of multimodal literacy educators invites students to create book trailers, public service announcements, digital stories, graphic novel projects, blogs, podcasts, comics, slide presentations, animation, interactive fiction, and more. In the 1970s, when Donald Murray wrote "Our Students Will Write—if We Let Them," the field of composition studies emerged as a discipline separate from its parent discipline of English and its allied discipline of education. The compositionists helped expand the concept of literacy to include writing as a literacy practice, and they were among the first to carefully articulate a new role for the teacher. Writing teachers generally don't lecture from behind the podium; they sit next to their students, discussing their writing as a process of discovery (Ballenger 2008). Writing scholars are thus inevitably focused on practices of teaching and learning, even though they may sometimes distance themselves from the discipline of education.

In Chapter 13, Jeremiah Dyehouse, a professor of writing and rhetoric at the University of Rhode Island, introduces readers to the work of John Dewey, one of the grandparents of media literacy who made major contributions to the fields of philosophy, communications, and education. Dewey challenged narrow conceptualizations of education and communication and reimagined concrete ways in which these institutions could more fully support democracy. Could new forms of writing and technologies of mass communication help to bring about broadly democratic social transformations? Or was social change best brought about through the creation of embodied, multisensory, and collaborative approaches to schooling? Dewey showed us the problems that result when what happens in school is mismatched with the needs and cultural practices of society. Dyehouse deconstructs one of Dewey's most pertinent insights for educators with deep interests in communication: he shows how the development of shared understanding is "not the *cause of* but rather a *result of* successful cooperations in action."

Media literacy teachers use the power of collaborative learning and want the literacy practices that happen in schools to be more deeply connected to the literacy practices used at home and in the community. Media literacy educators aim for schools to be an intermediary of sorts between home and mass media, popular culture, and digital media. Media literacy educators want to enact literacy and learning through accessing, analyzing, creating, reflecting, and taking action in the world. That's why the practices of inquiry and collaboration are so central to this work (Castek et al. 2012). When learners participate in a common activity—when they analyze or create media—the pleasure of co-constructing meaning results in not only a feeling of accomplishment but also a type of shared understanding that we call learning. That's why collaborative media production activities are a central pedagogical practice of digital and media literacy education.

The discourses of communication and education, which are fundamentally tied together in a complex relationship, have not yet been fully explored in contemporary scholarship. This book aims to advance and deepen the dialogue between the two knowledge communities. In Chapter 14, I introduce readers to the work of Jerome Bruner, who celebrated his hundredth birthday in 2015. Bruner is one of the architects of a learning theory known as constructivism: the idea that people learn by constructing new knowledge that builds on what they already know and can do. Bruner defined intelligence as "the internalization of 'tools' provided by a given culture, including not only technological hardware but symbolic systems as well" (quoted in Cole and Scribner 1974, 24). Bruner recognized the power of learning through language, visual media, and various gestural and enactive forms of expression and communication. As a developmental psychologist, he recognized that children are naturally inclined toward physical and social activities through which they develop attention, self-control, and problem-solving skills. The role of the teacher is to support this natural growth by creating learning environments that enable learners to discover ideas, concepts, and principles for themselves through well-structured and well-sequenced knowledge and meaningful activities that enable learners to explore, manipulate, and test ideas. Influenced by John Dewey, Bruner identified the powerful interplay between working with cultural objects and materials and working with symbolic representations and ideas. These are fundamental learning practices—and not just for young children. Media literacy educators insist on emphasizing creative-media production (in print, visual, sound, and digital formats) as a core element of pedagogical value, reflecting a Brunerian line of inquiry where learning is understood as a socially, culturally, and materially embodied symbolic process.

Few people have influenced the field of media literacy more than Neil Postman, whose work demonstrates the practice of media literacy by modeling the reasoning process with engaging, playful prose. When I met Postman in the summer of 1993, I was struck by his charisma, intelligence, and, especially, his relational depth; he has influenced a generation of students who are now professors themselves. In Chapter 15, Vanessa Domine, an education professor at Montclair State University, reflects on her relationship with Postman, describing the dialogical learning process of actively co-constructing knowledge along with him as a doctoral student.

Postman's students thrived because he created a true learning community. His inquiry-oriented perspective built on the significant connective tissue between the humanities, media studies, and education—he was a bridge builder, indeed. Postman's rhetorical skills were considerable: he knew how to create engaging arguments that simply captivated you, grabbing you by the throat. His fundamental claim in *Amusing Ourselves to Death* (1986) is that television is at its most dangerous when it tries to do good. As I recall, the very argument left us breathless at the time. How could educational television be a bad thing? How could TV news be dangerous? One simply had to read to discover the powerful and persuasive reasoning at work. Postman's way of inverting people's expectations truly captured the imagination.

Part of the challenge we have in the field of media studies and communication comes from the divorce with the humanities that has occurred as colleges and universities created separate programs that emphasize professional preparation for jobs in journalism, media, marketing, and industry. Most communications and media faculty will agree: our students no longer get rich, deep exposure to literature, history, and the arts. Can that be restored in the twenty-first century? Postman hoped so. But Postman's attitudes toward the humanities and technology were complex. I remember the whiplash I felt when reading *Teaching as a Subversive Activity* (1971), which Postman wrote with Charles Weingartner, and then, during Reagan's back-to-basics revolution, Postman's *Teaching as a Conserving Activity* (1982). It turns out that those dialectically opposed ideas were profoundly linked. Perhaps Postman's protectionism was actually a result of living so optimistically and having such high hopes for the future. Postman's work has helped me understand that my mission, as an educator, is to activate learners' power of communication, critical thinking, and imagination to challenge (and help transform) the inequities of the social status quo while at the same time enabling the next generation to appreciate and value those profound and fertile ideas that have withstood the test of time.

Engaging the Head, Heart, Hands, and Spirit

> Remember that values questions have a you in them. The goal is to involve people in relating what they see on the screen to their own lives, not to analyze the filmmaker's technique or to engage in intellectual criticism. Allow the conversation to flow along a values and feelings track.
>
> —Elizabeth Thoman, "Use TV to Exercise Values"

Media literacy has a powerful way of engaging the head, heart, hands, and spirit. Elizabeth Thoman, founder of the Center for Media Literacy in Los Angeles, certainly appreciated the cognitive, emotional, and even spiritual dimensions of media literacy. Recognizing education as a political act, Thoman understood that media literacy addressed issues of social justice, including inequality, poverty, racism, and sexism. She was deeply influenced by the work of Paulo Freire, a Christian socialist who helped thousands of Brazilians to learn to read and, thereby, to gain their political rights. As Thoman understood it, media literacy could create a "jolt in awareness" to inspire people to care about addressing social issues "that were caused, reinforced, perpetuated or exacerbated by objectionable media practices" (RobbGrieco 2014, 185).

Another of the pioneers of American media literacy, Jean Kilbourne, discovered the power of psychological reactance as she found that she could activate strong emotional responses from audiences by deconstructing magazine advertising images of gender. We experience reactance when we sense that our freedoms or choices are being limited or taken away. Kilbourne's audiences get angry when they learn about all the different ways in which advertising manipulates us. That anger may sometimes be channeled into activism; other times, it simply makes insight on the value of media literacy unforgettable. Her film *Killing Us Softly* (1979) shows how advertising uses powerful human drives for love, belonging, and status to sell products. By linking products to human values and ideals, advertisers activate and intensify our sense of discomfort with ourselves. Kilbourne believes that advertising's objectification of the body dehumanizes women and represents a form of symbolic violence. Scholars including Renee Engeln-Maddox at Northwestern University have developed measures of media literacy to examine how critical-analysis skills may be activated by an understanding that beauty images are fake, too thin, or even harmful to women (Engeln-Maddox and Miller 2008).

For many years, I was deeply opposed to using my authority in the classroom for persuasion, moralizing, or advocacy. I had experienced a bit of that kind of teaching as an undergraduate, as liberal professors persuaded undergraduate students of the 1970s to march in support of the Sandinistas in Nicaragua, the right to have an abortion, or some other cause. Perhaps because I was active in political causes, faculty exhortations generally felt patronizing (at best) or coercive (at worst). But although I did not directly advocate in the classroom, this did not stop me from finding engaging ways to activate students' own sense of civic engagement with issues that mattered to them. I also made it clear that I had an emotional involvement with the ideas of media literacy. Teaching students to question and create media was both joyful and hard. I was regularly surprised by what happened in the classroom as I worked to select relevant print, visual, and electronic texts; considered how to analyze and discuss them; and designed writing and media-production activities to challenge and support learning. I listened carefully to my students. I created a space where students could try out ideas and take risks. It seemed that the more open I was to encountering students as human beings, the more authentic and profound our conversations became. I continue to be mesmerized by the unpredictability of the classroom as different minds engage with each other in sometimes tentative, unexpected, and often lyrical ways. In the beginning, as a teacher, the mind-bending questions, the flashes of insight, and even the occasional bursts of anger or frustration (from students and from myself) were ever so mysterious to me. Over time, I discovered the magic that comes, in the seminar room, from trusting one's students—and oneself—with the organic process of wrestling with ideas to stitch together some bits of truth.

When I stumbled on the work of Parker Palmer, I felt I had discovered a guide to making sense of the emotional and spiritual dimensions of teaching and learning, which is "a living relationship with the subject at hand" in which students are invited into that relationship as full partners (1983, 115). Palmer writes, "Education is not just a cognitive process, not just the transmission of facts and reasons. It is a process that involves the whole person, and so involves deep feelings as well" (115). When students feel valued, teachers can be "vulnerable to the ways students may transform the teacher's relationship with the subject" while "stretching and testing" ideas through creative tension (103–104).

Digital and media literacy engages, empowers, and motivates learners. In *The Aims of Education* (1929), Alfred North Whitehead explained that the first stage of the education process is romance, when the student's own interest is aroused in encountering the thrill and mystery of the subject matter. In Chapter 16, Peter Gutierrez, a comics writer and curriculum development professional, shares with us his deep emotional attachment to comics and graphic novels and how this brought him into the world of media literacy. When he read Scott McCloud's *Understanding Comics* (1993), it legitimized the object of his love and helped him share his passion and connect with others. The book enabled him to suture his two identities, as a writer and editor of comics and as a freelance developer of curriculum and instructional materials; now, his approach to media literacy education is rooted in a deep appreciation of popular culture. Gutierrez is eager to respect the knowledge and insights that children and young people have in making sense of the stuff they love: pop music, sports, television, music, social media, and videogames. His approach elevates forms of culture that have been marginalized or even denigrated. As Gutierrez shows, moving effortlessly between the worlds of popular media and high art deepens our appreciation of both.

Engaging the head, heart, hands, and spirit means linking learning to what really matters. Media literacy education enables us to address one of the most fundamental challenges of being human: dealing with time, death, and loss. In Chapter 17, Susan Moeller, a professor of media and international affairs at the International Center for Media and the Public Agenda at the University of Maryland, offers us the ultimate example of how media literacy can inform one's understanding of the very essence of humanity. In reflecting on Roland Barthes's *Camera Lucida*, she recognizes how Barthes brings disparate fields of knowledge to bear on core questions: "Why do certain images seize our attention? What power is present in certain photographs so that we keep looking?" As we make sense of images, we dance with them, she explains. We bring our whole self into the reading process. That's how images can move us emotionally, viscerally, and with tenderness or awe.

Moeller's essay reminds me of Brian Stonehill, a professor at Pomona College, a media literacy colleague with a deep interest in visual communication who died in a tragic accident in 1997. Stonehill was the founder of the media-studies program at Pomona and a creative academic who was exploring how to use educational technology for teaching media literacy ("Brian Stonehill" 1997). His CD-ROM projects, *Screen Smarts* and *House of Visual Literacy*, were based on his book projects, and *Understanding D. W. Griffith* was an amazing interactive, scholarly, archival multimedia project. In considering the process of using the power of personal memory to elucidate the theoretical and historical roots of media literacy, I reflect on Stonehill and other media literacy colleagues who are "here" in memory alone. Remembering the past with knowledge of the present and anticipation of the future is, as Barthes writes, a "viewing moment" (1989, 79), a time machine of sorts that connects memory and imagination.

When we invest the mental effort that's necessary to really think and feel in responding to media messages, we may have an experience of the sacred and the sublime. Thornton Wilder tells us, "All the greatest people ever lived have been telling us that for five thousand years and yet you'd be surprised how people are always losing hold of it. There's something way down deep that's eternal about every human being" ([1938] 1998, 88). In the pages that follow, the distinguished authors of this book generously reveal themselves to us, helping us appreciate something of the eternal. Through the practice of digital and media literacy, we are invited to be alert to the constructed, the ephemeral, the subjective, and the eternal in human experience and all its mediated forms and representations.

REFERENCES

Alvermann, D., and D. Hayes. 1989. "Classroom Discussion of Content Area Reading Assignments: An Intervention Study." *Reading Research Quarterly* 24 (3): 305–335.

Arnheim, R. (1932) 1957. *Film as Art*. Berkeley: University of California Press.

———. (1957) 1974. *Art and Visual Perception: A Psychology of the Creative Eye*. Berkeley: University of California Press.

Barthes, R. (1957) 2012. *Mythologies*. Translated by Richard Howard and Annette Lavers. New York: Hill and Wang.

———. 1989. *The Rustle of Language*. Translated by Richard Howard. Berkeley: University of California Press.

Ballenger, B. 2008. "Reconsiderations: Don Murray and the Pedagogy of Surprise." *College English* 70 (3): 296–303.

Bazalgette, C. 1974. "The Myth of Transparency." *Screen Education* 10–11:11–19.

Beach, R. 2007. "CI5472 Teaching Film, Television, and Media, Module 5: Studying Media Representations." Available at http://www.tc.umn.edu/~rbeach/teachingmedia/module5/4.htm.

Bormuth, J. 1973. "Reading Literacy: Its Definitions and Assessment." *Reading Research Quarterly* 9 (1): 7–66.

Braudy, L. 1977. *The World in a Frame*. Chicago: University of Chicago Press.

"Brian Stonehill; Started Pomona Media Program." 1997. *Los Angeles Times*, August 12. Available at http://articles.latimes.com/1997/aug/12/news/mn-21819.

Castek, J., J. Coiro, L. Guzniczak, and C. Bradshaw. 2012. "Examining Peer Collaboration on Online Inquiry." *The Educational Forum* 76 4: 479–496.

Chandler, D. 2002. *Semiotics: The Basics*. London: Routledge.

Cole, M., and S. Scribner. 1974. *Culture and Thought: A Psychological Introduction*. New York: John Wiley and Sons.

de Beauvoir, S. 1948. *The Ethics of Ambiguity.* Translated by Bernard Frechtman. New York: Citadel Press.

DeFleur, M. L., and M. DeFleur. 2010. *Mass Communication Theories: Explaining Origins, Processes, and Effects.* Boston: Allyn and Bacon.

Engeln-Maddox, R., and S. A. Miller. 2008. "Talking Back to the Media Ideal: The Development and Validation of the Critical Processing of Beauty Images Scale." *Psychology of Women Quarterly* 32 (2): 159–171.

Flint, K., and D. Needham. 2007. "'Framing' Lifelong Learning in the 21st Century: Toward a Way of Thinking." In *Philosophical Perspectives on Lifelong Learning,* edited by David Aspin, 85–108. Dordrecht, Netherlands: Springer.

Fornet-Betancourt, R., H. Becker, A. Gomez-Muller, and J. D. Gauthier. 1987. "The Ethic of Care for the Self as a Practice of Freedom: An Interview with Michel Foucault on January 20, 1984." *Philosophy and Social Criticism* 12:112–131.

Hall, J., and N. Baym. 2012. "Calling and Texting (Too Much): Mobile Maintenance Expectations, (Over)Dependence, Entrapment and Friendship Satisfaction." *New Media and Society* 14 (2): 316–331.

Hall, S. 1980. "Encoding/Decoding." In *Culture, Media, Language,* edited by S. Hall, D. Hobson, A. Lowe, and P. Willis, 128–138. New York: Routledge.

Hall, S., and P. Whannel. 1967. *The Popular Arts.* Boston: Beacon.

Hediger, V. 2013. "Do Media Make a Difference? A Few Random Thoughts on the Attitudes and Assumptions Underlying Cinema and Media Education." In *Il cinema si impara? Sapere, formazione, professioni* [Can we learn cinema? Knowledge, education, the professions], edited by A. Bertolli, A. Marinari, and M. Panelli. Udine, Italy: Forum Editrice. Available at http://bit.ly/1TicC3c.

Hobbs, R., J. Stauffer, R. Frost, and A. Davis. 1988. "How First Time Viewers Comprehend Editing." *Journal of Communication* 38 (4): 50–60.

Jenkins, H., M. Ito, and d. boyd. 2015. *Participatory Culture in a Networked Era.* London: Polity Press.

Jenkins, H., and W. Kelley. 2013. *Reading in a Participatory Culture.* New York: National Writing Project and Teachers College Press.

Kilbourne, J. 1979. *Killing Us Softly.* Directed by M. Lazarus and R. Wunderlich. Cambridge Documentary Films.

Laughey, D. 2011. "Back to Basics: Education First, Then Media Education." *A Manifesto for Media Education.* Available at http://www.manifestofor mediaeducation.co.uk/2011/03/dan-laughey/.

Leavis, F. R., and D. Thompson. (1933) 1973. *Culture and Environment: The Training of Critical Awareness.* New York: Praeger.

Levine, L. 1990. *Highbrow/Lowbrow: The Emergence of Cultural Hierarchy in America.* Cambridge, MA: Harvard University Press.

Mahn, H., and V. John-Steiner. 2005. "Vygotsky's Contribution to Literacy Research." In *Multidisciplinary Perspectives on Literacy Research,* edited by R. Beach, J. Green, M. Kamil, and T. Shanahan, 77–100. Cresskill, NJ: Hampton Press.

Marvin, C. 1988. *When Old Technologies Were New*. New York: Oxford University Press.

Masterman, L. 1989. "Media Awareness Education: Eighteen Basic Principles." Center for Media Literacy. Available at http://www.medialit.org/reading -room/media-awareness-education-eighteen-basic-principles.

McLaren, P., and P. Leonard. 1993. *Paulo Freire: A Critical Encounter*. London: Routledge.

NAMLE (National Association for Media Literacy Education). 2007. "The Core Principles of Media Literacy Education." Available at http://namle.net/ publications/core-principles/.

National Council of Teachers of English. 1975. "Resolution on Promoting Media Literacy." Available at http://www.ncte.org/positions/statements/ promotingmedialit.

Noddings, N. 1984. *Caring: A Feminine Approach to Ethics and Moral Education*. Berkeley: University of California Press.

Ong, W. 1982. *Orality and Literacy: The Technologizing of the Word*. New York: Routledge.

Palmer, P. 1983. *To Know as We Are Known*. New York: Harper One.

Paluck, E. 2009. "Reducing Intergroup Prejudice and Conflict Using the Media: A Field Experiment in Rwanda." *Journal of Personality and Social Psychology* 96 3: 574–587.

Polan, D. 2007. *Scenes of Instruction*. Berkeley: University of California Press.

Postman, N. 1982. *Teaching as a Conserving Activity*. New York: Delacorte Press.

———. 1986. *Amusing Ourselves to Death*. New York: Penguin.

Postman, N., and C. Weingartner. 1971. *Teaching as a Subversive Activity*. New York: Delta.

RobbGrieco, M. 2014. "Media for Media Literacy: Discourses of the Media Literacy Education Movement in *Media & Values* Magazine, 1977–1993." Ph.D. diss., Temple University.

Striphas, T. 2009. *The Late Age of Print*. New York: Columbia University Press.

Thoman, E. 1987. "Use TV to Exercise Values." *Media & Values*, no. 40–41. Available at http://www.medialit.org/reading-room/use-tv-exercise-values.

Thompson, D. 2003. "SolPix Interviews: An Interview with Todd Gitlin." *SolPix*. Available at http://webdelsol.com/SolPix/sp-toddinterview.htm.

Vertov, D. 1929. *Man with a Movie Camera*. Directed by D. Vertov. Available at https://www.youtube.com/watch?v=z97Pa0ICpn8.

Whitehead, A. N. 1929. *The Aims of Education*. New York: Macmillan.

Wilder, T. (1938) 1998. *Our Town*. New York: Harper Collins.

2 /

David Weinberger
on Martin Heidegger

DAVID WEINBERGER

The lack of digital-media literacy is bemoaned by educators, parents, and others who worry about The Kids and Their Future. The moans are familiar, which is not to say that they're unwarranted: we need to teach The Kids what we used to call "critical thinking," by which we mean how not to fall into the traps others set for us to sway our beliefs and behavior. It's true that we need a focus on digital-media literacy because the Internet opens up a whole new set of traps, many due simply to the unprecedented nature of the net: content can float free of its attribution more easily than ever, content is corrupted as it passes from one hand to another like in a global game of Telephone (or Gossip), you can always find others to encourage your belief in some crazy idea, and the list goes on and on.

The type of media literacy that teaches critical thinking with regard to the net is, of course, important, but it's not my primary interest. As a writer and researcher, I personally am more interested in how digital-media literacy addresses the changing nature of knowledge. In some ways, the net pulls apart ideas, connecting them loosely through links. In this environment of many small pieces loosely joined, how should we be putting ideas together? The "how" in that question means both "How do ideas fit together?" and "What's the best process by which we can find that fit?"

To put it too briefly, before the Internet, the book was the medium of knowledge, and knowledge took on the properties of that medium. Knowledge became a particular type of content that we wrote down, so we thought of it as settled and unchanging, the way books don't change after you print them. Knowers would work in private (perhaps with a small, trusted group) and wouldn't get credit for their work until they published it; the rhythm of knowledge (work in relative private until you're sure) became exactly the same as the rhythm of publishing. Knowledge was divided into disciplines and topics, the way that books put a topic between covers.

Now, in the Age of the Net, knowledge is taking on the properties of the network. Knowledge is highly connected. It has no edges. It is always unsettled and subject to further argument. And, with links, it has no natural boundaries. There's good and bad to this, of course, although overall I think it's safe to say that this is the greatest time in human history to be someone who wants to know things. It's also the greatest time to be a total idiot, unfortunately—which is why we need the sort of digital-media literacy that keeps us from falling into traps of thought. In this essay, I discuss one important part of our understanding of knowledge that I think we need to rethink: communication. If knowledge is becoming networked, it's hard to understand the effect of that networking if we're thinking about the net as a communications medium in a pre-networked way.

Surprisingly, it was the work of a philosopher, written about sixty years before the World Wide Web was invented, that has influenced me the most on this topic.

Nowadays, the term *identity* usually refers to something that can be stolen: a credit card or Social Security number that lets someone else incur debts or obligations in your name. But when I was a lad, an identity was a solid sense of self that teenagers tried to grow into, often going through an identity crisis along the way.

My identity crisis was a doozy. It was 1968. I was a freshman in college. I couldn't tell how much of me was an act for other people and how much of it was real. I could spend a long time weighing every thought, assessing whether it expressed something really real about me or was just another shiny surface in my mind's hall of mirrors. That was fairly typical of identity crises, but for whatever quirk, I experienced mine as despair that all meaning is a human projection. See that fork lying over there? It's only a fork because we happen to take it as a fork. If we were the size of field mice, it'd be a seesaw. (It didn't help that 1968 was the year I started smoking pot.) See that tree? We say it's a tree, but that's because we choose to see it as something separate from the ground and air. We only think it's a whole, complete entity with leaves and roots because we choose to see the roots as distinct from the molecules constantly going across its "borders." In fact, we can see the tree in its entirety only when it has been uprooted. Our meaning of things (that's "meaning" as a verb) comes from uprooting them. Meaning is an act of violence. Dude.

The positive side of this was that it fueled my early pacifism: if humans are the source of all judgments about meaning and value, to kill a person is to kill the most valuable thing there is. This—plus principled opposition to the Vietnam War and a huge dose of cowardice—led me to apply to my local Draft Board to be classified as a conscientious objector. (They granted my application, and a few months later I won the newly instituted draft lottery, thus avoiding military service.) My identity crisis also made me a certain type of boy that a certain type of girl found appealing.

I am not proud of any of this.

Nor was it fun. If a fork had no real meaning, how could life? Why should I decide to become a doctor instead of a bank robber? Why should I butter my toast instead of feeding it to the ants? At least the ants knew what to do with it. Why should I get up? Or go to sleep? If killing myself had held any more meaning than living, I would have been suicidal.

Fortunately, mine was an equal-opportunity nihilism. My pacifism told me that I was the source of all the value I experienced, and my nihilism told me that for that very reason, the value wasn't real.

I was brought out of this funk by Martin Heidegger, thanks to a course I took a course from Professor Joseph P. Fell at Bucknell University. Professor Fell was interested in the Big Questions—and he still is—but not in the way freshmen sitting around a dorm room are. Professor Fell is a scholar who reads Greek, Latin, German, and French and has read deeply in Western philosophy. His course was rigorous, informed by the great minds of our culture, and was a model of what it means to seek to understand something. From that course, I began to see how much of my despair was, in fact, a silent inheritance from our intellectual history.

Professor Fell taught a course on Heidegger's *Being and Time* ([1927] 2010), which is a fairly ridiculous thing to do at a small college that graduated only a handful of philosophy majors. *Being and Time* is notoriously difficult. For one thing, it only makes sense as a response to mistakes made by our philosophical tradition. For another, it addresses the broadest question there is: What does it mean for anything to be? For yet another, Heidegger uses many words in peculiar ways because he doesn't want us to assimilate his ideas to our existing, corrupt way of understanding.

Also, Heidegger was a Nazi. An official, card-carrying member of the Nazi party. In 1968, we generally believed that he joined only as a formality to save Freiburg University from the *real* Nazis. It was only in the 1980s that new research showed that Heidegger's beliefs were more in line with the Nazi's romanticism about peasant life, and also possibly with their virulent anti-Semitism, than we'd thought. The debate about just how much of a Nazi Heidegger was continues to rage, but in 1968 Heidegger's party membership was written off as well-intentioned misjudgment by a terminally naive philosopher.

So, how did Heidegger come to my rescue?

My problem was that I assumed that we are all locked inside our own heads. Through this lens, everything we see is an inner picture of an outer reality. Once that picture is inside your head, you attach a meaning to it. We never get out of our own heads. And inside your own head, you have too much freedom to give things the meanings that you want.

It seemed obvious to me that this was simply the way consciousness works. It turns out that this picture wasn't my invention. It is the logical outcome of two-and-a-half thousand years of Western philosophy. The crisis got particularly severe in the seventeenth century when the distinction between the body and the mind was drawn most dramatically. The more different from the physical world the mind was perceived to be, the more difficult it became to explain how our minds know anything at all about the world. With the realm of thought severed from the physical world, what we know of the physical world must be just a mental reconstruction of it.

Heidegger was writing in response to that schizophrenic tendency of our philosophical tradition. Because he thought that the normal words for *mind* are infected by their philosophic history, what others call the *mind*, the *person*, or *consciousness*, he called *Dasein*, a German word that literally means being (*Sein*) there (*Da*). This new word helps us look with fresh eyes about how we actually experience the world.

What he finds—what he points out to us—is that we don't experience our world as being inside our own heads, except in rather exceptional experiences when we feel abstracted from the world and sit alone in a corner like an eighteen-year-old undergoing an identity crisis. Instead, think about the 99.999 percent of the rest of the time when you're making breakfast, ducking your head to avoid a branch, lowering a phonograph needle onto an LP (it's 1968, remember), or even listening to Professor Fell lecture. In all of these cases, we don't experience the world as inside our heads. Rather, our consciousness is out in the world, filled with the things of the world understood in terms of what it is that we're trying to do: eat breakfast, walk down a sidewalk, listen to music, understand some passage in Heidegger. We only have the locked-in-our-head experience when we sit down to think about it. The rest of the time we're engaged with the world, doing some form of purposive activity. Philosophy only thinks that we're separated from the world because philosophy occurs when you aren't engaged in the world but are thinking about it.

That was helpful to the eighteen-year-old me. Even more important, however, was Heidegger's observation—obvious though it now sounds—that if we look at how we experience the world, we realize that we are already in a world not of our own choosing. We are, in Heidegger's word, thrown into a situation that has arisen because of history, culture, language, and the particularities of our own lives ([1927] 2010). I was born in 1950 in America, not in 1450 in Mongolia. You can work on transforming yourself, but not all that much; even if I succeed in becoming a back-to-the-earth farmer who eschews modern technology, I can only do so as a twenty-first-century American. We're thrown and we're stuck with what we've been thrown into. We are, in a word, situated.

This, for Heidegger, is not just cold beans you have to eat. Being situated isn't simply a limitation on your experience and understanding; it makes experience and understanding possible. If you were not born into any situation (whatever that might mean), you'd stare blankly at the fork, not understanding what it is for. Things have meaning because we are thrown into those meanings. (And what's true for a fork is obviously true for what you read or view online.)

For Heidegger, those meanings are not intellectual definitions that one can formalize and be done with. Rather, the meaning of a thing is its position within a vast context of meanings. To understand a fork the way we do within our shared situation, you also have to understand which food can be forked, that there are a set of cultural norms about how forks are handled, that forks are designed for hands like ours, that we are creatures that enjoy eating and thus are capable of physical and social pleasure, that food comes to us through complex biological and economic processes, that we are biological creatures that need to eat, and that the world will continue without us as it managed before we existed. In short, you need to understand everything in order to understand anything. Of course, understanding everything does not mean that you know all the details of agricultural engineering or of cellular metabolism. Rather, the meaning of the fork is connected to a web of interrelated meanings, and nothing we encounter is outside that web; even if we find a scrap of metal in the street and we have no idea where it came from, we identify it as a scrap of metal and as something a human made for some purpose. That all-encompassing web is what Heidegger means when he refers to "the world" ([1927] 2010).

This was a radical idea because the world had been assumed to consist of all the Real Stuff—atoms, matter, energy—that exists independently of us. In contrast, Heidegger tells us that the world is the set of meanings in which we always already have found ourselves as situated creatures. Now, *meaning* here is definitely not capital-M Meaning, as in the Meaning of Life. Rather, it is the simple, everyday meaning we assume when we reach for the fork to twirl some spaghetti around. This lowercase meaning is expressed by the word *as*, as when we say that we experience the fork *as* a tool for eating, or we take the object we find in the road *as* a scrap of metal from some larger assemblage. Part of Heidegger's insight is that these simple *as*'s are only possible within a seamless and inexhaustible context of *as*'s: the world in which we exist.

Thus, Heidegger gets over the mind-body conundrum by saying that before we abstract ourselves into that problem, we already live in a world of meaning. We have been thrown into a world that matters to us in particular ways. In fact, meaning is so fundamental to this world that Heidegger points to it as the very heart of human existence. While the Western tradition focused on how we can know our world, Heidegger says that knowing the world is just one way of being in the world. It is, of course, an important mode, but it is not that which explains all other modes. Rather, *Dasein*—consciousness, if you prefer—is fundamentally characterized by the fact that we care about what happens to us. You go to pick up the fork because you want to eat. You use a fork instead of your hands because you care about what other people will think, or perhaps because you care about avoiding grease stains on your sleeve. Ultimately, you want to eat because you care about living. Human consciousness runs on care. Even the act of knowing the world is based on care. It's the fact that we care that causes us to take things *as* what they are; if you truly didn't care, you wouldn't be interested in eating or anything else, so the fork wouldn't show itself to you *as* anything in particular. It would truly be meaningless.

It's important to note that this did not make Heidegger into a preacher or narcissist. Looking at our experience, he concluded that we care not only about ourselves but also about others. We recognize that we have been thrown into a world that contains other people who care about themselves and about others. We are not isolated, selfish, lonely people. We share a world and share a caring about that world and others.

The ways in which we care lead to a history that results in our tending to see things some ways rather than others: we're more likely to take the fork as a way to eat than as a weapon or as a way to comb our hair because that's where our history has led us. That history is expressed by language. Except that, for Heidegger, that's a terrible way to put it. Language is, for Heidegger, not merely an expression of meaning; it is the shape of meaning itself. Just as the fork only has meaning within a web of references, so does the word *fork*. For Heidegger, the two are, in important ways, the same.

To make sense of this, it's important to distinguish language as a set of arbitrary squawks and squiggles from language as the set of meanings expressed in those squawks and squiggles. For Heidegger, language articulates meaning in the sense of drawing circles around things and drawing the links among the circles. That we have the words "plates" and "saucers" draws a distinction among these two similar sorts of eating equipment, but to understand what either is, one must see its position in the complex set of relationships that constitute the world. Language is that articulation. It generally happens to be expressed in squawks and squiggles (but also sometimes bumps on paper or hand motions).

It is a mistake, of course, to look for meaning in the squawks and squiggles of language, for they are arbitrary. But, for Heidegger, it's also a mistake to look for meaning in some easily expressed definitions of those squawks and squiggles. The meaning of a thing is its position in a complex, messy web of situated relationships that no one can ever make fully explicit. In my adolescent identity crisis, I made both mistakes. Particularly in situations where I was expected to be especially social—parties, for instance—I suffered a mild form of aphasia: I was unable to speak. Or I lacked the motivation to speak. The squawks were just squawks, and their definitional meanings seemed too impoverished. Speaking just wasn't worth the effort, and nothing that speech could utter seemed to be the truth.

Heidegger helped cure me of that symptom. He helped by *not* offering a theory of communication. *Communication* is one of those loaded terms that Heidegger is right to avoid. Our idea of it is quite modern. John Durham Peters in *Speaking into the Air*, writes, "Technologies such as the telegraph and radio refitted the old term 'communication,' once used for any kind of physical transfer or transmission, into a new kind of quasi-physical connection across the obstacles of time and space" (1999, 5). This idea gained an even greater hold on us, thanks to the invention of information by Claude Shannon in 1948, about twenty years after Heidegger's *Being and Time* was published in Germany.[1] (Heidegger, who died in 1976, wrote about computer technology a bit in the 1950s but did not show any evidence of understanding anything about Shannon's work.)

Shannon worked in Bell Labs, the research and development branch of the telephone company. That company had a large interest in trying to ensure that what went into one end of their lines came out the same at the other end. Shannon's theory of information—a relatively novel use of the term *information* at the time—provided a mathematical framework for measuring the amount of information that could be put through a medium and the inevitable noise that would deform it along the way. Although Shannon opens his initial article on the topic by telling readers that it is not meant to have anything to do with meaning, his theory was quickly taken as applicable not just to pulses of electricity moving over telephone wires but also to every human attempt to share meaning.

The impact of Shannon's theory of information was huge, which is remarkable given that its math was beyond all but the most expert. But it came with a diagram that seemed to be within everyone's reach. At one end, a message is encoded into a set of signals that go over a line, which might be a telegraph or telephone wire, and are decoded at the receiving end. Noise is depicted as an arrow pointing into the middle of the wire. Picture people talking into tin cans connected by string and you have the basic image.

This simple picture fit in perfectly with our idea of ourselves as locked in our own heads. We take our meanings, turn them into arbitrary sounds and scribbles, and send them out over some medium in the hope that someone else will receive them and decode them at least partially correctly. That's communication.

But this picture suffers from the same problems as the traditional picture of knowledge we've painted for ourselves. That picture leads us (and me, during the worst of my identity crisis) to think that communication is the process by which what's in your head gets into my head, and that process consists of moving arbitrary symbols through a medium. That picture isn't wrong so much as misleading. It's like saying that the experience of love consists of the firing of particular neurons. Neurons do fire when we experience love, but that doesn't tell us what love means or is like.

So drop the Shannon picture of communication, and look again. I say, "Beautiful morning," and you respond, "Too bad we have exams." Yes, these are particular squawks that have moved through the air (more exactly, they've caused changes in the pressure of the air between us), but that doesn't tell us what it means to communicate. Heidegger's approach provides an alternative way to understand what's going on. You and I share a world in which we are situated. We understand this world in terms of what we care about, what matters to us. When you and I talk, we are not moving inner pictures from one head to another. Rather, we are each turning the other to the world itself, disclosing our understandings in terms of what matters to us. When I say "Beautiful morning," I'm turning your attention to the weather. When you say, "Too bad we have exams," you're pointing to a feature of our shared world—exams are coming—that matters to us in a shared way and that has implications for what we're going to do today. In conversation, we turn each other toward aspects of the world that matter to us. We do so within a situation that shares not only a language but also a domain (school) with its own features (exams) about which we care.

So, rather than thinking of language as a vehicle for communication, and communication as a process of re-creating in your mind the picture I have in my mind, Heidegger thinks of speaking (and writing and painting and dancing) as turning us toward our shared world, disclosing its possibilities based on what we care about.

This is entirely consistent with the rest of Heidegger's thought. Language is something we find ourselves thrown into; we already speak at least one language. (Heidegger doesn't provide a theory of how we get into that situation.) Language is already something we share, just as we always already experience the world itself as shared. The elements of language only have meaning because they are embedded in a relational context as extensive as the world itself. And language, like our life in the world, is saturated with care: I only speak if there's something I care about, and in disclosing the world together we are making what we care about manifest.

This view of communication rejects the fundamental premise of the prevalent abstract understanding of communication, which sees it as overcoming disconnectedness: you and I are fundamentally isolated (the theory suggests) unless and until we communicate. Even at that point, we are isolated individuals who happen to have the same mental content at the same time. Against this, Heidegger proposes the concept of the *always already*: before we ever think that we are isolated consciousnesses, we have always already found ourselves in a shared world that is rich with meaning—where *meaning* means the *as*-ness of things ([1927] 2010). That *as*-ness—seeing the fork as a way to eat some peas instead of as something to comb your hair with or as a mouse's seesaw—occurs within a complex, messy set of relationships (a.k.a. the world).

This is just what eighteen-year-old me needed to hear and to accept. My experience of isolation and of meaninglessness was looking for Meaning that was independent of all situations. I could not find it because understanding is always situated, always a part of its culture, language, and history. I so mourned Meaning's absence that I missed the world full of meaning that we all always already inhabit.

In short, I was taking the unusual experience in which meaning seems to withdraw as especially revelatory. But that mood is deceptive. The proof of this is that if we experience the temporary withdrawal of meaning as a loss, it's because we are care-based creatures living in a language-soaked, shared world. If, in your despair, you pick idly at your food with a fork, the forkiness of that fork proves Heidegger's point. In fact, Professor Fell's work over the years has repeatedly come back to the question of the always already. He finds the idea in Aristotle's sense of the prior community of nature that allows us to understand a world that is in many ways very much unlike our understanding of it.[2] He finds it in the thinking of his own teacher, John William Miller, when he writes about the mind world (Fell 1990). The awareness of the mystery of the always already was a great gift for which I continue to thank Professor Fell. In practical terms, I was on the student-faculty committee at Bucknell that first allowed students to create their own major, and I was one of the very first to take advantage of the opportunity. I graduated as a Meaning major.

So, thanks to Professor Fell's patience, clarity, and wisdom, Heidegger brought me out of my teenage angst. I saw that the world wasn't the illusion. The illusion was that I lived inside a hollow skull, trying to wring meaning from meaningless experience and from the echoes of arbitrary squawks and squiggles emitted from other hollow skulls. As a result of questioning the idea that communication overcomes fundamental isolation, I was reminded of the more important truth: we are always already together in a shared world about which we all care, but care differently.

What does this reunderstanding of the nature of communication mean for digital-media literacy? The prior idea of media literacy pictured students reading a newspaper (ah, the old days!) or watching TV by themselves, prey to all the ways that advertisers and propagandists lie to us. We still need to learn how to encounter media on our own, but we should also recognize that generally we now read in a shared space, with other people. What we read comes from them, via links and tweets and all the other ways we recommend places on the net to one another. What we read comes filtered through others who often comment on it, guiding our understanding and attitude. Our network does much of the hard work of spotting traps and exposing liars, whether it's through a Reddit thread contradicting a hyperbolic headline or a response on Facebook that links to a contrary source.

So, while we still need to sharpen our skills, we also need to figure out how to make the networked space better at discovering the truth and swerving around the lies. Our fundamental image should no longer be that of an isolated student facing an onslaught of lies. Rather, it should be that of a shifting network of people with a shared interest, showing one another how the world looks to them. Media literacy needs to produce not just literate individuals but networks that are better at telling the truth—which means they're better at letting us see the world together and helping us care about it more.

NOTES

1. I write this with the understanding that it's usually taken as obvious that information has been with us throughout time. I disagree, except in the sense that one could also say that miles and centigrade degrees have been with us forever. But that's not our topic.

2. "For interaction between two factors is held to require a precedent community of nature between the factors." Aristotle 1997, chap. 4.

REFERENCES

Aristotle. 1997. *De Anima* [On the Soul]. Bk. 3. Translated by J. A. Smith. *Classics in the History of Psychology.* Available at http://psychclassics.yorku .ca/Aristotle/De-anima/de-anima3.htm.

Fell, Joseph P. 1990. *The Philosophy of John William Miller.* Lewisburg, PA: Bucknell University Press.

Heidegger, Martin. (1927) 2010. *Being and Time.* Translated by J. Stambaugh. Albany: State University of New York Press.

Peters, John Durham. 1999. *Speaking into the Air: A History of the Idea of Communication.* Chicago: University of Chicago Press.

Shannon, Claude E. 1948. "A Mathematical Theory of Communication." *Bell System Technical Journal* 27:379–423, 623–656.

3 /

Lance Strate on
Marshall McLuhan

LANCE STRATE

I can't say when I first heard the name Marshall McLuhan. Growing up in the sixties, there were some names that were simply environmental, part of the cultural (and countercultural) backdrop—names like Timothy Leary, Bob Dylan, Jane Fonda, Ken Kesey, Jerry Garcia, Twiggy, Tom Wolfe, John Lennon, and Yoko Ono. Marshall McLuhan was one of them. I may have first seen the name when I was seven years old on a magazine cover or in a newspaper article, following the explosion of publicity that surrounded the publication of *Understanding Media: The Extensions of Man* (1964). Maybe I first saw the name on the pocket-sized paperback edition of that book that was published the following year. Unlike today, when larger, trade paperbacks are the norm, at that time smaller and relatively inexpensive books in the format pioneered by Pocket Books were plentiful, sold in many different types of retail outlets, stationary stores, five-and-dimes, drug stores, supermarkets, newspaper stands, and the many small, independent bookstores that once were commonplace. Admittedly, it was most likely to have been a collection of *Peanuts* cartoons or *Mad* magazine material that caught my attention, but there were many intellectual, indeed scholarly, books included in the mix, and I did have a wandering eye when it came to reading material. It is most likely that I first heard the name on television or maybe even saw McLuhan in one of his many talk show appearances (in those days authors were featured routinely on such programs). Since my parents were in the habit of watching television news every night, I would have heard the report on November 26, 1967, about McLuhan undergoing what was at the time the longest continuous brain surgery ever attempted, which successfully removed a large, benign brain tumor. If nothing else, I am certain I would have heard Henry Gibson recite the line "Marshall McLuhan, what are you doin'?" in the fall of 1968 while watching the NBC comedy program *Rowan and Martin's Laugh-In*.

All this speaks to McLuhan's celebrity, of course, and not his ideas. Media was not a topic that came up much when I was in elementary school (Public School 99 in Kew Gardens, part of the New York City school system). I do remember going to the auditorium with my class where a television set was placed on stage, so that we could watch some live event—I think it was a NASA rocket launch. And I was particularly struck by the fact that all of us kids burst out laughing when a commercial for some beauty product came on. It was the kind of commercial that we would watch without reaction when sitting in front of the tube by ourselves at home, but something about seeing it in the school context made it absolutely hilarious. And somehow this never happened when we had radio programs piped into our classroom over the PA system or were shown educational filmstrips or movies. There was something different about the television medium and something different about school as a situational context. But we never talked about television as a medium.

We did, however, talk about the press, and I recall learning about the trial of John Peter Zenger as part of American history, and with it the idea of freedom of the press. I think that was in fourth grade, and I believe it was in sixth grade that we had to subscribe to the *New York Times* for a month. I remember being taught how to read the newspaper, learning that the most important story on the front page appeared in column eight (there were eight columns in those days, as opposed to six now), and practicing the straphanger fold (a technique for reading the paper on a crowded subway or bus). We also had a class trip to the newspaper's headquarters in Manhattan and received souvenirs in the form of bits of metal type used for printing.

Of course, elementary school back then was mainly about the three Rs—reading, 'riting, and 'rithmetic—which is to say that the focus was on language, literacy, and numeracy. Grammar came as second nature to me, and I was fortunate that the dialect of English that I knew was more or less the standard dialect being taught in school. The formal qualities of the written word were the subjects I had greatest difficulty with—specifically, spelling and handwriting—and this heightened my consciousness of the differences between spoken language and its written representation. And while I had no difficulty with the rules of grammar, diction was another matter altogether, and in fourth grade I was sent to speech class to learn how to make the *th* sound. My parents were immigrants from Eastern Europe, and substituted a *zh* or *dzh* sound for *th*; consequently, I learned to speak in that way as well and needed instruction on how to put my tongue up against my upper front teeth to make the *th* sound, a phoneme that is not used in many other languages. On the other hand, I was entirely familiar with the hard *ch* sound that is entirely absent from English, but commonly used in German, Yiddish, Hebrew, and Scottish. This served to instill in me an early awareness of speech and language as modes of communication. I should add that I grew up in a multilingual environment, my parents both speaking many different languages and my neighborhood populated by Jewish immigrants from many different nations. My parents spoke German to each other when they didn't want me to understand what they were saying, so naturally I started to pick up the language when I was very young, although I never actually learned to speak it. I also gained a limited familiarity with another German dialect, Yiddish, which was a lingua franca spoken in many contexts when I was growing up; relatives and friends of my parents often expressed disapproval that I didn't speak Yiddish, but in those days immigrants, no matter their origin, wanted their children to speak English and English alone, to become fully American. Nevertheless, I would hear my mother speaking Polish to her sister, my father speaking Hungarian to his friends from the old country, and both parents speaking Romanian to other friends and relatives. And around the time I was sent to have my speech deficiency "cured" in public school, I began my formal religious education with Sunday school on Sunday mornings and Hebrew classes twice a week after school. Learning Hebrew involved not only learning another language but also learning another alphabet, learning the difference between a spoken language and a writing system, and learning how the same writing system could be used to represent the sounds of different languages. Moreover, the most sacred object in the synagogue is the Torah, a parchment scroll handwritten by a specially trained religious scribe, written in an ancient Hebrew that used no vowels, very limited forms of punctuation, and a special, calligraphic style; this introduced me, in a profound way, to a kind of book that existed before printing, before book-binding, and before the introduction of paper as a writing surface. I should also note that not long after I started my religious education, I bought a book at one of the Scholastic book fairs, held periodically at our public school, that put all of this in context for me: it was *What's Behind the Word*, by Sam and Beryl Epstein (1964), and it told the story of the evolution of the English language, the nature of words, and the roles played by writing, the alphabet, and printing.

Language and literacy, speech and writing, and even typography all are topics that were not typically associated with the idea of media, at least not before McLuhan published his two major works, *The Gutenberg Galaxy* (1962) and *Understanding Media: The Extensions of Man* (1964). McLuhan's background was quite different from mine, as he was an English-speaking Canadian born almost half a century before me (1911 versus 1957). His mother was an elocutionist, which undoubtedly provided him with an early awareness of speech as a form of expression. As a youth, he was befriended by a young S. I. Hayakawa, who went on to become the best known proponent of general semantics, devoted to raising our consciousness of language as a means of mapping reality (Haslam and Haslam 2011). And as an English major who went on to get his doctorate in the subject from Cambridge University, he was particularly drawn to poetry and prose that exhibited a self-reflexive quality, such as the writing of the French symbolists and James Joyce (by way of contrast, I was deeply moved by J.R.R. Tolkien, whose fantasy was based, significantly for this discussion, on his background as a scholar of philology (Strate 2011). At Cambridge, McLuhan studied with I. A. Richards, whose approach to English emphasized an understanding of how symbol, referent, and reference form a semantic triangle (Ogden and Richards 1923) and, therefore, an understanding of how language functions as a medium of expression, a view echoed by the anthropologist Edward Sapir (1921) whose linguistic relativism had a major impact on McLuhan's thinking (see also Lee 1959; Whorf 1956). Also quite importantly, it was during McLuhan's years as a doctoral student that he converted to Catholicism, embracing an experience that emphasized an ancient and somewhat alien language. Praying in Latin placed greater emphasis on the sound of the prayer rather than the verbal content, enhancing the spiritual and mystical quality of the experience, and McLuhan was not in favor of the Second Vatican Council's move away from the Latin Mass. The cathedral itself represents a physical environment that is quite distinct from everyday settings, which includes the powerful medium of religious iconography, stained glass windows, statues, and so on that Saint Gregory the Great had characterized as the books of the illiterate. McLuhan came to his understanding of media through the lens of a medievalist, both intellectually and religiously.

Following the end of the World War II, colleges and universities in the United States began to form Departments of Communication, bringing together scholars in areas such as speech, rhetoric, English, psychology, sociology, and political science. For example, my department at Fordham University was founded in 1946 by merging programs in theater, radio, and journalism. McLuhan joined the faculty at the University of Toronto that same year, having previously taught at Saint Louis University (like Fordham, a Jesuit school) and Ontario's Assumption University. At Toronto, he was influenced by Harold Innis, a senior scholar of political economy and author of *Empire and Communications* (1950) and *The Bias of Communication* (1951); there he began a close collaboration with the anthropologist Edmund Carpenter. Both Innis and Carpenter had much to do with McLuhan turning his attention from literary criticism and popular culture, the latter the subject of McLuhan's first book, *The Mechanical Bride: Folklore of Industrial Man* (1951), to an emphasis on communication and media. Carpenter and McLuhan worked together to publish nine issues of the interdisciplinary journal *Explorations* and an anthology based on the periodical *Explorations in Communication* (Carpenter and McLuhan 1960), which brought together essays by independent and innovative thinkers such as the noted sociologist David Riesman, literary theorist Northrop Frye, seminal nonverbal communication researcher Ray L. Birdwhistell, historian and medievalist H. J. Chaytor, pioneering popular culture scholar Gilbert Seldes, architectural critic Sigfried Gidion, famed modernist painter Fernand Léger, and well-known humorist and radio personality Jean Shepherd. McLuhan's collaboration with Carpenter also led to a grant from the National Association of Educational Broadcasters, supplemented by funding from the United States Office of Education, which resulted in his *Report on Project in Understanding New Media* (1960), on which his subsequent work was based. The report was very much concerned with media literacy education and later became the basis of a textbook he coauthored, intended for use in secondary schools (McLuhan, Hutchon, and McLuhan 1977, 1980), which emphasized having students go beyond the classroom to research the components of their media environments, such as light bulbs, newspapers, and, especially, television. I can only guess at what a high-school class based on that curriculum might have been like.

High School Communication Arts

Language, speech, and symbols, as well as writing and printing, are areas of interest in the field of communication and in the broader study of media that McLuhan introduced, but the only experience I had with any formal study of communication before college was when I took two classes in communication arts (on a quarterly system, the equivalent of one semester), which were offered as English electives in my high school. I should note at this point that I was in the first graduating class at Hillcrest High School in Queens, New York (TV stars Fran Drescher and Ray Romano were both a year behind me), which followed an innovative curriculum and structure based on the educational reform movement of the sixties and early seventies. Many in this movement were influenced by McLuhan's comments about the difficulty that young people, having been born into a media environment dominated by television and electronic technologies, faced in adjusting to a school environment shaped by print media and mechanical technologies.

As a high-school student, I was unaware of the larger context of the educational reform movement—that reformers had been arguing for greater relevance in the curriculum, as well as for more flexible structures—but I was impressed with all the talk about how innovative Hillcrest High School was. By senior year, however, it became clear to me that the innovations that had been introduced were either not particularly substantial (e.g., instead of semesters, the school year was divided into four quarters) or resulted in a less rigorous and effective form of schooling.

In any event, one aspect of Hillcrest's innovative approach was to offer elective courses in place of a traditional English curriculum. To be honest, it was only in my last quarter that I took a course on Shakespeare's comedies, realizing how ridiculous it would be to graduate high school without ever taking any Shakespeare at all. Sadly, I did graduate having studied almost no literature, as I was allowed to take mostly creative writing classes instead, as well as those two English electives in communication arts, a subject I had never heard of before. (Later on, educators would refer to that sort of class as "media literacy," but that designation was hardly a blip on the academic radar at that time.) The first quarter was on radio, the second on television. I imagine some mention was made of McLuhan at that time, but I can't remember anything specific, so I doubt there was anything more than a passing reference. All that I recall was being tested on our ability to memorize terms such as *pan, zoom, fade,* and *dissolve,* making communication arts a progressive subject approached in a regressive manner. I also remember the teacher setting up a video camera and monitor, giving us all a chance to look through the viewfinder, and to stand in front of the camera and see what we looked like on TV, which was quite new and exciting at that time. It was fun, but there was not much there that was particularly stimulating, intellectually. It probably was good preparation for working as a camera operator.

While I was in high school, I discovered another one of those pocket-sized paperbacks: *Future Shock,* by Alvin Toffler (1970). I bought my copy in a neighborhood candy store, and, incredibly, you could buy the book with a cover in one of four different colors. This seemed altogether futuristic, in keeping with the theme of the book, although it also illustrated one of the characteristics of the syndrome that gave the book its title: overchoice, having too many choices and no basis of deciding on one or another. But the book was exhilarating in its description of the massive social and cultural changes we were experiencing during the mid-twentieth century on account of technological innovation, scientific discovery, and innovations in communication. I found it very exciting to learn that I was coming of age during a pivotal moment in human history. *Future Shock* was the perfect work to ignite my teenage imagination, as a relatively accessible, popular work. Only later would I learn that it was somewhat derivative and something of a simplification of the work of media-ecology scholars such as McLuhan (and that the term *future shock* was first introduced by Neil Postman [see Postman 1988]). But Toffler got my feet wet and whetted my appetite for more, and I would eventually discover that many others found their way to McLuhan's ideas through such popularizations of his thought. Toffler's concept of future shock was included in an Introduction to Communication Theory course I took in my first semester of college at Cornell University, taught by the late Jack Barwind. It was in that same course that I was introduced to McLuhan's ideas for the first time, and I immediately found them appealing and inspiring. Also in that same course, I was introduced to related concepts from Harold Innis, Jacques Ellul, and Daniel Boorstin, as well as general semantics, general systems theory, and relational communication. It was not until I became a doctoral student, studying with Postman, that these and other ideas were tied together within the field of media ecology (see Strate 2006, 2014), but this first undergraduate course served as my formal introduction to an approach that McLuhan shared with several other scholars. As the field was unnamed, and its scholars not formally listed under the same heading or placed in the same category, all that could be said at the time was that they shared a common sensibility. And they were grouped together with other concepts and theories in communication studies that I found interesting, if nowhere near as heady. I had enrolled as a biology major, but after a few semesters in which I found the subject too technical for my tastes, I changed my major to communication arts and never looked back.

Reading McLuhan

And now I come to the confessional part of this chapter. My first confession is that when I first read McLuhan's *Understanding Media* in an upper-level undergraduate communication theory course, I had considerable difficulty understanding his writing. This was a great disappointment for me. When I first was introduced to McLuhan's basic ideas in Barwind's introductory lecture course, they made a great deal of sense to me. I could relate to the perspective and, in fact, embraced it beyond any other set of ideas I had encountered in my education. But McLuhan's writing style was oblique, full of puns, allusions, metaphors, non sequiturs, paradoxes, and paralogisms, and I had never encountered anything like it. Stylistically influenced by Joyce as he was, my own lack of literary education put me at a distinct disadvantage, although I was far from alone in finding him to be a challenging read. Jerome Agel, who produced McLuhan's best-selling book *The Medium Is the Massage: An Inventory of Effects* (McLuhan and Fiore 1967), would later tell me the following joke from the sixties: "Did you know that *Understanding Media* has been translated into over a dozen languages?" "Oh yeah? Has it been translated into English yet?" And speaking of *The Medium Is the Massage*, that book was on sale in our college bookstore, not as an assigned text for any course but just in the general reading section (college bookstores used to be more like neighborhood small or midsized bookstores, with only a small amount of space devoted to clothing and collegiate paraphernalia), so I decided to buy a copy. It was very intriguing in being full of illustrations, photographs, cartoons, and novel forms of typography. I had never seen anything like it, and indeed it was an unprecedented kind of book. Some dismissed it as a nonbook, but its innovations in graphic design proved to be enormously influential, not least in inspiring the look of *Wired* magazine a quarter of a century later.

Of course, I had no idea about any of this; I just hoped the book would provide me with a more accessible introduction to McLuhan's thought than *Understanding Media*, so I took it back to my room to read. And now comes my second confession. By the time I got to college, smoking marijuana was pretty much a commonplace activity that most students indulged in at least once or twice. Many indulged in the drug use purely for recreational pleasure, but some were also interested in using altered states of mind to better understand consciousness, both individually and collectively. I did not know it at the time, but Timothy Leary, the great proponent of the much more powerful psychedelic drug LSD, had claimed that McLuhan had given him the slogan "Turn on, tune in, and drop out." McLuhan denied the connection, but certainly the "tune in" part was derived from McLuhan's emphasis on the mind-altering qualities of the television medium, and McLuhan did coauthor a book titled *Take Today: The Executive as Dropout* (McLuhan and Nevitt 1972). The point of all this is that I inhaled, as the saying goes (or as Barack Obama put it in response to a query, "I inhaled. That was the point" [Seelye 2006]). And I inhaled *The Medium Is the Massage* as well, reading it in about half an hour.

And at that moment, I was able to say, "I got it! I got McLuhan!" The experience of suddenly *getting* McLuhan has been described as akin to a religious experience by some or in more general terms as an epiphany; to use a term popular during the sixties, I was able to *grok* McLuhan (*grok* was coined by the science-fiction writer Robert Heinlein in his novel *Stranger in a Strange Land* to refer to an extreme form of understanding and empathy). In visual terms, it was the kind of experience depicted in comic strips of a light bulb being switched on over a character's head, which would certainly be fitting, given that McLuhan argued that electric technology and electronic media constituted the basis of a revolution that was reversing the course of some three millennia of Western civilization. Television was the specific electronic medium that had pushed our culture over the edge, he argued, and one of the characteristics of television was its low resolution image, which McLuhan compared to that of the printed cartoon, which elevated the comics medium in importance (see Scott McCloud's insightful, McLuhan-inspired graphic nonfiction, *Understanding Comics* [1993]). This idea had no small significance for me because I had been reading comics since before I could read (my parents read them to me), despite the fact that the hybrid medium was often disparaged by teachers and others arguing in defense of elitist literary culture. The fact that comics crossed—or, if you like, transgressed—the boundary between literate and pictorial media contributed to my own developing awareness of differences among media, differences in their biases towards different types of content, differences in their effects on the ways we think, feel, act, perceive, and organize ourselves, differences that McLuhan famously summed up by saying, "The medium is the message" (1964, 7).

The image of a light bulb turning on is a visual metaphor for an idea (the word is derived from the Greek term for *seeing*) and perhaps the most basic way of describing the effect of my reading *The Medium Is the Massage* was that I was suddenly able to see the world from an entirely new perspective (in addition to being a field or intellectual tradition, media ecology has often been referred to as a perspective, although I prefer to use *approach* in order to avoid the visual metaphor). Or, to invoke Aldous Huxley's (1954) well-known phrase, used to describe his experiments with hallucinogens, the "doors of perception" suddenly opened for me. The reference to perception is particularly significant because McLuhan's specific approach to media ecology emphasized the primary role that sensory organs play in our thought processes.

In this, he followed the philosophy of the medieval Roman Catholic theologian, Thomas Aquinas, who argued that all that we know is based on what we take in through our senses, a position that resonated powerfully with the mid-twentieth-century zeitgeist that McLuhan was a part of. McLuhan characterized Western civilization as one in which alphabetic literacy had placed unprecedented emphasis on the visual sense alone, training the eye to focus on the world from a fixed point of view, stressing the linear and sequential and a one-thing-at-a-time mentality. Before writing and the alphabet, the different senses functioned in a balanced and coordinated manner worked out by biological evolution, one in which hearing had particular prominence as the sense through which the word, language in the form of speech, was communicated. Then came the silence of the literate world, which was broken by the electronic media, with its transmission and playback of sound; the linearity of the alphabet was disrupted by the electronic circuit and rippling broadcast waves, restoring some element of sensory balance and giving rise to new forms of tribalism on a massive scale—the "global village," as McLuhan (1962, 36) put it. This was entirely consonant with the world of record albums, stereo systems, and electronically amplified instruments that I inhabited as a college student. Coming to a clear understanding of the distinct differences between hearing and seeing, between the ways in which the ear and the eye mediate our experience of the world, is essential to unlocking McLuhan's approach to understanding media (Strate and Wachtel 2005).

One of the currents that ran through this period was the importance of retrieving a prelinguistic state of mind. It was the understanding that our thought processes were mediated and dominated, if not entirely monopolized, by language and that thinking was a kind of inner dialogue or monologue, a narration that interfered with pure perception, with seeing things in a relatively unmediated, novel, and creative way. Many advocated getting back to viewing the world without immediately attaching names and labels to the objects of our perception, from physicists such as J. Robert Oppenheimer to celebrants of psychedelic experience like Huxley and Leary, as well as practitioners of Transcendental Meditation and other New Age mavens (including Carlos Castaneda, whose books made a strong impression on me as a teenager and who turned out to be one of Edmund Carpenter's students). Through my own experimentation, I learned how to achieve a quiet state of mind and to concentrate on sense perception alone, and that experience with altered states informed and enabled my understanding of McLuhan when I first sat down to read *The Medium Is the Massage.*

I hasten to add that much of the credit goes to the innovative graphic design of the book itself, which helped show, illustrate—indeed, embody—McLuhan's ideas in ways that I could relate to and readily absorb, independent of any particular mental state. And by reducing his prose down to smaller, more manageable chunks, like poetry, I could make sense of his philosophy of media. Reading McLuhan otherwise has quite accurately been described as trying to drink from a fire hose. I also want to stress that this was the beginning, not the end, of my story. The door was open, but to enter required many years of study, and as I progressed from undergraduate to graduate work and from an M.A. to a Ph.D. program, I found that I needed a clear head and unimpeded linguistic ability both for reading and for writing. I came to the conclusion that McLuhan's thought, and the insights of other media-ecology scholars, can be explained in clear and logical terms (see, for example, Strate 2005, 2008). The kind of quantum leap that so many of us had experienced was necessary because of the way that McLuhan communicated, and it was the kind of intellectual slap in the face that was needed at that time to wake us sleepwalkers up from the dream state that three millennia of alphabetic culture had imposed on Westerners. But I suspect that kind of wake-up call is less necessary these days, and I also have found that it is possible to generate the same kind of shift in orientation and approach through less drastic means, by unpacking McLuhan's ideas and presenting media ecology as a field and intellectual tradition in a straightforward manner (see, for example, Strate 2006, 2014). But McLuhan's writings remain a great source of scholarly ferment, as well as creative inspiration (e.g., Strate and Karasick 2014), and I take great pleasure in introducing students to books like *Understanding Media*, *The Gutenberg Galaxy*, *The Mechanical Bride*, *Media and Formal Cause* (McLuhan and McLuhan 2011), and of course, *The Medium Is the Massage.*

Lessons Learned

What I have learned from McLuhan is first and foremost how absolutely essential media education is, not just in producing well-rounded individuals properly prepared for successful careers in a world dominated by electronic and digital communications but for the future of citizenship, justice, and democracy in a society in which public discourse, political action, and our collective business in its entirety is conducted through or with the aid of various forms of new media. Indeed, media education is essential to our reclaiming some measure of control over our world and may well be the key to our ongoing survival as a species. McLuhan made it clear that this has to begin with a wake-up call. Along with other media-ecology scholars, he used the metaphor of the invisible environment to refer to the fact that we tend to focus on the content of communication and ignore the medium used to convey those messages. We are conscious of the medium itself when it is brand new, but as soon as the novelty wears off, the medium becomes part of a routine, fading into the background and becoming functionally transparent to us. Typically, the medium itself will be brought back into our awareness only when it breaks down or becomes obsolete. The first goal of media education is to restore the sense of novelty, that experience of strangeness, that we so easily lose regarding our modes of communication, to distance ourselves from our media and learn to look at them rather than through them.

The second goal is to focus on their differences and, following Gregory Bateson (1972), those differences that make a difference. As

I have noted, this can begin with an understanding of how different modes of sense perception yield different experiences of the world: for example, the differences between seeing and hearing. The body and the nervous system are our primary media, and differences in biological structure lead to differences in perception, cognition, emotion, and behavior. Language is the mode of communication that is most distinctive to the human species, providing us with our tools for thought and shaping our attention, perception, and memory. It follows that different languages provide us with different ways of viewing and experiencing the world and, thus, different ways of thinking and feeling and acting. One of McLuhan's basic points is that languages are a form of media, and that a medium can be understood as a language in its own right, with its own particular vocabulary and grammar and its own way of helping us to know about the world and ourselves. *Media* is a plural noun, and each medium has its own biases towards certain forms of expression and understanding.

I prefer not to use terms like *media literacy* and *digital literacy* in my approach to media education because I am concerned that they obscure the distinctive quality of *literacy* as it refers to the ability to read and write—that is, to work with the written word as a medium. When it comes to differences that make a difference, there is no sharper contrast than that between words and images (Strate 2014), which is why a phrase like *visual literacy* strikes me as a contradiction in terms. Moreover, understanding the differences between speech, the acoustic medium that forms the basis of all human languages, and writing, the visual medium used to represent, preserve, and transmit the spoken word, is central to McLuhan's approach (see also Ong 1982). For McLuhan, it was language, not literacy, that was the key metaphor, although he was certainly sympathetic to the idea behind media literacy, and his work constitutes an important foundation for the field and movement. McLuhan was, in fact, very sensitive to the role that metaphors play in our thinking about the world, and he argued that media themselves constitute metaphors (e.g., a person is like an open book, life is like a movie, the mind is like a computer) and that technology is a means of translating experience (as, for example, a lever is used to translate force, amplifying it from the arm to the object to be moved). It might follow that I would prefer a term consistent with the view of media as language, and in this respect *media fluency* comes to mind (which has a nice resonance with the use of *flow* as metaphor for electricity), but I think the clearest and most straightforward phrase to use in this context is simply *media education.*

I have also used the term *media ecology,* in conjunction with McLuhan, to suggest a particular approach and field of study in which media are studied as environments. This is another metaphor, to be sure, but one that emphasizes the idea that media are not only tools that we use but also environments that envelop us, that we find ourselves immersed within, which underscores the fact that they influence and shape us individually and collectively. Language and symbolic communication are what makes us human, and we depended on speech alone for tens of thousands of years, living in tribal societies. The invention of forms of notation, and especially writing, has been associated with the development of complex societies in the ancient world, and the specific form of writing called the alphabet was the basis of the distinctive characteristics of Western cultures. The modern world began with the printing revolution begun by Gutenberg in the fifteenth century, continued with electronic technologies beginning with the telegraph in the early nineteenth century, and culminated with television in the mid-twentieth century. Television brought the modern era to a close and thrust us into an entirely new moment in human history, one that continues to evolve through the addition of various forms of digital technology. Media education, in my view, is about much more than learning how to use and decode various types of media; it is about understanding how media have affected and continue to alter the human psyche, society, and culture.

For me, the foundation of media education is the idea that the medium is the message, which I take to mean that we should pay attention to the question of *how,* that the way that we do things has much to do with what we end up doing and what we end up with when we do them. It means that we need to stop ignoring form in favor of content. We need to learn to recognize the patterns and relationships that surround us by understanding *media* as a term that refers to all codes and modes of communication: face-to-face situations and actual locations as well as gadgets and devices. It also means attending to methods, to all manner of technology and technique, as they mediate between ourselves and our environment. Media function as our environments because they are the means through which we relate to our world; they are the ways in which we perceive and experience our environment and the ways in which we act on and modify our environment, and they constitute the artificial environment that we have constructed to shield us from the world as it might otherwise exist. For me, then, media education is essential to fully understanding our world, its history, and its future and our place in it as human beings, not to mention what the prospects are for the survival of our species and how we might sustain ourselves without sacrificing our humanity.

REFERENCES

Bateson, G. 1972. *Steps to an Ecology of Mind: Collected Essays in Anthropology, Psychiatry, Evolution, and Epistemology*. New York: Bantam Books.

Carpenter, E., and M. McLuhan. 1960. *Explorations in Communication*. Boston: Beacon Press.

Epstein, S., and B. Epstein. 1964. *What's Behind the Word?* New York: Scholastic.

Haslam, G., and J. Haslam. 2011. *In Thought and Action: The Enigmatic Life of S. I. Hayakawa*. Lincoln: University of Nebraska Press.

Huxley, A. 1954. *The Doors of Perception*. New York: Harper and Row.

Innis, H. A. 1950. *Empire and Communications*. Oxford: Clarendon Press.

———. 1951. *The Bias of Communication*. Toronto: University of Toronto Press.

Lee, D. 1959. *Freedom and Culture*. Englewood Cliffs, NJ: Prentice-Hall.

McCloud, S. 1993. *Understanding Comics: The Invisible Art*. New York: Paradox Press.

McLuhan, M. 1951. *The Mechanical Bride: Folklore of Industrial Man*. New York: Vanguard.

———. 1960. *Report on Project in Understanding New Media*. Washington, DC: U.S. Department of Health.

———. 1962. *The Gutenberg Galaxy: The Making of Typographic Man*. Toronto: University of Toronto Press.

———. 1964. *Understanding Media: The Extensions of Man*. New York: McGraw-Hill.

McLuhan, M., and Q. Fiore. 1967. *The Medium Is the Massage: An Inventory of Effects*. New York: Bantam.

McLuhan, M., K. Hutchon, and E. McLuhan. 1977. *City as Classroom: Understanding Language and Media*. Agincourt, ON: Book Society of Canada.

———. 1980. *Media, Messages, and Language: The World as Your Classroom*. New York: National Textbook.

McLuhan, M., and E. McLuhan. 2011. *Media and Formal Cause*. Houston: NeoPoiesis Press.

McLuhan, M., and B. Nevitt. 1972. *Take Today: The Executive as Dropout*. New York: Harcourt Brace Jovanovich.

Ogden, C. K., and I. A. Richards. 1923. *The Meaning of Meaning: A Study of the Influence of Language upon Thought and of the Science of Symbolism*. New York: Harcourt, Brace.

Ong, W. J. 1982. *Orality and Literacy: The Technologizing of the Word*. London: Routledge.

Postman, N. 1988. *Conscientious Objections: Stirring up Trouble about Language, Technology, and Education*. New York: Alfred A. Knopf.

Sapir, E. 1921. *Language: An Introduction to the Study of Speech*. New York: Harcourt Brace Jovanovich.

Seelye, K. Q. 2006. "Barack Obama, Asked about Drug History, Admits He Inhaled." *New York Times*, October 24. Available at http://www.nytimes.com/2006/10/24/world/americas/24iht-dems.3272493.html.

Strate, L. 2005. "Media Transcendence." In *The Legacy of McLuhan*, edited by Lance Strate and Edward Wachtel, 25–33. Cresskill, NJ: Hampton Press.

———. 2006. *Echoes and Reflections: On Media Ecology as a Field of Study*. Cresskill, NJ: Hampton Press.

———. 2008. "Studying Media *as* Media: McLuhan and the Media Ecology Approach." *Media Tropes* 1:127–142.

———. 2011. *On the Binding Biases of Time and Other Essays on General Semantics and Media Ecology*. Fort Worth, TX: Institute of General Semantics.

———. 2014. *Amazing Ourselves to Death: Neil Postman's Brave New World Revisited*. New York: Peter Lang.

Strate, L., and A. Karasick. 2014. *The Medium Is the Muse: Channeling Marshall McLuhan*. Seattle: NeoPoiesis Press.

Strate, L., and E. Wachtel. 2005. *The Legacy of McLuhan*. Cresskill, NJ: Hampton Press.

Toffler, A. 1970. *Future Shock*. New York: Random House.

Whorf, B. L. 1956. *Language, Thought, and Reality*. Cambridge, MA: MIT Press.

4 /

Dana Polan on Roland Barthes

DANA POLAN

During my junior-high and high-school years, I had had two leisure pursuits: amateur radio and moviegoing. In engaging in the latter, I could see from the films of the moment, which increasingly were coming to challenge both older proprieties (with new subject matter dealing with violence and sexuality, among other issues) and older storytelling norms, that something was going on with the art form that merited attention. The newest cinema was, in fact, increasingly getting attention from critics who had to deal not only with common Hollywood fare but also with cutting-edge experimentation. But these critics didn't seem so much to be studying cinema as responding to it intuitively, directly, and even viscerally. Pauline Kael, the standout critic who most seemed alive to new currents in movies, wrote bristling essays that were quickly collected into books with kinetic, physical, and dynamic titles like *Kiss Kiss Bang Bang* (1968). She also, in a sort of potential anti-intellectualism, notoriously attacked scholars like the émigré intellectual Siegfried Kracauer, who had dared—scandal of scandals, as Kael saw it—to offer up a full-length *Theory of Film* (1960).

Not seeing from the critics how film could be an object of study, I didn't imagine it as a career path for me (I wasn't interested in production, just cinema appreciation), and my high-school guidance counselor concurred that this was not something for me to pursue, with the additional assumption on her part that, in any case, film was too much a form of popular diversion or escapism to even be worthy of study. Instead, she locked onto the fact that I also did amateur radio and suggested that, since it involved wires and vacuum tubes and the like, I should go into electrical engineering. Such were the arbitrary decisions that made many career paths in those days of guidance counseling in small-town America. I began a B.S. in engineering at Rensselaer Polytechnic Institute (RPI) in Troy, New York.

I made two discoveries pretty quickly. First, I had no aptitude for math, which you need a lot of to be an engineer. Second, RPI had two professors who taught film classes (they were not full-fledged cinema scholars but were branching into this hot new area from more traditional parts of the humanities), which suggested that somehow film could be studied. Of course, that fact, in itself, didn't suggest how one prepared for film study or even how film study itself should proceed. Indeed, one of the two professors (whose name I've forgotten) did little in his course but show films and ask us about particular shots and how they were, to his mind, composed according to classic art precepts. We looked at balance and harmony in the frame and things like that, and while it all was no doubt useful in getting us to think of the visual aspects of cinema (whereas the tendency for the young student—still apparent today in our students—was to focus on plot and character), it didn't go beyond simple appreciation of compositional design. I remember, for instance, wondering about the moving images that clearly made up films and how that dynamism might change the meanings we could attribute to static scenes. Although I now understood that one could teach cinema, I wasn't yet convinced that this commentary on single images was the only way to do it. And even had I liked the art-history angle, it seemed to involve little more than just saying what you saw on the frozen screen before you, which didn't seem very analytic. I wasn't satisfied with the RPI professor's approach and was perhaps already sensing, although I wouldn't have been able to formulate the thought at the time, that humanistic study needs both a coherent method *and* the underlying principles that give that method purpose and reach.

At the beginning of the 1970s, when I transferred to Cornell University in search of a liberal arts education that would give grounding to my budding interest in cinema appreciation, it turned out that French theory, which at that point primarily meant structuralism and semiotics with some beginning glimpses of the poststructuralism that would challenge the claims to objectivity of these methods, was all the rage in cutting-edge departments in the humanities. This was true even in disciplines that might have claimed a greater adhesion to social-science principles than those of the humanities. I remember, for instance, one session of Dominick La Capra's course, Twentieth-Century Intellectual History (which met on Thursdays), when he breathlessly announced that the previous Tuesday he had started reading the just-published translation (in the French-inflected journal *New Literary History*) of Jacques Derrida's "White Mythology" and wanted to talk about this important work a bit, although his first impressions were still inchoate. To be there as ideas seemed literally to be brewing before you was intensely inspiring for young scholars (and I've tried over the years to replay that breathless enthusiasm at first contact with great thoughts as I work with my own students).

My film study at Cornell came to entail not only extensive viewing but, in the energetic context of Cornell's investment in French theory, intensive reading. (Reading was something I hadn't really realized you needed for film appreciation; I assumed you watched the films and their resonant power announced itself to you directly, and it's true that there was an energy and mix of viscerality and cerebrality to the cutting-edge films of the times that meant they often did seem to speak in direct fashion to the hip viewer.)

Structuralism and Mass Culture

Structuralism captured how diverse cultural productions shared regularities in their makeup (that is, in their underlying structure), whether it be Tzvetan Todorov on the codified pivotal moments in the literature of the fantastic, Vladimir Propp on the narrative consistencies in Russian folktale, or Umberto Eco on the basic formula for James Bond stories. Many of these texts were appearing in English translation at just the moment when I was beginning my study, so, even though I could read French, there was the excitement of the newly new, the immediately available, coming onto the scene with direct impact. Of the influential texts that I would characterize as structuralist, the most significant one wouldn't have its translation until the 1980s, so I had to slog (and it often indeed was a slog) through its recondite, even dry French prose: this text was *Système de la mode* (*The Fashion System*) by Roland Barthes, which set out to establish some fundamentals of structuralist methodology by taking fashion slogans (i.e., the captions that accompanied fashion photos in popular magazines) and submitting them to extended analysis. Barthes examined how the captions commonly designated an object (say, a sweater) and a support for a variant (say, a collar which could either be wide or narrow or lacy or solid or whatever), and I've always thought his attempt to render the regularity of the structure by the abbreviation OSV (object/support/variant) offered resemblance to the basic structure of a sentence (SVO: subject/verb/object). In other words, it seemed to me that Barthes was suggesting that fashion statements were modeled on the more fundamental form of statement that is the linguistic utterance per se. For all its user-unfriendly dryness, Barthes's argument that phenomena of everyday life other than direct linguistic communication—in this case, discourses of advertising in the world of fashion—were basic acts by which a society spoke to itself and spoke of its values struck me as exciting and still does.

Even more consequential for me, though, was another of Barthes's books, which I encountered early on in my time at Cornell: *Mythologies* ([1957] 2012), a book that made him known to a wide part of the French public and thereby made him an important public intellectual. Significantly, I came to read Barthes in one of the courses for the basic French language sequence: compared with usual suspects like Ionesco's *The Bald Soprano*, *Mythologies* was much more in keeping with the sense, at Cornell, that Theory was everywhere and could help you at everything, even basic language instruction with its rote drills and so on.

Bringing together most of a series of essayistic reflections that Barthes had been fashioning on a monthly basis for the journal *Lettres Nouvelles* (plus two pieces from other publications) on objects, phenomena, and key practices of contemporary mass culture, *Mythologies* stands as one of the first concerted modern attempts to attend closely to the concrete operations of mass culture as ideological practice. The volume gains additional value from a long theoretical postscript, "The Myth Today," that Barthes penned in 1957 after he had concluded his series of little examinations of French everyday life. He appended the postscript to these mini-studies, the individual "mythologies" of French life, to seem to grant them the rigor of quasi-scientific method: although the analyses themselves tended to eschew jargon and high theoretical formulation for more journalistic commentary, "The Myth Today" claimed that underlying each of Barthes's disquisitions on specific practices of mass culture was a grounding of analysis in that fairly new methodology known as semiology (the science of signs, here understood as the taking of mass cultural phenomena as so many loaded messages addressed to everyday citizens). Barthes had, in fact, been grappling with semiological theory from the end of the 1940s, when Claude Lévi-Strauss and A. J. Greimas had first recommended some key readings to him, and *Mythologies* certainly can give the impression of a gap between the essayistic mythological readings themselves and the more formal, even dogmatic theoretical framework offered up by "The Myth Today."

Overall, it is the book's combination of the very concrete in its often harsh reflections on individual practices of mass culture and its appeal to a very modern theoretical apparatus that it claimed anchored those reflections in rigorous methodology that has made the book a canonic work of mass culture analysis. This combination pulled me to it immediately.

Close Reading

One of the most-famed mythological analyses, "The Great Family of Man," which comes toward the end of *Mythologies*, can serve as a useful condensation of many of the operations and arguments that Barthes brings to bear on contemporary mass culture. Often singled out in studies on Barthes—rightfully so, since it does capture his ideological critique at its sharpest—the piece takes as its target a traveling exhibit by the American photographer Edward Steichen that originally bore the name *The Family of Man* but was retitled *The Great Family of Men (la grande famille des hommes)* when it came to Paris in 1956. The exhibit offered images of humans from around the globe, being birthed, laboring, sustaining themselves, loving each other, and dying.

In Barthes's analysis, the exhibit's intent is to deny specific human situations (for example, the quite pointed differences in the ways diverse populations come into the world and live and die within it) for the sake of a generalization about a supposed universal human condition. In his sardonic summary of the exhibit's ideology, "man is born, works, laughs and dies in the same fashion everywhere; and if in these actions some ethnic particularity subsists, there is now some understanding that there is deep inside each one of us an identical 'nature,' that their diversity is merely formal and does not belie the existence of a common matrix" ([1957] 2012, 196–197). The effects of this universalization are several. First, the human adventure (along with the very idea that, indeed, there is one single such adventure) is rendered in sentimental terms (we all are born, we all die; that's what human existence is all about). Second, by assuming we are all put on the earth in the same way and to the same ends, the exhibit can easily slide beyond mere sentiment toward religiosity—what Barthes terms a "pietistic intention" that readily imagines we are all here for one purpose: in Barthes's words, "God is reintroduced into our Exhibition: the diversity of mankind proclaims his richness, his power; the unity of its actions demonstrates his will" (197).

Finally, and most importantly, the assumption of a universal human condition—across time, across cultures—encourages passivity: if this is our fate, if this is our nature, then there is no reason to try to change things. But, as Barthes counters, even if we all are born, live, and die, we don't always do so in equivalent ways, and we don't necessarily have to do so in the ways that this or that society has tried to determine for us. We can fight to change our destiny. As Barthes proclaims, "Whether or not the child is born with ease or difficulty, whether or not he causes his mother suffering at birth, whether the child lives or dies, and, if he lives, whether he accedes to some sort of future—this, and not the eternal lyric of birth, should be the subject of our Exhibitions. And the same applies to death: Are we really to sing its essence once again and thereby risk forgetting that we can still do so much against it?" ([1957] 2012, 198). Thus, in a blunt example, Barthes cites the savage lynching at the hand of Southern white racists of the African American boy Emmett Till the year before the *Family of Man* exhibit came to Paris: yes, Till died, and we all will, but his early, horrific death had fully historical, fully social causalities behind it—ones that shouldn't have existed in a society that declares itself democratic, ones that should no longer exist and that one might fight to make sure no longer exist.

The great resonance of *Mythologies* within the history of mass-culture study derives first of all from the sheer mass, the very diversity, of commodity practices that Barthes draws on from across a vast range of modern everyday life. To the extent that dominant ideology operates by means of the grafting a set of very specific (and circumscribed) values onto the objects and practices of the world, semiology becomes interlinked with ideology critique: the mythologist studies bourgeois acts of signification—especially in their internal workings in the construction of socially tendentious meanings—in all sort of things, from words and pictures to gadgets and gizmos to comestibles. As Barthes himself asserts, "The whole of France is steeped in this anonymous ideology: our press, our films, our theater, our pulp literature, our rituals, our Justice, our diplomacy, our conversation, our remarks about the weather, a murder trial, a touching wedding, the cooking we dream of, the garments we wear, everything, in everyday life, is dependent on the representations which the bourgeoisie *has and makes us have* of the relations between the man and the world" ([1957] 2012, 252; emphasis in original). That every practice of the social world could be read as ideological was a first attraction of *Mythologies* for a budding theorist like myself.

But Barthes continues, "It is through its ethic that the bourgeoisie pervades France: practiced on a national scale, bourgeois norms are experienced as the evident laws of a natural order—the further the bourgeois class propagates its representations, the more naturalized it becomes" ([1957] 2012, 252), and here we see a second, consequential aspect of Barthes's volume. It is not just that he analyzes lots of different phenomena from modern French life but that he incessantly brings them back to a common core: whether foods or cars or faces in mass periodicals, the objects of French middle-class life, when consumed, endlessly convey a common and circumscribed set of significations. Whatever the diversity of things that embody it, the dominant system of French values is an insistent, even overwhelming, repetition of the same (of the same values, that is, and of the same ideological operations).

Although *Mythologies* appeared more than a decade earlier than the famous argument by the French Marxist Louis Althusser (1971) that ideology operates by means of an interpellation of social subjects, a hailing by which they are made to assume proper position in the dominant order of things, Barthes's work anticipates Althusser's in viewing mass culture as a set of insistent intentions that work effectively on social subjects in ways that are hard to resist. As Barthes puts it, "Myth has an imperative, buttonholing character. . . . It is *I* who it has come to seek. It has turned toward me, I am subjected to its intentional force, it summons me to receive its expansive ambiguity. . . . [T]his interpellant speech is at the same time a frozen speech" ([1957] 2012, 234–235).

At this moment in his writerly trajectory, Barthes was very much inspired by a Marxist theory of alienation in which, under capitalism, the meaningfulness of human labor is taken away from the laborer to return to him or her in alienated form (for example, a separation of the worker from any real say in the making of the products of his or her labor or the uses to which they are to be put). Contrasting such capitalist alienation, Barthes asks the reader to imagine what he claims is the unalienated labor of a "woodcutter": "If I am a woodcutter and I am led to name the tree I am felling, whatever the form of my sentence, I 'speak' the tree, I do not speak about it. This means that my language is operational, transitively linked to its object; between the tree and myself, there is nothing but my labor, that is to say, an action" ([1957] 2012, 258). (One inspiration for Barthes might be the famous encounter in Jean-Paul Sartre's 1938 novel *Nausea* of the existentially questioning protagonist-narrator Roquentin with a tree that comes to stand for him as ultimate fact of the primal, fundamental being of the world, beyond all sociality, beyond all humanly imposed meanings.)

Where I found Barthes's targeting of the ideological operations of everyday culture eye-opening, I couldn't help but find the idea of a realm supposedly outside ideology, like that of the woodcutter off in some idyllic communion with nature, potentially quite troublesome. In Marxist terms, the claim here is that the woodcutter engages in a direct, unmediated, unalienated, and, therefore, authentic praxis. Needing to intervene directly in the world, the woodcutter, for Barthes, moves in a realm outside ideology. But we might well question whether such a realm of supposedly pure and pristine labor as the woodcutter's exists, at least in any substantial, meaningful way after the mid-1950s. Perhaps there were such pure woodsmen here and there within the space of modernity, but the image seems out-of-date, mythicized in its own manner.

As became clear to me as I read more semiological theory, much of the problem in Barthes's approach derived from the very semiological model that Barthes employed in the 1950s in *Mythologies* and into the 1960s; specifically, Barthes took from the Danish linguist Louis Hjelmslev an opposition between denotation as the literal, first meaning in a signification and connotation as new values added in particular situations to primary meaning and sending it in new directions. Barthes then grafted this opposition onto the theorization of ideology defined as the adding of tendentious, unnatural signification to a more primary, more primal relation to the natural. To take the most famous example from *Mythologies*, a photograph of a young black man in a French uniform saluting the flag appears on the cover of an issue of *Paris-Match*, which Barthes comes across in a barber shop. The photograph uses a first level of truth—insofar as he was photographed, it would seem true that this black man actually did salute the flag—to build up and shore up a tendentious, underlying message that goes something like "Being part of the imperial nation of France is natural, even for a colonized subject" ([1957] 2012, 225).

The conceptual (and political) problem here is not in the assumption that social connotations are always being added to first-level significations but in the idea that the latter are somehow initially free of connotation and start out from some level of pure denotation. In the example of the young, saluting black man, Barthes wants to argue that there are meanings to this figure (for instance, the irreducible details of his life) that exist prior to his embodiment on the *Paris-Match* cover, some of which the cover needs to gloss over in order to do its ideological work. This glossing over is necessary, since if the viewer focuses too much on the details of the first level of meaning—for instance, on contingent details in the photo or wondering too much about those irreducible life details—it becomes harder for the image to abstract away from it to make generalizable ideological assertions. A photograph appears to capture more of the surface truth of the world than, say, a verbal phrase or a drawing, and that is both its power and its weakness when marshaled in the cause of broad arguments. But in using a before-after model (connotation builds on denotation and thus comes after it), Barthes risked the implication that there was a first realm that could have ever been free of social meanings, that somehow signified the world directly and not through context. Quite the contrary, the young black man certainly gains new social meanings when he is put on the cover of a mass-market periodical, but he already would have had social meanings in the contingency of his life: how he came into French imperiality and what that says about the life he has been able to lead is already social, through and through.

By the time Barthes had completed his book *S/Z*, at the beginning of the 1970s, he was still insisting on the theoretical value of the concept of connotation, as well he should have, but he was also beginning to reject the power of the concept of denotation, as well he also should have. As he now put it, "Denotation is not the first meaning but pretends to be so; . . . it is ultimately the last of connotations . . . , the superior myth by which the text pretends to return to the nature of language, the language of nature" ([1970] 1975, 7, 9). In other words, all meanings, all human acts, are social and contextual. There is no pre-social meaning that would be literal and free of connotation.

I read *S/Z* in my senior year at Cornell in a graduate seminar devoted just to it, and it soon became the decisive Barthes text for me. We might contrast the short and pithy readings Barthes enacts in *Mythologies*, finding the recurrent operations of bourgeois everywhere, to his slow-motion dissection of a single Balzac story over hundreds of pages in *S/Z*: there, Barthes uses close reading to capture Balzac's text as caught between realism and modernism, between representation and its delirious breakdown, and between depiction of an older social order's stability and the invocation of the new, unfixed social relations of an expansive capitalism geared to creative destruction. I had taken to heart Barthes's insistent demonstration in *Mythologies* of the incessant operations of ideology in mass culture, but *S/Z* offered nuance, detail, a concern with contradiction, and a deeper sense of history (not all texts across time are ideological in the same way and to the same degree).

Roland Barthes has stayed with me as an inspiration (although I generally find his writings after *S/Z* up to his death in 1980 much less useful to the project of historical and ideological analysis that I continue to engage in). I've taught seminars on him over the years, and each time I see the spark that occurs when students engage with works like *Mythologies* and *S/Z*. But I also feel the spark anew myself, as I find myself learning again and remembering why Theory mattered—and continues to matter.

REFERENCES

Althusser, L. 1971. "Ideology and Ideological State Apparatuses." In *Lenin and Philosophy and Other Essays*, translated by B. Brewster, 85–126. New York: Monthly Review Press.

Barthes, R. (1957) 2012. *Mythologies*. Translated by R. Howard and A. Lavers. New York: Hill and Wang.

———. (1970) 1975. *S/Z*. Translated by R. Miller. New York: Hill and Wang.

Kael, P. 1968. *Kiss Kiss Bang Bang.* Boston: Little, Brown.

Kracauer, S. 1960. *Theory of Film: The Redemption of Physical Reality.* New York: Oxford University Press.

5 /

Cynthia Lewis on Mikhail Bakhtin

CYNTHIA LEWIS

When I was an undergraduate literature student at the University of Illinois, I fell in love with Fyodor Dostoevsky. I was attracted to all nineteenth-century Russian literature, perhaps because my grandparents, who lived with my family, were turn-of-century immigrant Russian Jews whose interactional dynamics resonated, for me, in these novels. Reading them was an aesthetic, personal, and pleasurable experience, as I became immersed in the characters' cadences that fueled my childhood memories. And even after later learning about Dostoevsky's anti-Semitism, I continued to feel a strong connection to Dostoevsky's novel *The Brothers Karamazov* ([1880] 1992) for its narrative point of view and uses of dialogue, which continue to connect me to my childhood— in particular, to the tradition of D'var Torah as part of the Bar/Bat Mitzvah ceremony. This tradition involves thirteen-year-olds interpreting portions of the Torah. The young interpreters are taught that they are entering a conversation that includes two thousand years of interpreters—rabbinical scholars—whose competing perspectives and translations are an expected and accepted part of the dialogue. In other words, the presence of other interpreters always already exists in the words, the language of the text, and the interpreter. As Mikhail

Bakhtin would have it, "The word in language is half someone else's," meaning that language is foundationally dialogic, intertextual, and heteroglossic and that every utterance contains the traces of prior and future utterances (1982, 294). Thus, there were connections, for me, from Dostoevsky to my family's conversations—rife with overlapping turns and competing perspectives—to Bakhtin and back again to Dostoevsky (whom Bakhtin explicates in his book *Problems of Dostoevsky's Poetics* [1984]).

In graduate school, my interest in literature turned to teaching and learning, specifically how young people make meanings of literature and other signs, both as reader-interpreters and as writer-producers. Thus, my thoughts about Bakhtin are connected to my interests as a researcher whose work uses sociocultural theory, ethnography, and discourse analysis to study literacy, media education, and learning. When I read *The Dialogic Imagination* and *Speech Genres*, I understood, through Bakhtin's lens of dialogism, not only how heteroglossic voices converge and collide in literature but also how all signs are thus constituted. In this way, Bakhtin's philosophy of language mirrors that of his close colleague Valentin Voloshinov (1973), who argues that the sign is inevitably a site of struggle. As Janet Maybin puts it in her explication of Bakhtin's philosophy of language, "Language originates in social interactions and struggle and these are always implicated in its use and meaning" (2001, 64). In *Speech Genres*, Bakhtin makes it clear that genres arise and shift in and through these struggles. The "signs" of faith, doubt, responsibility, morality, and so on are all sites of struggle played out through language in *The Brothers Karamazov*—with each utterance responding to and anticipating other utterances in a polyphony of voices.

In Bakhtin's world, polyphonic texts are not benignly so. Evaluations are produced through double-voiced texts, in which meanings are refracted through authorial interventions such as parody or irony. The same is true in social settings outside the novel, in our everyday reporting of the speech of others—the way we animate, as though we are the speakers, inflecting the speech with our own ideological formations. For example, a teacher who participated in an ethnographic study I conducted in a high-school classroom was helping students understand an indigenous scholar's perspective on the 1995 Disney film *Pocahontas*. As part of her pedagogy, she used direct and indirect forms of reported speech (see Bakhtin 1982) to position herself in relation to the scholar's text and the film:

Okay, so back when the Europeans came, they considered themselves superior—better than—the Native Americans. Okay. They said, "Well, look at us; we're civilized," 'kay. "We live a certain way. We—we consider ourselves to have the correct religion. We consider ourselves to be—we're gonna all go to heaven because we believe in a certain kind of god," right.

Here, she animates the speech of the colonizers through her own voice, inflected with sarcasm to make sure it is understood that she did not author these words. She surrounds these utterances with indirect reporting (e.g., "they said" and "right") to remind her students of her own distance from the colonizers. Her evaluation is clear and she has positioned her students not only to understand the scholar's ideology but to see that ideology as the one that is most aligned with the position of indigenous people who were oppressed by the colonists.

Bakhtin was interested in signs within their social contexts—language in use, in all its complexity. He and his circle were responding to the literary and semiotic theories of their time. Conventional scholarship viewed signs as having arbitrary meanings, positioned literary texts as linguistic artifacts with language separate from social context and use, and conceptualized the author (in the case of literature) as an individual psyche. But if signs are sites of struggle, then meanings are motivated rather than arbitrary. This Bakhtinian philosophy of language—a sociological and linguistic philosophy—views signs as complexly motivated, literary texts as nested in social contexts, and the author as a socio-ideological self.

Given where I come from, my own socio-ideological self, perhaps my attraction to this line of thinking is not surprising. As a child, I was taught to distrust authority, especially institutions that could potentially be anti-Semitic, and I grew up with the tacit knowledge that fixed discourses without nuance and multiple perspectives were, more often than not, to be challenged. I brought these assumptions to my work as a teacher and have since taught the interpretations of all texts and signs, from middle school through graduate school, using the same three principles of critical literacy (Lewis, Pyscher, and Stutelberg 2015). I'm interested in (1) how signs position readers/ viewers, (2) how readers/viewers position signs, and (3) how signs and readers/viewers are positioned within social, political, cultural, and spatial contexts. The first dimension addresses signs as mediational means whose effects on readers are often inscribed within the sign (e.g., who does this film address, and what ideologies are present in the film?). The second addresses the ideological formations and identity affiliations of the reader. The third addresses the sociocultural placement of texts and their consumption in particular sociocultural and spatial contexts.

To demonstrate the salience of these dimensions of critical literacy, I often begin teacher workshops with a clip from the 2007 film *Freedom Writers* that shows the shock of the protagonist, a teacher, when her students devalue her worth in their lives and claim to "hate white people." We ask questions (e.g., Who does this film think you are? What does this clip make you desire? What ideologies have shaped this desire?) to discuss ideologies of texts and readers/viewers that inscribe and respond to dominant fantasies about teaching in urban schools. We look also at the DVD cover to talk about the inter-semiotics of signs, such as the large, central positioning of the actor Patrick Dempsey (famous for his portrayal of Derek Shepherd, also known as "Dr. McDreamy," on the prime-time TV show *Grey's Anatomy*) despite his small role in the film. The concept of sign selection is also relevant in what gets foregrounded (McDreamy) and backgrounded (the urban youth) within the physical and social space of the DVD cover. To consider the third dimension, we each discuss different experiences we have had as teachers, such as one that emerged for me out of a meeting with an African American mother who preferred that her son have opportunities to read "melting pot" (Sims 1983) books that had African American characters living middle class lives, rather than books raising critical issues of discrimination or oppression. The mother's predominately white, rural community served as an important backdrop for this decision, a sociopolitical context that we, as educators, needed to consider as we thought about what critical literacy meant in that context and whose interests it would serve (Lewis, Ketter, and Fabos 2001).

Bakhtin proposes that speakers and audiences address one another by producing utterances that are constituted in an awareness of the expectations of others in the interactional context. However, authoritative discourse does not allow for the give-and-take between social voices that leads to appropriation and change. Visiting an urban charter high school that emphasizes the recording arts, I was reminded about the central role that address and authoritative discourse play in media communication and audience response. The school, with an enrollment mostly of African American males, had received some media attention that the school viewed as positive. A small national magazine had celebrated the school's success in using hip-hop as part of the curriculum with students whom the magazine characterized as would-be dropouts. I recall that the article's headline included the words "Hip Hop" and "Dropout" printed in large, bold font. Noticing the article displayed on a table during an all-school meeting, a soon-to-graduate African American student read the article's headline and quietly remarked that this school was neither a school for dropouts nor one that focused on hip-hop. He did not agree with the broad sweep of these generalizations about the identity of his school and its students. The school's administration, on the other hand, was pleased with the publicity and its positive focus on the school's successes.

This strikes me as a useful anecdote because it so clearly demonstrates that texts have little meaning outside the particularly contextualized lives and identities of their readers. Although meanings are produced, in part, through reader-text transactions, both readers and texts are situated within social, cultural, and institutional frameworks that both constrain (close) and destabilize (open) meanings. The article in the anecdote was shaped by the discourse of structural racism that participates in "framing dropouts" (Fine 1991) as black and interested in hip-hop. The young man refused to be addressed by those dominant discourses. He was an accomplished young man who had, in fact, just been awarded a college scholarship. As Garrett Duncan argues, "By critically reading the world, Black teenagers construct their identities through redefining what it is that constitutes respectable thinking and behaving in a racist society" (1995, 58). This student redefined respectable thinking and provided a corrective to the way in which the article frames black youth identity.

It is entirely possible that some teachers and administrators at the school would have a response to the article similar to this young man's; however, a given text can engender an open set of contradictory interpretations that depend on how and to what effect the text will be read by others—in other words, on whom the text addresses. In this case, the potential for what could be viewed as positive publicity for the school may have resulted in a positive official school response to the article. Given a national climate in which schools are generally the object of negative media attention and increasingly subject to free-market principles, it is not surprising that the article represents a school identity that could be viewed as strategically desirable. This media text was linguistically heteroglossic, with language that contained competing discourses (authoritative and persuasive) and meaning potentials. Even in this brief example, we can see how language can contain traces of prior and future utterances, simultaneously answering past utterances and addressing those to come.

These examples—the film *Freedom Writers* and the magazine article—highlight what Bakhtin refers to as the "centripetal" or homogenizing effects of texts existing in tension with their "centrifugal" or heterogeneous effects (1982, 272). Throughout my career, I have been interested in studying how textual ideologies are shaped by multivoiced responses and meanings that can't be controlled by teachers or assessments. By way of illustration, I'll return to my previous example of the teacher who animated the speech of colonists. Later in the unit on Disney's *Pocahontas*, she read aloud from an article by an indigenous author who was critical of the film's representation of native women as sexually free in contrast to white women. An African American female student asked what the article meant by the phrase "sexually more free" (Pewewardy 1996–1997, 22). The teacher explained that it might mean that native women are not as bound by the rules that would bind a white woman, and the student quipped with sarcasm, "So the white woman is holier than holy," and followed with, "I don't agree with that." The teacher asked the student if she agreed that this is what the movie shows. The white students were disturbed that the author of the critique and the students in class (the African American, Latina, and Native American students, all of whom agreed with the author of the critique) were ruining an "innocent" movie for little kids. They felt that if the movie addressed issues of racism and genocide, it would not be suitable for kids.

For the African American student who spoke up, this discussion was not a scholarly exercise. It was about her embodied identity as a young African American woman in the face of mediascapes and social spaces that cast her as hypersexual. For this student, the film carried dominant racist views about black female sexuality, despite its explicit reference to Native American women, and the article—although it was a trenchant critique of the film—somehow coded and ultimately reified these dominant views for her.

This placed the teacher in an awkward position. She had chosen the article because it so effectively critiqued the Disney film, and she wanted her students to see that the author was not saying that white women are truly purer or less overtly sexual than women of color but rather that the film portrays Native American women in this way. In this case, the student translated the critical scholarly text in a way that marshaled or mobilized her indignation about the film and, more directly, about the language that constructs women of color as deviant ("sexually free").

Bakhtin teaches us that dominant discourses are not sufficiently attuned to the incredible dialogic complexity of social worlds. More importantly, however, Bakhtin teaches us that critiques of dominant discourses are also inadequate in the face of the heteroglossic complexity that exists in the classroom I have described and in the social worlds where all of us live our lives. In the end, I am interested not only in Bakhtin's obvious attention to structure and ideology. What really draws me to his work is the truth it seems to speak about the dense and complicated language of my childhood, resulting in a healthy (I hope) disequilibrium in relation to identity and discourse that Bakhtin so perfectly addresses. For it is this dynamic function of language that allows each of us to "create new ways of being" as Dorothy Holland and her colleagues (1998, 5) put it, to reinvent ourselves in relation to media texts and continuously emerging contexts.

REFERENCES

Bakhtin, M. M. 1982. *The Dialogic Imagination*. Translated by C. Emerson and M. Holquist. Austin: University of Texas Press.

———. 1984. *Problems of Dostoevsky's Poetics*. Translated by C. Emerson. Minneapolis: University of Minnesota Press.

Dostoevsky, F. (1880) 1992. *The Brothers Karamazov.* Translated by R. Pevear and L. Volokhonsky. New York: Knopf.

Duncan, G. A. 1995. "What Is Africa to Me? A Discursive Approach to Literacy and the Construction of Texts in the Black Adolescent Imagination." In *Toward Multiple Perspectives on Literacy: Fifty-Ninth Yearbook of the Claremont Reading Conference,* edited by P. H. Dreyer, 46–62. Claremont, CA: Claremont Reading Conference.

Fine, M. 1991. *Framing Dropouts: Notes on the Politics of an Urban Public High School.* Albany: State University of New York Press.

Holland, D., W. Lachicotte, D. Skinner, and C. Cain. 1998. *Identity and Agency in Cultural Worlds.* Cambridge, MA: Harvard University Press.

Lewis, C., J. Ketter, and B. Fabos. 2001. "Reading Race in a Rural Context." *International Journal of Qualitative Studies in Education* 14 (3): 317–350.

Lewis, C., T. Pyscher, and E. Stutelberg. 2015. "A Critical Sociocultural Approach to English Education." In *Reclaiming English Language Arts Methods Courses: Critical Issues and Challenges for Teacher Educators in Top-Down Times,* edited by J. Brass and A. Webb, 22–39. New York: Routledge.

Maybin, J. 2001. "Language, Struggle and Voice: The Bakhtin/Voloshinov Writings." In *Discourse Theory and Practice: A Reader,* edited by M. Wetherell, S. Taylor, and S. J. Yates, 64–71. London: Sage.

Pewewardy, C. 1996–1997. "The Pocahontas Paradox: A Cautionary Tale for Educators." *Journal of Navajo Education* 14 (1–2): 20–25.

Sims, R. 1983. "Strong Black Girls: A Ten Year Old Responds to Fiction about Afro-Americans." *Journal of Research and Development in Education* 16 (3): 21–28.

Voloshinov, V. N. 1973. *Marxism and the Philosophy of Language.* New York: Seminar Press.

6 /

Srividya Ramasubramanian
on Gordon Allport

SRIVIDYA RAMASUBRAMANIAN

Gordon Allport remains one of the most influential, oft-cited, and leading social psychologists of the twentieth century. His scholarship is marked by its empirical rigor, breadth, pluralism, social impact, and ethical concerns; he boldly experimented with new methodologies and topics of study with the aim of bringing about social change. His landmark books, *The Psychology of Radio* (with Hadley Cantril; 1935), *The Individual and His Religion* (1950), and *The Nature of Prejudice* (1954), created a paradigm shift that enabled future researchers to make significant developments in the field. As foundational classics for contemporary social scientists, Allport's research on stereotyping, intergroup relations, personality, radio studies, and religion continue to influence media scholars even today.

Allport took a pragmatic and applied approach to the social sciences, one that was deeply rooted in the political, cultural, and social issues of his times. He had a broad approach to psychology that accommodated multiple theoretical and methodological perspectives. He embraced major theories from a variety of fields, such as anthropology, sociology, theology, literature, and history. Although he was an experimental social psychologist, Allport was fascinated by biographies and case studies, both from a literary and scientific standpoint, throughout his life. Therefore, it is only fitting that I use personal narrative and autoethnography to pay tribute to my "academic grandparent," Gordon Allport, by examining his contributions to media literacy. In this chapter, I examine the key ideas and life events that shaped my work, as well as those that shaped Allport's, to highlight the sociocultural and historical contexts that play a significant role in shaping the media literacy discipline. In other words, I examine how scholarship on media literacy is socially constructed and embedded in the ideological values of the historical contexts in which it is situated.

Radio Research and Its Influence on Contemporary Media Literacy

In the 1930s, Allport was the first major scholar to examine the sociopsychological effects of mass media by conducting research on popular radio. Radio emerged as a powerful medium during this time, dramatically affecting the sociocultural, political, and economic milieu. By 1935, when Allport and his former student Hadley Cantril coauthored their pioneering book, *The Psychology of Radio*, almost 70 percent of U.S. households had a radio set and close to 78 million Americans were dedicated listeners (Cantril and Allport 1935; Pandora 1998). For the first time ever, broadcast programs could reach mass audiences from various regions, social classes, races, and ethnicities.

Allport's choice of examining contemporary popular culture through his research on radio was pathbreaking and radical. During his time, psychologists were modeling their research agendas on the pure sciences by focusing on scientific objectivity, academic pursuits, and theoretical contributions (Pandora 1998). *The Psychology of Radio* (Cantril and Allport 1935) stands as a classic example of how social-science scholarship can connect to the wider social arena, contemporary social issues, political activism, and social democracy. By declaring that "the really important problems of the radio are now psychological problems" (4), Cantril and Allport were setting the foundation for the new applied field of media psychology and legitimizing it as a valid field of serious scientific study. Cantril's

(1940) detailed analyses of the effects of the radio broadcasting of the Martian invasion continues to be used by present-day media-effects scholars to highlight the situational contexts that lead to powerful effects of radio on mass audiences.

As a child growing up in India, I witnessed how color TV became popular in the 1980s and how satellite television dramatically affected our family media habits in the 1990s; as a young adult, I witnessed how the rise of digital and social media in the new millennium drastically shifted the nature of mediated communication. By focusing my scholarship on the stereotyping effects of popular media, I was following the path pioneered by Allport and Cantril (1935), which was then furthered by media psychologists Jennings Bryant and Dolf Zillmann (1986, 1994) in the second half of the twentieth century. These founding figures of the media-effects tradition examined how popular culture and media entertainment influenced audiences' attitudes and behaviors. When I arrived at Pennsylvania State University to get a Ph.D. in interdisciplinary mass communication, I was fortunate to inherit this rich legacy of empirical rigor, social-science research methods, and media-effects theories when I was adopted into the academic lineage of the Zillmann-Bryant school of media psychology as the first advisee of Mary Beth Oliver and as a student of S. Shyam Sundar.

Media Stereotyping and Prejudice Reduction

Intergroup harmony and peaceful coexistence among various ethnic and racial groups were central to Gordon Allport's scholarship. Even as a young man, Allport had an open mind, a big heart, and a strong conscience (Bruner 1968). He often visited the Department of Social Work at Harvard University to assist scholars on field visits, and he volunteered his time for social work and to help foreign students. In 1919, right after completing his undergraduate degree, he spent a year in Turkey during the tenure of the last sultan. Additionally, after receiving his Ph.D., he spent a year in Germany and another year in Cambridge, UK. He also assisted professors who moved to the United States to escape Nazi persecution.

The early twentieth century was marked by several social, economic, and political inequalities between colonizers and the colonized in various parts of the world, between Nazis and Jews in Europe, and between white people and racial and ethnic minority groups in the United States. Discrimination, bigotry, hostile prejudice, and other forms of antagonisms toward racial and ethnic minorities were openly practiced and institutionalized through segregation and political exclusion.

Allport took a complex and interdisciplinary approach to the study of prejudice. His extensive and brilliant volume on prejudice titled *The Nature of Prejudice* (1954) remains one of the most influential and foundational works in intergroup relations. He brought the subject of racial and ethnic stereotyping to the mainstream in the social sciences by examining it from a multilayered cognitive, functionalistic, motivational, and affective approach. His definition of prejudice as an irrational and faulty generalization was significantly different from how prejudice was conceptualized during his times. He is credited for organizing the scholarship on prejudice into categories of individual, internal personality structures; psychological functions; and external societal determinants of prejudice. His work examined the causal determinants, affective content, cognitive dimensions, motivational factors, personality characteristics, and psychological effects of prejudice. His research on right-wing authoritarianism, for instance, provides deep insights into the relationship between personality and prejudice.

True to his optimistic outlook on life and socially relevant approach to scholarship, Allport's research on prejudice focused as much on theoretical explanatory analyses as it did on reflecting on remedial solutions to the social issue. He recognized that discriminatory behavior was not just a product of individual hostile attitudes but also influenced by situational factors such as social norms and the influence of authority figures. He also observed that state laws, segregation, and other discriminatory institutional policies obstructed racial equality.

Allport is credited with developing the contact hypothesis, also known as intergroup contact theory, which argues that interpersonal contact is one of the most effective ways to reduce prejudice. By communicating with others, people are able to understand and appreciate different points of view involving their ways of life. This theory continues to be one of the most studied aspects of intergroup relations. Taking a multilevel approach, Allport suggests that not just any type of contact between majority and minority group members is effective. Specifically, he outlines four conditions that are needed for reducing intergroup bias and promoting positive attitudes toward out-groups: equal status between minority and majority groups, opportunities to cooperate, interdependence of goals, and support of institutional authority figures.

My family history is rooted in research and practice in media and communication. A contemporary of Allport's on another continent, my great-grandfather P. Vishwanatha Iyer, a journalist and freedom fighter, was working as an associate editor of a leading national newspaper, the *Hindu*. Although I never met him, his inspirational rags-to-riches story played an important role in shaping my decision to choose communication as my major. He pioneered research on media history in India by editing several volumes, including *The History of Indian Journalism*, which remains an important reference collection. When Mahatma Gandhi walked across India from village to village to resist salt taxes imposed on the common people, Iyer joined this civil disobedience movement and wrote about it for the *Hindu*.

Gandhi's effective communication efforts toward raising consciousness among colonizers and unifying and mobilizing Indian citizens to fight for their freedom using nonviolent means remain a source of inspiration for people around the world, especially for scholars committed to social justice and nonviolence. Core Gandhian principles such as *ahimsa* (nonviolence), *satyagraha* (civil disobedience), and self-sufficiency are founded in universal positive human values. These principles of inclusiveness, diversity, and intergroup harmony have had a significant impact on my scholarship on media literacy.

Guided by Allport's foundational scholarship on intergroup relations and my great-grandfather's association with Gandhian values, my scholarship has focused on media literacy, intergroup harmony, and social change. Specifically, my research examines media portrayals of race and gender, the effects of positive and negative stereotypes on audience attitudes, and the effectiveness of counter-stereotypical media exemplars and media literacy training in prejudice reduction. It has theorized about the complex affective, cognitive, and policy-decision-making effects of stereotypes and addressed conceptual issues in media literacy education and prejudice reduction (Martinez and Ramasubramanian 2015; Ramasubramanian 2007, 2010, 2011; Ramasubramanian and Oliver 2007; Ramasubramanian and Sanders 2009).

A Multidisciplinary and Inclusive Approach to Research

Allport's primary legacy is that of an inclusive, applied, and multidisciplinary approach to the social sciences. He was anything but a traditionalist and was way ahead of his time. No wonder he declared himself quite accurately as a "maverick" (Hiltner 1969, 66). Although he conducted rigorous lab experiments, he also believed that clinical approaches using case studies were very important. This was a unique position during his time, when there was a lot of debate and polarization within the field between clinical and experimental approaches. He was an expansionist and inclusive scholar who fought against dogmatic extreme theoretical or methodological stances with the view of bringing a balance to the field (Pettigrew 1999). He emphasized the uniqueness of each human being and resisted the idea of measuring people as intersections of multidimensional factors. He advocated strongly for the comprehensive study, with respect and dignity, of the individual as a whole (Clark 1967).

An openness to various methodological approaches and multidisciplinary perspectives on scholarship has also played an important role in my journey into media literacy. Although my training in high school was in the natural sciences, I grew up in a family that was devoted to music, dance, theatre, and the arts. My artistically gifted mother and scientifically oriented father encouraged me to take up communication as my major, as they believed it would allow me to foster my creative expression as well as scientific approach. In my hometown in India, this program of study was offered only in a men's college. The experience of being one of the few women in a men's college was eye-opening in terms of gender and sexual relations, which shaped my scholarship on intergroup communication. Eventually, when I moved to the United States for my Ph.D., once again my identity as a minority, this time as a South Asian non-Christian female scholar, became salient, especially after the September 11,

2001, attacks. It was within this context that my scholarship on media stereotyping was shaped.

Allport was particularly concerned about the negative effects of the World Wars. He wrote about morale, rumor, public opinions, propaganda, and prejudice. In the postwar era, Allport's work on social ethics and religion also intensified. His conviction that social psychology should be morally rooted and be of service to the society as a whole was strengthened. It is in the context of war and destruction that questions about the role of mass communication in persuasion, propaganda, and peace relations were examined. Allport was concerned about aggression, anxiety, and other negative effects of combat on people's psyches. The contemporary digital-media literacy movement has similarly been concerned about the impact of media violence, health, and stereotyping.

Much of my own scholarship on media literacy education is similarly issue-driven, with social change as the overarching goal. I believe that media practitioners, parents, and educators will find it more useful to learn about practical and effective media-based strategies to undermine and eliminate prejudice than to merely learn about their prevalence and effects on audiences. My applied projects in this area identify two media-based strategies for stereotype inhibition and change (Oliver, Ramasubramanian, and Kim 2007; Ramasubramanian and Kornfield 2012; Ramasubramanian and Oliver 2007; Ramasubramanian 2007, 2011, 2013). The first is an audience-centered approach that focuses on developing critical-viewing skills, and the second is a message-centered approach that presents audiences with stereotype-disconfirming information. Using both of these strategies simultaneously is most effective in achieving prejudice-reduction goals.

Inspired by Allport and other scholars committed to public scholarship who take a socially conscious, applied approach to their research, in 2013 I established Media Rise, a global alliance for media, art, design, and storytelling for social good. The alliance brings together media educators, artists, activists, and community leaders who are committed to using media to accelerate social change. Our mission is to promote meaningful media creation and consumption that focuses on universal human values, such as respect and dignity. We foster partnerships and collaborations among various sectors:

media industry, academia, government, and nongovernmental organizations. Through a weeklong annual festival and monthly meet-ups around the world, we hope that digital-media scholarship is able to reach the citizens and public at large.

Conclusion

Allport's socially relevant, solution-driven, and theoretically grounded empirical approach to the study of social sciences has served as an inspiration to contemporary media scholars to explore the role of digital media in addressing real-world social problems. Throughout his life, Allport championed several humanitarian causes and conducted research with the purpose of promoting greater intergroup harmony. His rigorous scholarship, sense of wisdom, open-minded pluralism, courage, and passion for accelerating social change make him a role-model academic ancestor for digital-media scholars, especially those studying media literacy and prejudice reduction.

REFERENCES

Allport, G. W. 1950. *The Individual and His Religion.* New York: Macmillan.

——. 1954. *The Nature of Prejudice.* Reading, MA: Addison-Wesley.

Bruner, J. S. 1968. "Gordon Willard Allport: 1897–1967." *American Journal of Psychology* 81 (2): 279–284.

Bryant, J., and D. Zillmann. 1986. *Perspectives on Media Effects.* Hillsdale, NJ: Lawrence Erlbaum.

——. 1994. *Media Effects: Advances in Theory and Research.* Mahwah, NJ: Lawrence Erlbaum.

Cantril, H. 1940. *The Invasion from Mars: A Study in the Psychology of Panic.* Princeton, NJ: Princeton University Press.

Cantril, H., and G. W. Allport. 1935. *The Psychology of Radio.* New York: Harper and Brothers.

Clark, W. H. 1967. "Gordon Willard Allport, 1897–1967." *Journal for the Scientific Study of Religion* 6 (2): 281.

Hiltner, S. 1969. "Gordon W. Allport—In Memoriam." *Pastoral Psychology* 19 (2): 65–67.

Martinez, A., and S. Ramasubramanian. 2015. "Latino Audiences, Racial/Ethnic Identification, and Responses to Stereotypical Comedy." *Mass Communication and Society* 18 (2): 209–229.

Oliver, M. B., S. Ramasubramanian, and J. Kim. 2007. "Media and Racism." In *Communication and Social Cognition: Theories and Methods,* edited by

D. R. Roskos-Ewoldsen and J. Monahan, 273–294. Mahwah, NJ: Lawrence Erlbaum.

Pandora, K. 1998. "'Mapping the New Mental World Created by Radio': Media Messages, Cultural Politics, and Cantril and Allport's *The Psychology of Radio*." *Journal of Social Issues* 54 (1): 7–27.

Pettigrew, T. F. 1999. "Gordon Willard Allport: A Tribute." *Journal of Social Issues* 55 (3): 415–428.

Ramasubramanian, S. 2007. "Media-based Strategies to Reduce Racial Stereotypes Activated by News Stories." *Journalism and Mass Communication Quarterly* 84 (2): 249–264.

———. 2010. "Television Viewing, Racial Attitudes, and Policy Preferences: Exploring the Role of Social Identity and Intergroup Emotions in Influencing Support for Affirmative Action." *Communication Monographs* 77 (1): 102–120.

———. 2011. "The Impact of Stereotypical versus Counter-stereotypical Media Exemplars on Racial Attitudes, Causal Attributions, and Support for Affirmative Action." *Communication Research* 38:497–516.

———. 2013. "Intergroup Contact, Media Exposure, and Racial Attitudes." *Journal of Intercultural Communication Research* 42 (1): 54–72.

Ramasubramanian, S., and S. Kornfield. 2012. "Japanese Anime Heroines as Pro-social Role Models: Implications for Cross-cultural Entertainment Effects." *Journal of International and Intercultural Communication* 5 (3): 189–207.

Ramasubramanian, S., and M. B. Oliver. 2003. "Portrayals of Sexual Violence in Popular Hindi Films, 1997–99." *Sex Roles* 48 (7–8): 327–336.

———. 2007. "Activating and Suppressing Hostile and Benevolent Racism: Evidence for Comparative Stereotyping." *Media Psychology* 9 (3): 623–646.

Ramasubramanian, S., and M. S. Sanders. 2009. "The Good, the Bad, and the Ugly: Exploring the Role of Emotions in Understanding the Appeal of Video Game Characters." *American Journal of Media Psychology* 2 (1–2): 148–169.

Sanders, M. S., and S. Ramasubramanian. 2012. "Stereotype Content and the African-American Viewer: An Examination of African-Americans' Stereotyped Perceptions of Fictional Media Characters." *Howard Journal of Communication* 23 (1): 17–39.

7 /

Michael RobbGrieco
on Michel Foucault

MICHAEL ROBBGRIECO

My path to media literacy education wound through my experiences as a media artist and literature student and my days as a high-school English teacher before arriving at my current roles of media-education scholar and teacher educator. In the middle of this journey, in 1992, I encountered the work of French philosopher-historian Michel Foucault, which, ever since, has inspired and challenged me to rethink and think anew about what I have done and what I will do with media and literacy. From the early 1960s until his death in 1984, Foucault used historical research to investigate how language, power, and knowledge work through flexible systems of discourse in society. He wrote books on the histories of madness, clinical medicine, human sciences, prisons, and sexuality in addition to sharing political ideas in essays and many interviews during his life as a high-profile public intellectual in Europe.

However, Foucault himself rarely mentioned media and never formally studied it. Furthermore, his ideas about education mostly connected with his notions of surveillance and governmentality in the discipline of subjects—positioning education as an oppressive and conservative institution. I do not connect to education in this way at all; rather, I strive within formal education to afford students opportunities for intellectual growth and freedom. So how could Foucault be my intellectual grandparent for my work in media literacy? Foucault seemed to change his path with each step but chose to see his prior work as preparing him for his next challenge—as something to build on. In his last completed book, *The Use of Pleasure: The History of Sexuality*, Foucault made sense of his work, much as his critics and followers would later, in three phases: (1) showing that knowledge and truth are constructed of historical contingencies and not inevitable, (2) developing an analytics of power, and (3) understanding subjectivity, or how it is we come to know ourselves in particular ways (Foucault 1990, 6). Each phase proceeded from and incorporated the work of the prior phase(s).

I have found myself making sense of my own experiences with media as a learner, an artist, and a teacher by incorporating each into my work in media literacy education—work that revolves around finding ways to seek and share understandings about three main themes that parallel Foucault's: (1) the constructedness of media in relation to knowledge, truth, and reality; (2) power in relation to media and literacies; and (3) identity in relation to media. By sharing some of my own path to media literacy education and how Foucault's work has inspired and challenged me along the way, I hope to illuminate some of the ways Foucault's thinking may connect to media literacy and be useful for the growth of our field and practices.

Confronting "Power/Knowledge" and Discourses through Media Literacy

In his early work, Foucault used a historical approach to critique modern ideas about a range of topics—madness, clinical medicine, human sciences—by tracing the conditions of their emergence and development in the eighteenth and nineteenth centuries in order to disrupt their contemporary status as truths taken for granted. When I first encountered media literacy as a high-school English teacher in 2000, I saw much of what was being done by my colleagues in media literacy–themed classes with texts and meanings as analogous to what Foucault had done with conceptual truths and historical contingencies in his early books. Through critical inquiry with our students, we were disrupting the common-sense truths and taken-for-granted values communicated through various media.

Foucault's *Madness and Civilization: A History of Insanity in the Age of Reason* (1992)[1] describes systems of discourse, ways of thinking and speaking, that developed into rules for labeling and dealing with madness in various ways—as an illness, a threat, a disorder, and so on—asserted through emerging institutions of medicine and psychoanalysis in the 1700s and 1800s. The work emphasizes how ways of thinking and talking about madness were produced through the convergence of historical contingencies rather than by a progressive march of humane advancements in understanding the truth or reality of the human body and the psyche. For example, the end of leprosy in Europe left a vacancy in leper houses, many of which became asylums for the mad, who, for the first time, were confined, treated, and studied en masse away from their communities. The new occupants of these asylums inherited the discourse of exclusion, disease, and fear that surrounded lepers:

> What doubtless remained longer than leprosy, and would persist when the lazar houses had been empty for years, were the values and images attached to the figure of the leper as well as the meaning of his exclusion, the social importance of that insistent and fearful figure. (Foucault 1992, 6)

By showing how contingencies contributed to the historical formation of discourses around madness that persist today, Foucault does not uncover the buried truth of the past, but rather recovers the possibility for thinking differently about inherited "regimes of truth" by tracing the construction of knowledge. In a similar way, my high-school media literacy students and I, in our English classes, focused our inquiry on the constructedness of media messages rather than using analysis to uncover true meanings or correct interpretations. Although this sort of critical thinking about media is often positioned as a way to interrupt the processes of media influence through awareness and active reasoning, the critical function of interrupting taken-for-granted meanings can also be seen as productive—a way of opening up space to think and communicate differently. In response to detractors who claimed that his work took apart truth without asserting any alternatives, Foucault emphasized this productive role of intellectual criticism:

> The question of what reforms I will introduce is not, I believe, the objective that an intellectual should entertain. His role, since he works in the register of thought, is to see just how far thought can be freed so as to make certain transformations seem urgent enough so that others will attempt to bring them into effect, and difficult enough so that if they are brought about they will be deeply inscribed in the real. (Quoted in Rabinow 2009, 32)

Foucault's conception of the intellectual as freeing thought so that others may take transformative action, without imposing or prescribing particular reforms oneself, continues to resonate with my preferences for best practices in media literacy pedagogy, which include creating opportunities for reflective media practice using critical thinking tools to facilitate student-led inquiry toward social action.

When I first encountered Foucault, as an undergrad in a course in intellectual history at Bucknell University, his project of problematizing taken-for-granted truths and disrupting naturalized knowledge resonated with my tastes and experiences in literature, film, art, and, especially, music. As a preteen and teen through the 1980s, I had musical tastes that wandered through many outsider forms: the transgressive, violent posturing of heavy metal; the gender-bending pleasures of glam rock; and the aggressive resistance to meaning itself in punk. Reading Foucault, I saw my years of playing in bands of these styles as various ways of trying to make space for new articulations of thought and feeling by disrupting and subverting older forms. Through the 1990s, I developed an affinity for something we called "lo-fi indie rock," which basically involved playing with pop, rock, and folk-song forms in ways that stretched, inverted, disrupted, or repurposed their expected effects. Whether through self-reflexive lyrics, unpolished vocals, droning minimalist progressions, haphazard improvisation, bursts of noise, partial homages, sampled juxtapositions, willful sloppiness in performance, or hissing low fidelity in recording, I was constantly attracted to music that showed its seams, that used inconsistencies in structure and meaning to show me how

I made sense of my experience using them and, in turn, attempted to transcend them in some way.

My professors cultivated this affinity and extended it across a variety of media. The discontinuities in the images of surrealist film, such as Luis Buñuel and Salvador Dalí's *Un Chien Andalou* (1929), called my attention to how my mind automatically tried to create logical and narrative connections, even where there was obvious intention to subvert and avoid them. Looking at surreal art, such as Marcel Duchamp's readymade sculptures like *Bicycle Wheel* (1913), constructed of a bicycle wheel fused to a stool, I connected with theater artist Robert Wilson's idea that a baroque candelabra on a baroque table is less striking and effective in communicating the essence or meaning of each element than a baroque candelabra on a rock (Shevtosa 2007, 56). From the juxtaposition of incongruous elements, I felt myself learning about the webs of meaning that had been constructed in my mind around each object. Gertrude Stein's experimental writing, Samuel Beckett's absurdist plays, and John Cage's music composed by chance operations all had similar effects on me. As I took classes in film, literature, and theater that traced the emergence and development of genres and styles in each medium, I maintained a keen interest in the avant-garde attempts to expose, subvert, exceed, and transcend the constraints. Foucault reminded me that those constraints were always historical and seldom, if ever, inevitable. In media literacy education, I found a way of sharing tools for inquiry about media that created a similar effect as the music, art, and film that I loved and that worked in the same productive critical spirit as Foucault's historical research. My teaching and learning in media literacy continues to revolve around this experience of seeing how meaning is constructed through a confluence of historical forces, media techniques, and compulsions to make sense of images, sound, language, and information.

Why interrupt the flow of automatic meaning-making? The interruption allows us to ask questions about whom these meanings benefit and harm, where they come from, how they might be understood differently, what purposes and political projects they serve, and how they relate to reality; in short, interruption allows us to ask questions about power. When I began teaching in 1999, I found that negotiating power relations is just as important in the classroom as it is in the analysis and production of media texts, and Foucault's tools for analyzing power became most useful for me in developing media literacy pedagogy.

In the second phase of his work, Foucault developed an analytics of power that avoided notions of power as primarily repressive or held by certain people, groups, and institutions. For Foucault, power circulates through discourses, which constitute the rules of communicating and thinking in particular ways (Foucault 1980b, 93). Although institutions may try to rigidly propagate certain rules of discourse to freeze or shift power relations in particular forms of knowledge, with the publication of *Discipline and Punish: The Birth of the Prison* (1977) and his series of lectures on "governmentality" in 1978 (see Foucault 1991), Foucault emphasized that discourses emerge and develop by way of people using them in practice. Power operates not only from the top down but also from the bottom up as people embody discourses and reproduce power-knowledge formations in their communications and actions. This suggests, for media literacy, the importance of balancing media inquiry about power among questions aimed at political economy, authors, institutions, texts, systems of representation, and audiences. Most of my English-teacher colleagues gravitated toward addressing power as held in one area and moving in one direction. In English, it's easy to privilege the power of the text, the sign system, the author's intention, or the reader's response. Foucault pushed me to find ways to use the key questions of media literacy—about authors and audiences, messages and meanings, and representation and reality—as a way to see how power is exercised in a multidirectional, living system. When students pursue questions of power in media communication, I find the notion of power as circulating through networks of discourses and constructed knowledge to be a useful way to avoid the "blame game" of simply pointing to bias, political interests, and profit motives of authors, institutions, and markets.

Rather than a repressive, sovereign power that Foucault finds explicit in torture and other bodily punishments of the pre-Enlightenment period, modern power takes the form of disciplines, which Foucault finds most explicit in the penal system of criminalization and rehabilitation (Foucault 1977). These disciplines operate through discourses that govern our understandings of ourselves in particular ways of thinking, acting, and speaking. We take up subject positions in discourse—teacher and student, doctor and patient, parent and child—through which we reproduce particular power relations, forms of knowledge, and ways of being. Thus, power is productive as discourses produce people (at least in terms of how they understand themselves, each other, and their world) and people produce discourse.

By thinking of power and knowledge as both disciplinary and productive, as exerting control and enabling participation, I am sensitized to the effects of my media literacy pedagogy as a practice that both asserts particular ways of thinking and acting, and enables students to participate in discourses from which they may benefit. For me, the trick in pedagogy is to balance at least three vectors of power in the classroom: (1) valuing and supporting students' growth in their own primary discourses (what they know and like, and who they feel they are); (2) offering access to discourses that the teacher, school, and community believe will facilitate students' participation in greater power; and (3) creating opportunities for students to transform discourses and challenge power relations. For media literacy, this balance means creating situations for students to learn informally (following and sharing their interests, knowledge, and skills in various media with peers), formally (learning established knowledge about media as well as skills for effective communication), and critically (problematizing and challenging media texts, institutions, and media-use practices that perpetuate injustice as the status quo). However, Foucault's research on prisons and governmentality leaves little room for individual agency.

Foucault emphasizes how institutions, like media industries and education, perpetuate particular forms of knowledge and relations of power that, since the eighteenth century, have produced the options for selfhood.[2] For a teacher, this view seems particularly bleak. It paints informal learning as likely to reproduce the status quo, formal learning as the perpetuation of dominant discourses, and critical inquiry as another disciplinary discourse that we train students to take up in hopes of shifting power relations by promoting subjugated discourses.[3] Where is agency? How do individuals and groups make change? How can students learn to exercise the critical autonomy that has been central to media literacy education, from Len

Masterman's foundational *Teaching about Television* (1980) through Henry Jenkins's "transparency problem" and "ethics challenge" in new media literacies (Jenkins et al. 2006, 3)? In the last years before his untimely death, Foucault began to address questions about agency through his volumes on the history of sexuality and a series of lectures on "subjectivation," wherein "he searched amongst the ancients for the answer to this question: how do subjects become active, how are the government of the self and others open to subjectivications that are independent of the biopolitical art of government?" (Lazzarato 2002, 106). What is media literacy if not the quest to become more active (strategic and effective) in the relations between our media and ourselves?

Care of the Self: Identity and Agency in Media Literacy Education

When I have introduced Foucault's ideas about discursive power to high-school and college students, they have not reacted pessimistically at all. In 2001, I introduced my high-school juniors to some basic language of sociolinguistic discourse theory, which students applied in sociocultural analysis of interaction, speech acts, and personal identity. With the film *Six Degrees of Separation* (Schepisi 1993) as our central text, we discussed how the character Paul, a destitute African American street hustler, gains access and acceptance into the wealthy society of New York through a contrived comembership in the discourse communities of a particular wealthy white couple. We find, in flashback segments of the film, that a privileged young white man had tutored Paul in the diction, manners, and conversational knowledge of high society. Together, my students and I mapped a web of notes detailing the various discourse communities through which Paul found comembership or alienation. Parallel to our analysis of the film, students used these new conceptual tools to analyze their own social identities. They created personal "identity maps" by creating conceptual webs, in which they laid out various discourse communities they saw as part of their own "identity kits" while listing signifiers comprising these discourses.[4] Using these new conceptual tools, some students saw the available identity positions that they occupied as sufficient, or even overwhelming; they used media literacy to strengthen their understandings and uses of the discourses that situated their identities. Others saw themselves as able to combine aspects of the available subject positions into identities that were new and fresh, using their own sense of style and innovations in communication (lingo, images, music, etc.) as expressions of their freedom to be who they want to be and to influence others to recognize and share their values, politics, and ways of being. Still others saw identity as a playground and used media literacy, along with their intellectual curiosity, to explore new discourses and "try on" new identities.

In Foucault's final years of work, he was particularly interested in how people become tied to their identities, accepting certain categories of individuality and performing within certain moral codes. He studied historical articulations of sexuality to analyze how we come to know ourselves and act as subjects of particular power relations, noting:

> Power applies itself to immediate everyday life which categorizes the individual, marks him by his own individuality, attaches him to his own identity, imposes a law of truth on him which he must recognize and which others have to recognize in him. It is a form of power which makes individuals subjects. There are two meanings of the word *subject*: subject to someone else by control and dependence, and tied to his own identity by a conscience or self-knowledge. (Foucault 1983, 212)

Although cautious about the notion of individual agency, Foucault's work was moving in the direction of discovering how individual subjects may willfully affect change in power relations organized by discourses (Rabinow 2009, 33). Consistent with his earlier analyses of the disciplinary function of institutional discourses, Foucault finds that the self does not emerge from the will of the individual alone. The individual enters into power relations through the process of subjectivation, which Foucault sees as involving intersections of personal, social, and cultural uses of discourses on morality and law.

> In short, for an action to be "moral," it must not be reducible to an act or a series of acts conforming to a rule, a law, or a value.

> Of course all moral action involves a relationship with reality in which it is carried out, and a relationship with the self. The latter is not simply "self-awareness" but self-formation as an "ethical subject," a process in which the individual delimits that part of himself that will form the object of his moral practice, defines his position relative to the precept he will follow, and decides on a certain mode of being that will serve as his moral goal. And this requires him to act upon himself, to monitor, test, improve, and transform himself. There is no specific moral action that does not refer to a unified moral conduct; no moral conduct that does not call for the forming of oneself as an ethical subject; and no forming of the ethical subject without "modes of subjectivation" and an "ascetics" or "practices of the self" that support them. (Foucault 1990, 28)

While the core concepts and questions of media literacy may be seen as tools for inquiry and reflexive (thoughtful and strategic) media practice, they are also "practices of the self," ways in which we act upon ourselves, "to monitor, test, improve, and transform." Media literacy education acts as an intervention in power relations by asserting knowledge, skills, and habits of mind to protect from media effects and influence, to emancipate from oppressive ideologies, or to facilitate participation in digital cultures. Personally, I value all of these interventions for what they offer students, as long as we strive to make media literacy's interventions in power relations transparent to our students and to ourselves as part of our inquiry. I do not want to be limited to playing the role of socializing agent on behalf of the community, the government, or other hegemonic institutions my school is enmeshed with. I want to serve individuals with opportunities to understand how they may direct their own identities through mindful action. However, I can't shake the recognition of "power/knowledge" and of subjectivity that Foucault has shown me. So I look to add agency where Foucault left off. I seek to support a strategic awareness of how my students' participation in group and cultural discourses constitute their personal senses of themselves. Media are an integral part of this process, and discussing the processes of media communication are a useful way to learn how power works in order to gain conceptual tools for making strategic choices in our social and cultural participation, through media and otherwise.

My journey with Foucault continues. As an artist, I do noise improvisation with non-musicians to explore how our tastes and meaning-making might open up through a refusal of established forms. I play with digital remix to inhabit and subvert the identities constructed by familiar media texts. As a teacher, recently I have explored how analysis and production of digital remix create opportunities to learn through the juxtaposition of discourses associated with elements of different media texts. As a scholar, I have followed Foucault more directly in my dissertation research on the history of media literacy in *Media & Values* magazine (RobbGrieco 2014). By looking at how notions of media literacy emerged and developed from past discourses of media studies, education reform, and popular culture, I hope to lend perspective to the current tensions and illuminate opportunities for synergy in our disparate contemporary field of media literacy education.

As I strive to contribute to new knowledge, Foucault keeps me mindful of how my work has implications for power relations and identity positions among teachers, students, and media. I locate my own agency in the possibility of affecting the formation of discourses through my production of knowledge as a scholar and my media production as an artist, which I strive to align with the intellectual curiosity central to media literacy pedagogy. Foucault wrote:

> As for what motivated me, it is quite simple; I would hope that in the eyes of some people it might be sufficient enough. It was curiosity—the only kind of curiosity, in any case, that is worth acting upon with this degree of obstinacy: not the curiosity that seeks to assimilate what is proper for one to know, but that which enables one to get free of oneself. After all, what would be the value of the passion for knowledge if it resulted only in a certain amount of knowledgeable-ness and not, in one way or another and to the extent possible, in the knower's straying afield of himself? There are times in life when the question of knowing if one can think differently than one thinks, and perceive differently than one sees, is absolutely necessary if one is to go on looking and reflecting at all. (Foucault 1990, 8–9)

In media literacy education, I find an opportunity to share this motivation, inherited in part from Foucault, to find new ways of knowing and being.

NOTES

1. The book was first printed in 1961 as *Folie et déraison: Histoire de la folie à l'âge classique.*

2. Foucault calls these options "technologies of the self," which work as the microprocesses or "capillaries" of power (Foucualt 1980a, 39); these self-disciplines are articulated by subjects taking up identities within networks of available institutional and social discourse, a mutually constituting process (the rules of discourse make thought and communication possible, the performance of discourse reconstitutes and reifies the rules, albeit imperfectly, which thus allows for change).

3. Or as David Buckingham calls it, teaching kids to "talk posh" about media (Buckingham 2003, 110).

4. The "identity kit" concept is adapted from Gee 1998.

REFERENCES

Buckingham, D. 2003. *Media Education: Literacy, Learning and Contemporary Culture.* Cambridge, UK: Polity.

Buñuel, L., and S. Dalí. 1929. *Un Chien Andalou.* Directed by Luis Buñuel. Paris: Studio de Ursulines.

Foucault, M. 1977. *Discipline and Punish: The Birth of the Prison.* New York: Random House.

———. 1980a. "Prison Talk." In *Power/Knowledge: Selected Interviews and Other Writings, 1972–1977,* edited by C. Gordon, 37–54. New York: Pantheon Books.

———. 1980b. "Two Lectures." In *Power/Knowledge: Selected Interviews and Other Writings, 1972–1977,* edited by C. Gordon, 78–108. New York: Pantheon Books.

———. 1983. "The Subject and Power." In *Michel Foucault: Beyond Structuralism and Hermeneutics,* 2nd ed., edited by H. L. Dreyfus and P. Rabin, 208–226. Chicago: University of Chicago Press.

———. 1990. *The History of Sexuality.* Vol. 2, *The Use of Pleasure.* Translated by Robert Hurley. New York: Random House.

———. 1991. "Governmentality." In *The Foucault Effect: Studies in Governmentality,* edited by G. Burchell, C. Gordon, and P. Miller, 87–104. Chicago: University of Chicago Press.

———. 1992. *Madness and Civilization: A History of Insanity in the Age of Reason.* Translated by Richard Howard. London: Routledge.

Gee, J. P. 1998. "What Is Literacy?" In *Negotiating Academic Literacies: Teaching and Learning across Languages and* Cultures, edited by V. Zamel and R. Spack, 51–59. Routledge: London.

Jenkins, H. R. Purushotma, M. Weigel, K. Clinton, and A. Robison. 2006. *Confronting the Challenges of a Participatory Culture: Media Education for the 21st Century.* Cambridge, MA: MIT Press.

Lazzarato, M. 2002. "From Biopower to Biopolitics." *Pli, the Warwick Journal of Philosophy* 13:99–113.

Masterman, L. 1980. *Teaching about Television.* London: Macmillan.

Rabinow, P. 2009. "Foucault's Untimely Struggle: Towards a Form of Spirituality." *Theory, Culture and Society* 26 (6): 25–44.

RobbGrieco, M. 2014. "Media for Media Literacy: Discourses of the Media Literacy Education Movement in *Media & Values* Magazine, 1977–1993." Ph.D. diss., Temple University.

Schepisi, F. 1993. *Six Degrees of Separation.* Directed by Fred Schepisi. Los Angeles: MGM.

Shevtosa, M. 2007. *Robert Wilson.* Oxon, UK: Routledge.

8 /

Gianna Cappello
on Theodor Adorno

GIANNA CAPPELLO

R enee Hobbs's invitation to consider my media literacy "grand-parents" came at the very moment when I was trying to come to terms with my growing sense of uneasiness with the populist and technologist drift that is happening lately within the fields of media studies and media literacy. The uncritical celebration of audience sovereignty, as further enhanced by the infinite benefits of technological innovation, has brought a proliferation of educational-policy agendas in which digital skills are promoted as (and reduced to) readymade expertise for the job market and the critical-political thrust of media literacy is exchanged for a long-awaited legitimation within institutional settings (schools *in primis*). To counteract this drift, I have been developing the idea that we need to (re)theorize and (re)politicize media literacy by taking a detour through Theodor Adorno's critical theory (Cappello 2013).

"The splinter in your eye is the best magnifying glass" is an apho-rism from *Minima Moralia: Reflections on a Damaged Life* ([1951] 2005, 50), a small book Adorno started writing in 1944, while he was exiled in the United States, and completed in 1949. Despite his pessimistic views about the "damaged life" he happened to live, having just seen the horrors of the Holocaust, *Minima Moralia* is, in fact, a book about the hope and redemption achievable through knowledge and social commitment. To illustrate this, Adorno uses a powerful visual metaphor: the eye and the magnifying glass. Usually these are used to see and to improve seeing, but Adorno here shatters the lens and a splinter lands in the eye, magnifying the power of seeing in a totally new and non-instrumental way (Leppert 2002). Although the splinter hurts, Adorno believes that it is better to keep the eyes open wide and look rather than look away. Social redemption may only come from this kind of looking-knowing, and from the social uses we make of it. This is also the ultimate utopian function of art (and education, I would add): to stare at history straight in the eyes and then posit an "otherwise" that is currently unavailable. Art can help us understand not only what prevents utopia from happening but also how a utopian world might look and how we might fight for it. As Adorno puts it, "Art is the ever broken promise of happiness" ([1970] 1997, 136), "the promise of a life without fear" ([1952] 1981, 156).

A Nagging Presence

Adorno has basically accompanied my entire intellectual life, from my early high-school years, back in a small town in southern Italy, to my university time in Catania, when I was inspired by the devastating critique made by Jerzy Kosinski in his novel *Being There* (1970) and decided to write my thesis about television. Adorno's critical views about mass culture supported my argument against the negative effects of television and a national television system in which Silvio Berlusconi's commercial networks had definitely won it all, so to speak, against quite traditional (and, I must say, rather boring) public-service broadcasting (RAI) and were thus ready to support him in his rising political career. Right after, I encountered his ideas again during my graduate studies at the University of Illinois at Urbana-Champaign in the early 1990s. I thought I had gone there to study media and communication (which, in fact, I did, albeit with an unexpected approach), but instead, there I was, attending my very first cultural studies class, held by a ponytailed Larry Grossberg who, sipping a Diet Coke while sitting on his desk, introduced his syllabus by dropping names such as Baruch Spinoza, Immanuel Kant,

Theodor Adorno, Walter Benjamin, Louis Althusser, and Antonio Gramsci but also Umberto Eco, Michel de Certeau, Stuart Hall, John Fiske, Dick Hebdige, Angela McRobbie, David Morley, Gayatri Spivak, and many others. Some I already knew, but a lot of them were totally new to me. As I learned in the following weeks, these people were part of the "theoretical legacies" of cultural studies and were all somehow related to the notion of mediation, to the relationships between subjectivity and structure, culture and power. I learned that the media's negative effects and audiences' passivity could not be taken for granted (as I thought when I wrote my undergraduate thesis). I learned that popular culture—redefined as "lived experience" and "polysemic"—represents an important symbolic resource that people actively use in their everyday life to make sense of the world and "resist" dominant culture, as proved by innumerable ethnographic studies. It was indeed a huge sigh of relief to be able to slightly untighten the leash of puritanical critical theory toward the manipulative mechanisms of "the system" and the alienating ideology of the culture industry. That was when I started to question my Adornian views about popular culture, to "wrestle with my angel," as Stuart Hall would put it[1]—not so much in the sense that I wanted to give up on him but as a "problematic" (again, Hall's term) that is as much about struggling against the constraints and limits of Adorno's ideas as about the necessary questions I still felt he required me to address. Eventually, when I returned to Italy in the mid-1990s, I casually met Roberto Giannatelli, who—together with some colleagues from the Catholic University in Milan, a couple of media professionals from RAI (the Italian public-service broadcasting), and a group of gutsy middle-school teachers—was about to found the Italian Association for Media Education (MED).[2] At local and national levels, we then started to meet and train dozens of teachers, trying to convince them that their critiques of popular culture were in fact an act of cultural elitism toward their students, whom they snobbishly looked at as cultural dupes, and that we needed to think of them as actively committed in diverse and creative interpretations of media messages. And yet, although I am still fascinated by the notion of the "active audience," throughout these years I have always been somehow unsatisfied with the simplistic and somewhat caricaturist Adornian vulgate that this notion seems to assume. In other words, like a karstic river that you don't see but know it flows somewhere underneath, Adorno has always been there, a nagging presence to remind me that the story is a bit more complex and that we constantly need to reconstruct—beyond the traps of binary thinking (powerful media versus active audience, manipulation versus resistance, culture as ideology versus culture as lived experience, etc.)—the intricate interplay between popular culture and everyday life. Adorno has marked my entire intellectual life, fueling my uneasiness with the populist views about the power of the people to subvert or circumvent dominant structures of power and also reinforcing my conviction that education (like art) is the key to "a life without fear," as he would put it. Education (and art) can help us look history straight in the eyes—that is, lucidly look at the limits and constraints of contemporary popular culture (at a macro level) and yet be able to develop with our students (at a micro level) ways of interacting with it in more creative and critical ways and, in doing so, posit an "otherwise" that is currently unavailable.

The Challenges and Limitations of Popular Culture

Writers after the Holocaust were challenged by a profound moral and philosophical failure: How can one bear witness when left speechless? Adorno recognizes that such a failure was due to the assumption that reason could comprehend reality in its complexities and planes of development. Anticipating contemporary poststructuralist theory, he viewed ideas (and all the related paraphernalia of words, measurements, categories, indicators, etc.) as, at best, approximations of reality because they inevitably derive from some historical processes of representation. If reason is equated with reality, it inevitably becomes either a conformist and sterile academic exercise (at best) or an authoritarian act of power (at worst). In both cases, it objectifies reality by making it appear axiomatic and therefore indisputable; in both cases, it loses its critical, reflexive edge and its capacity to transform consciousness. Adorno is not at all interested in positivistic knowledge that reproduces general axioms rather than interrogate them; he seeks instead to look for and speculate about difference and contradiction—the aporia, the residual, the ill-fitting—in short, all that does not cohere with existing categories of thought. To Adorno, reason must be reconfigured as a constant negation of any attempt to reduce rational thinking into a reality made of givens, a negative dialectic challenging the habits of mind and stereotypes that replace lived, material experience with preordered "facts" that "simply exist" (Horkheimer and Adorno [1947] 2002, 24).

Adorno's critique of reason runs parallel to his critique of popular culture. He uses the term "culture industry" to acknowledge that standardized cultural goods like movies, music, and magazines were being produced in a factory-like manner, which contributed to audience passivity (Horkheimer and Adorno [1947] 2002, 94). Having very high expectations about the social role of culture, he harshly complains about its debasement at the level of the subjective—that is, as an expression of mere personal emotions and events with neither a connection to wider social and historical questions nor a cognitive function to play in terms of activating and transforming consciousness. According to Adorno, cultural products—insofar as they enable or constrain (through their specific formal and aesthetic properties) particular modes of production and consumption—can structure consciousness and, hence, produce particular social consequences. The culture industry can be dehumanizing. In particular, he writes, "the repetitiveness, the selfsameness, and the ubiquity of modern mass culture tend to make for automatized reactions and to weaken the forces of individual resistance" (1957, 476).

To make this clear to the teachers I work with, I usually make reference to Adorno's ideas about stereotypes. In the age of the culture industry, he argues, the standardization and stereotyped nature of cultural products conjure up a powerful system for social control through cultural consumption. The problem is not with stereotypes themselves. In fact, since they "are an indispensable element of the organization and anticipation of experience, preventing us from falling into mental disorganization and chaos, no art can entirely dispense with them" (Adorno 1957, 484). The problem arises when this organizing and simplifying function is turned into something else. Once stereotypes are adopted within the ideological and economic logic of mass production, this function is altered and exploited for quite different reasons. The more people consume representations of reality that are constantly and consistently clichéd and formulaic, the less they are likely to change their preconceived ideas; the more modern life gets complex and opaque, the more people are "tempted to cling desperately to clichés" to make sense of it. "Thus, people may not only lose true insight into reality, but ultimately their very capacity for life experience may be dulled by the constant wearing of blue and pink spectacles" (484).

Contrary to all this, Adorno believes that true experience (both aesthetic and of other kinds) arises from the tension or dialectic between the familiar and the unfamiliar, so that people are forced to actively speculate on (and eventually negate) what they are seeing, reading, or listening to; compare it with their past and future; and then think of possible alternatives. Mass culture, instead, limits consciousness as it offers predigested products that have already been conceptually and formally organized for easy consumption, undermining people's capacity to have new experiences by critically reflecting on things that do not fit into predetermined cognitive or cultural schemes. Both the products of the culture industry and the way they are consumed work against the mediation necessary for critical thought to deploy its emancipatory potential. As Adorno writes in *Minima Moralia*, "The value of a thought is measured by its distance from the continuity of the familiar. It is objectively devalued as this distance is reduced; the more it approximates to the pre-existing standards, the further its antithetical function is diminished" ([1951] 2005, 80).

Although Adorno offers many examples of how mass culture has given up on art's cognitive function (i.e., its power to produce social change), I want to focus on one of them that may prove particularly useful when working with young people in a media literacy class: popular music. In his well-known essay on popular music written in 1941, Adorno launches a caustic critique of the ways in which mass production negatively affects the political and cognitive potential of music by creating a tension between standardization and its "necessary correlate" (1990, 308), pseudo-individualism (or product differentiation, as marketers would call it today). To be mass-produced, a hit song must have at least one trait that distinguishes it from all the others and yet belong to the same conventional framework. Thanks to this tension, the song can be sold automatically as customers are seduced into believing that they are experiencing something unique when, in fact, they are not. As Adorno writes, "Structural standardization aims at standard reactions" to the extent that "popular music becomes a multiple-choice questionnaire" (1990, 305, 309), implying the dissolution of any critical capacities. He then concludes that the industrial standardization of popular music must be taken seriously if one wants to make a political assessment of it and give it back the power to transform consciousness.

This is how far I can get with Adorno's critique of popular music (and popular culture as a whole) before I start wrestling with him. As I mentioned, dozens of empirical studies have showed us that the relationships between texts, people, and contexts, as they deploy in daily life and not at the highly speculative level at which Adorno writes, are in fact much more nuanced and complex. I have learned that texts contain multilayered meanings depending on the circumstances of their use. They do not have one single meaning but rather a delimited a range of potential meanings: which meaning is preferred is determined as much by the reader as by the text in a constant process of negotiation between the two. But if this is true, do I ask media literacy educators to give up on critical textual analysis? Are texts imposing ideological meanings on people, and therefore, does media literacy have the task to teach them how to decode and criticize them? Or are people actively producing their own meanings, in which case media literacy has no role to play? In other words, if people are always already actively negotiating their own meanings, isn't the teacher's request to look for stereotypical, ideological meanings useless, if not an exercise of power over his or her negotiating students? In fact, both possibilities are true. Texts are ideologically constructed and tend to "close" meanings,[3] and, at the same time, readers have the capacity to creatively produce their own meanings. In both cases, media literacy educators have a major role to play: in the first one, they teach their students to deconstruct and distance themselves from the ideological nature of texts; in the second one, they teach their students how to turn their spontaneous activity of meaning-making (either as a symbolical activity of interpretation or, with the advent of digital media, as a practical activity of content production) into a more reflexive act of expression and participation in the public sphere, as I argue later.

So, to go back to Adorno, he is right to point out the alienating power of stereotypical media representations, and yet not only does he fail to recognize the negotiating power of the audience; he also fails to recognize that standardization and stereotyping may also be sources of pleasure as they are "somehow connected to deep and entrenched psychological dispositions" (Gendron 1986, 29) that the human ear learns and develops beginning very early in childhood.[4] The psychological pleasure of recognizing the familiar (and being reassured by it) is paired with the self-assurance derived from getting social recognition by sharing, commenting on, and reworking it with friends, family, and fellow fans. Adorno also fails to recognize that, diachronically, musical pieces (and cultural products in general) may be differently judged according to either the conventions and traditions dominating in a particular epoch or the connotations evoked. For example, let us compare, following Bernard Gendron, two different versions of the hit song "Blue Moon": the original one, recorded by Connee Boswell in 1935, and the version recorded in 1961 by the doo-wop group the Marcels. These two versions certainly share the same melody and harmony (suffering from standardization, as Adorno would promptly notice), and yet there are some remarkable differences—at the level of timbre and connotation—that do not simply amount to mere commodified "embellishments" (as Adorno would dismiss them). In Gendron's words, "Boswell gives us a muted torch song, while The Marcels do an upbeat number in which the soloist is constantly bombarded with an amazing variety of doo-wop sound from the backup singers.... Correspondingly, the connotations are radically different, though the lyrics are the same. The first is a song of pining world-weariness, the second a let's-have-fun song, resplendent of the innocent (though vaguely threatening) enthusiasm of fifties pop culture. The first song conjures up images of art-deco nightclubs; the second song, images of urban street corners" (1986, 30–31). A historical materialist like Adorno would explain change in one tradition in terms of its own conventions and practices, rejecting as repetitive and standardized all that does not fall within that tradition. Therefore, judging popular music from the standpoint of Western classical music, he would conclude that the two versions of "Blue Moon" are the same standardized product of the culture industry, opening himself to charges of ethnocentrism and elitism. Yet while melody and harmony are central features in Western classical music, rhythm and connotation are central in contemporary pop music. As Gendron continues, "It would be absurd for example to conclude that traditional African music is backward because its harmonic and melodic schemes are considerably more elementary than those of European classical music. Harmony is simply less important in African music than are rhythm, vocal expressivity, and participation" (1986, 31).

Gendron's reference to "connotation" as a defining characteristic of popular music brings us back to the complex interplay between texts, readers, markets, and society. In fact, the meaning of popular music (and culture) is both "writerly" and "readerly" defined, as Barthes (1975) would say. Meaning is the result of both the conventions and traditions to which creators more or less unconsciously conform and the reinterpretations and rewritings it undergoes once it enters into the practices and rituals of consumers. Although Adorno brilliantly shows how political economy must be combined with semiotics if we want to understand the successful production mechanisms of the culture industry, he fails to fully take into account what happens at the other end of them: consumption. Not only is he blind to any possible transformative activity of consumers, but he also presumes that the logic of culture can be read automatically from the logic of the industry. He also assumes a cultural homogeneity that is, in fact, the result of his own homogenizing theories. In short, he fails to acknowledge that culture is produced by both individual and collective actions, in more or less distinctive ways that are more or less free from the tentacles of the culture industry.

Media Literacy as Critical Cultural Analysis

I think that the grafting of ideas and practices from the field of communication research (particularly the "active" audience tradition) within the field of media literacy pedagogy has powerfully increased the capacity of media literacy educators to achieve a multidimensional understanding of the media's role in contemporary society and thus develop more effective classroom activities. At the same time, however, Adorno raises some important questions that are still relevant today, urging media literacy educators to look at popular culture in terms of the constant tension between production and consumption. The culture industry relentlessly recurs to standardization and stereotyping to make profit and reach consensus. To ignore this and celebrate the unconditioned creativity of the active audience is to ignore the paradoxical nature of media consumption as resulting from processes that are both hetero- and autodirected. As Roger Silverstone rightly argues, "In consumption we express at the same time and in the same actions, both our irredeemable dependence and our creative freedoms as participants in contemporary culture" (1994, 105).

Since the ways in which popular culture is subjectively experienced are inevitably connected with power and commodification, we cannot but conclude that popular culture is both self-empowering and manufactured, which requires us to account for how people experience it in their everyday lives and, at the same time, reconstruct how it is materially shaped by forces that go beyond their immediate comprehension and control. Pleasure—as audience studies have largely shown—is a key element here. Defined in dialectical terms, pleasure is an organized and organizing principle of social action, enabling and at the same time escaping control by social agents. As such, it produces (and operates within) certain "mattering maps" that direct people's investments in what they do and with what intensities, determining where and how otherwise-disparate individuals may locate themselves into certain configurations of social order, albeit temporarily, superficially, or inadvertently (Grossberg 1988, 55).

This is ultimately where media literacy meets critical cultural analysis. In other words, I think that media literacy educators, in order for their activities to have a real impact on their students' lives, should know not only how to decode media messages—how they convey meaning and produce certain effects—but also how this decoding process happens with reference to specific social relationships and contexts of action; how media provide both constraining and enabling resources for their students; and how media uses are negotiated within certain conditions of possibility. For example, if educators want to work with their students on video games (not just use them as teaching aids but work on and around them), not only do they need to look at what individual video games mean as texts (in terms of plots, characters, actions, settings, etc.), but, more importantly, they must look at how the video gaming experience is part of their students' everyday routines; where, when, and how video gaming occurs within the domestic economy of the family; how parents regulate it; how students negotiate and circumvent this regulation; how video gaming is constrained by the market or by technology (and to what degree students are aware of that); and how students use video gaming to develop social status among peers and to acquire expertise in domains such as retrieval of information about games and gaming on the Internet.

I know. That is a lot to do, and teachers are not trained for it (as they always tell me), at least in Italy, where teachers' media training is often narrowly defined as instruction for the use of educational technologies in the digital class. In our association, MED, throughout these years, we have been precisely trying to counteract this limitation by stressing the importance of adopting a more culturalist approach, which inevitably requires teachers to be able (and willing) to work as an interdisciplinary team with their colleagues, not only because they can get help and save time but, more importantly, because the complexities of popular culture inevitably demand a holistic and multidimensional approach.

Admittedly, Adorno would not be of much help here. His theories about the interplay between power, culture, and social control rest at the level of speculation; he is uninterested in verifying how abstract structures of domination are negotiated, resisted, or violated through the "logic of practice" enacted by individuals in their everyday lives, as Pierre Bourdieu ([1980] 1990) would say. To ignore this logic, as Adorno seems to do, may produce a "symbolic violence," to again use Bourdieu's words, that denies people's active participation in the social world ([1982] 1991, 170). But the contrary—that is, to celebrate the innumerable cases of activism that occur in media use—is also equally questionable. As a matter of fact, when looking at how empowering media use can be, cultural analysts do not always take into account Bourdieu's "insoluble contradiction" by which symbolic domination is reinstated at the very moment it is questioned. As Bourdieu explains:

> When the dominated quest for distinction leads the dominated to affirm what distinguishes them, that is, that in the name of which they are dominated and constituted as vulgar, do we have to talk of resistance? In other words, if, in order to resist, I have no other resources than to lay claim to that in

the name of which I am dominated, is this resistance? Second question: when, on the other hand, the dominated work at destroying what marks them out as "vulgar" and at appropriating that in relation to which they appear as vulgar (for instance, in France, the Parisian language), is this submission? I think this is an insoluble contradiction: this contradiction, which is inscribed in the very logic of symbolic domination, is something those who talk about "popular culture" won't admit. (1990, 155)

Similarly, when "messing around" with technology in the name of progress and digital learning, teachers do not always take the time to question and define the broader pedagogy of what they are doing. Think, for example, of a teacher proudly showing during a conference the school website his or her students have enthusiastically created for their media literacy class. At the end of the presentation, let's ask the teacher some very basic questions: Was the activity organically part of the school curriculum? Were all students involved in it, or were some of them were excluded, for whatever reason? What strategies did the teacher think of to overcome this exclusion? What, exactly, did the teacher want his or her students to learn? Some specific content from a discipline; some communication, cooperation, or metacognitive skills; or something else? Was this project also an occasion to think about the ways in which meaning is produced and presented in websites (including institutional ones) and for what reasons? What is the ideology behind it? What is the role of online advertising (when included)? What kind of assessment and evaluation of the whole activity was made? And what, exactly, needs to be assessed and evaluated? Can the apparent enthusiasm and motivation of the students be a good indicator of learning achievement? Can the activity be easily transferred to and repeated by students in some other class? We can imagine our teacher answering these questions with some embarrassment.

In other words, when cultural analysts (and teachers alike) celebrate engagement with the media as an act of resistance to the dominant order or as a learning experience, without ever taking into account either how the dominant order is more or less overtly and deeply affecting them or how the broader pedagogy of this learning experience ought to be defined, aren't they in fact celebrating their own empowering pleasure to act out their subjectivity as media consumers themselves? Aren't they simply enjoying the possibility to ease up the puritanical zeal of radical critical theory? As Judith Williamson acutely asks to those left-wing practitioners who, in the late 1980s, were accounting for people's pleasurable engagement with *The Price Is Right*, "How about a radical left critique of [it]? With all our education, have we nothing more to say than 'people like it'?" (quoted in McGuigan 1992, 78). Indeed, the risk is always there to turn cultural analysis (and media literacy) into yet another exercise of power.

Self-Reflection as Educational Liberation

A well-known thesis of Adorno is that, since the Enlightenment, society has increasingly become colder and more violent. Humans' first encounter with this coldness and violence is school—"virtually the prototype of societal alienation *per se*" (1998c, 186)—as it is based on an authoritarianism expressed through two forms of hierarchies, an official one "founded on intellect, achievement, and grades" and a latent one founded on "physical strength" and discipline (186). In "Philosophy and Teachers," Adorno offers an alternative by proposing self-reflection as a way for teachers to reflect on "their specialized discipline—that is, reflect upon what they are fulfilling—and in reflecting upon themselves transcend the bounds of what they have actually learned" (1998b, 21). Self-reflection has nothing to do with psychological introspection, as it always implies the reconstruction of the material conditions causing alienation in view of social change. Thus, "education must transform itself into sociology, that is, it must teach about the societal play of forces that operates beneath the surface of political forms" (1998a, 203). As Daniel K. Cho writes, "The practice [of self-reflecting] never stops at the level of the self or the individual; rather, it becomes an expansive form of thinking that maps the self within the conditions of society as a whole. It is a type of thinking that treats the self as a particular through which the whole is mediated" (2009, 76–77).

Only by self-reflecting on their work and its relationship with society at large may teachers be regarded as "intellectuals" and not "merely specialized technicians" (Adorno 1998b, 21) working for an institution that reifies consciousness into standardized and bureaucratized practices. This reifying process produces what Adorno calls "half-education" (*Halbbildung*), an example of which are those manuals that instruct readers to appreciate the so-called classical music by teaching them to recognize bits and pieces of well-known symphonic themes. Undoubtedly, these readers do gain some kind of knowledge of classical music, and yet what worries Adorno is their arrogant belief that they possess absolute knowledge of it, as if being able to recognize, name, and classify tunes represented knowledge per se. "The half-educated, unlike the merely uneducated, hypostatize limited knowledge as truth" (Horkheimer and Adorno [1947] 2002, 162) and thus are "at once intellectually pretentious and barbarically anti-intellectual" (Adorno [1959] 1993, 36).

In short, Adorno urges educators to call into question their work and teach their students to resist commonsensical knowledge and practices in any field. Although he is well aware that education played a crucial role in creating the psychological, intellectual, and social conditions that made Auschwitz possible, Adorno refuses to reduce education to an institution and a set of practices exclusively concerned with domination and social reproduction. This very basic lesson from Adorno has probably inspired my entire work on media literacy. Following him, I have always thought that education is part of the problem but also part of the solution insofar as it refuses to substitute critical learning (i.e., self-reflection) with mere training (i.e., half-education).

The fact that education is at the same time part of the problem and part of the solution is even more apparent these days, when formal education (at all levels) is embracing a kind of consumerist, instrumentalist, and administrative ideology claiming the cost-effectiveness of digital assessments of students' and teachers' performance, downsizing schools and universities to "factories" for training a digitally skilled work force, and ultimately reifying knowledge behind a pseudoprogressive discourse of student-centeredness and creativity, digital empowerment, job standardization, professionalization, and meritocracy. On the contrary, digital literacy requires education (redefined as media literacy education) to play a liberating and empowering role by which students can operate in full autonomy and agency for collectively building democracy. As

Henry Giroux puts it, Adorno's "call to refashion education in order to prevent inhuman acts has to take as one of its founding tasks today the necessity to understand how free market ideology, privatization, outsourcing, and the relentless drive for commodified public space radically diminish those political and pedagogical sites crucial for sustaining democratic identities, values, and practices" (2004, 18). In fact, if education has a political role to play, it cannot stop at criticism; it must also "imagine itself as a mechanism for changing the world . . . [and] engage democratic values, principles, and practices as a force for resistance and hope in order to challenge unquestioned modes of authority while also enabling individuals to connect such principles and values to 'the world in which they live as citizens'" (19).

The Adornian Detour of Media Literacy

For this to happen I think we need to retheorize and repoliticize media literacy via a detour through Adorno so that media literacy educators can gain new powerful insights to resist the populist and technologist drift dominating their field and also redefine one of the most challenging tensions they face daily in their work—that is, the nexus between critical analysis and creative production (Cappello 2010). I believe this tension is at the core of media literacy itself, as it ultimately points to the interplay that exists between the conditioning power of ideology and the subjective agency that people express when they use media in daily life. As I said, such tension has basically nagged at me my entire intellectual life, and I think it still somehow nags media literacy educators today. When I first started working with teachers (almost twenty years ago, when we founded MED), I met many who were eager to learn about how to deconstruct media (namely, soap operas, advertising, and the news) as ideological texts that manipulated the consciousness and cultural taste of their students; these teachers' ultimate concern was the location and critical assessment of meaning. Yet, over the years, I have been trying to explain that people (and youth in particular) do not primarily experience media as devices for conveying meaning and producing cognitive processes but rather as symbolic resources (and technical devices) providing opportunities for imaginative self-expression, play, and action that cannot be reduced to narrowly ideological formulas. Often, youth use media to pursue hobbies and sports, chat and exchange instant messages with friends, play games, download music and movies, and so on. Indeed, critical analysis—we have tried to explain to teachers—is not of much help for understanding all that. With the advent of digital media, teachers have discovered low-cost production opportunities to allow a refreshing immersion—after years of gloomy analyses of manipulative media texts—in the flux of students' emotions, lived experiences, and creative action. However, as I have previously said, there is always a risk that these activities may become a pedagogical goal per se, dominated by a technologist and instrumentalist orientation. Therefore, while critical analysis, taken alone, risks a focus on mere abstract knowledge far removed from students' lived experience, conversely, media production itself, taken alone, may result in a kind of self-referential and unproblematic activity emanating from an authentic self who can finally find free and creative expression. Ultimately, it "runs the risk of simply leaving students where they are" (Buckingham and Sefton-Green 1994, 130).

In fact, media literacy education is not an either/or choice. We need to recompose the schism between the two, between the macro level (media as a social institution structuring individuals' lives and consciousness) and the micro level (where individuals use the media as a source of pleasure and personal action). But how do we do that? How do we reconnect the macro with the micro? How do we help students interact more reflexively with media by learning to acquire, select, process, and create information on their own; generating critical knowledge; playing an active and poetic role in the construction of reality; and triggering a critical process of social inclusion and participation? Following Adorno, I argue here that critical analysis and media production, to be pedagogically valid as a form of self-reflection, should dialectically feed each other, originating a kind of reflexive practice (or, if you will, practical reflection) by which students can engage with media production as a legitimate source of pleasure and subjective empowerment and yet also with systematic reflection about the broader modes of knowledge and social structuring that construct them as citizens and consumers. As products of this practice, their media productions will be fraught with difference and contradiction as they simultaneously seem to reproduce and yet subvert dominant values and beliefs, offering new possible ways of expression and active participation in public discourse by using an aesthetic of montage, appropriation, fragmentation, and juxtaposition, constantly backboned by critical thinking. Ultimately, I think that if media literacy is to make a real difference in our students' eyes, it needs to establish a strong connection between critical analysis and those media uses to which students commit most of their passion and energy. Indeed, learning has to be meaningful to them in their own terms before it can become critical. And yet once their media habits, tastes, and preferences become a legitimate object of interest in the media literacy class, students must also be critically interrogated and used as a resource to make sense of broader modes of knowledge and social structuring. To put it briefly, when lived experience is evoked in the media literacy class, we must take a theoretical "detour" (Althusser 1987) and then develop a process of self-reflection and critique by which media literacy becomes an effective, transformative pedagogical praxis.

True, like Adorno's splinter in the eye, media literacy—redefined as reflexive practice and practical reflection—will painfully challenge students to engage the familiar and the unfamiliar, but while doing that, it will also magnify their power of seeing, and knowing, in a totally new and progressive way. That is ultimately art's (and education's) "broken promise of happiness."

NOTES

1. Going back to his early years as director of the Birmingham Centre for Contemporary Cultural Studies, Hall uses the metaphor of "wrestling with angels" to describe good theoretical work. "The only theory worth having is that which you have to fight off, not that which you speak with profound fluency" (Hall 1992, 280).

2. See the organization's website at http://www.mediaeducationmed.it.

3. Umberto Eco (1981) uses the term "closed" to refer to texts that try, through the way they are structured, to impose their influence on the reader. "Open" texts allow the reader a greater and more creative role in the negotiation of meanings.

4. Surprisingly, Adorno himself alludes in one passage to the process by which musical preferences are shaped and rigidified through "the nursery rhymes, the hymns [one] sings in Sunday school, the little tunes [one] whistles on [one's] way home from school" (1990, 307).

REFERENCES

Adorno, W. T. (1951) 2005. *Minima Moralia: Reflections on a Damaged Life.* London: Verso.

——. (1952) 1981. *In Search of Wagner.* London: Verso.

——. 1957. "Television and the Patterns of Mass Culture." In *Mass Culture: The Popular Arts in America,* edited by B. Rosenberg and D. M. White, 474–488. Glencoe, IL: Free Press.

——. (1959) 1993. "Theory of Pseudo-culture." *Telos* 95:15–38.

——. (1970) 1997. *Aesthetic Theory.* Minneapolis: University of Minnesota Press.

——. 1990. "On Popular Music." In *On Record: Rock, Pop, and the Written Word,* edited by S. Frith and A. Goodwin, 301–314. London: Routledge.

——. 1998a. "Education after Auschwitz." In *Critical Models: Interventions and Catchwords,* 191–204. New York: Columbia University Press.

——. 1998b. "Philosophy and Teachers." In *Critical Models: Interventions and Catchwords,* 19–36. New York: Columbia University Press.

——. 1998c. "Taboos on the Teaching Vocation." In *Critical Models: Interventions and Catchwords,* 177–190. New York: Columbia University Press.

Althusser, L. 1987. *A Detour of Theory.* New York: Verso.

Barthes, R. 1975. *The Pleasure of the Text.* New York: Hill and Wang.

Bourdieu, P. (1980) 1990. *The Logic of Practice.* Stanford, CA: Stanford University Press.

——. (1982) 1991. *Language and Symbolic Power.* Cambridge, MA: Harvard University Press.

——. 1990. *In Other Words: Essays Towards a Reflexive Sociology.* Stanford, CA: Stanford University Press.

Buckingham, D., and J. Sefton-Green. 1994. *Cultural Studies Goes to School: Reading and Teaching Popular Media.* London: Taylor and Francis.

Cappello, G. 2010. "Analisi critica vs. produzione creativa: Le nuove sfide della media education nell'era digitale" [Beyond the critical vs. creative debate: New challenges for media education in the digital age]. *Form@re* 70. Available at http://formare.erickson.it/wordpress/it/2010/analisi-critica -vs-produzione-creativa-le-nuove-sfide-della-media-education-nell%E2% 80%99era-digitale/.

——. 2013. *Ritorno al futuro: Miti e realtà dei nativi digitali* [Back to the future: Myths and realities of digital natives]. Rome: Aracne.

Cho, D. K. 2009. "Adorno on Education; or, Can Critical Self-reflection Prevent the Next Auschwitz?" *Historical Materialism* 17 (1): 74–97.

Eco, U. 1981. *The Role of the Reader.* London: Hutchinson.

Gendron, B. 1986. "Theodor Adorno Meets the Cadillacs." In *Studies in Entertainment,* edited by T. Modleski, 18–36. Bloomington: Indiana University Press.

Giroux, H. 2004. "What Might Education Mean after Abu Ghraib: Revisiting Adorno's Politics of Education." *Comparative Studies of South Asia, Africa and the Middle East*, 24 (1): 5–24.

Grossberg, L. 1988. *It's a Sin: Postmodernism, Politics and Culture*. Sydney: Power.

Hall, S. 1992. "Cultural Studies and Its Theoretical Legacies." In *Cultural Studies*, edited by L. Grossberg, C. Nelson, and P. Treichler, 277–294. New York: Routledge.

Horkheimer, M., and W. T. Adorno. (1947) 2002. *Dialectic of Enlightenment: Philosophical Fragments*. Stanford, CA: Stanford University Press.

Kosinski, J. 1970. *Being There*. New York: Harcourt Brace Jovanovich.

Leppert, R. 2002. *Theodor Adorno: Essays on Music*. Berkeley: University of California Press.

McGuigan, J. 1992. *Cultural Populism*. London: Routledge.

Silverstone, R. 1994. *Television and Everyday Life*. London: Routledge.

9 /

Douglas Kellner
on Herbert Marcuse

DOUGLAS KELLNER

My approach to media and media literacy was mediated through interaction with multiple grand- and godfathers, including critical theorists like Herbert Marcuse and Jürgen Habermas, proponents of a political-economy approach to media like Noam Chomsky and Herbert Schiller, and champions of a cultural-ecology approach like Marshall McLuhan and George Gerbner. I have always maintained that an important part of media literacy is a broad understanding of media and their significant economic, political, cultural, and social effects. Thus, understanding media and promoting media literacy in its contemporary moment led me to engage a variety of media, cultural, and social theorists. I developed a multiperspectival approach with focuses on political economy, media texts, audiences, and analyses of the multiple roles and impacts that make cultivating critical media literacy such an important part of citizenship in today's world. In this chapter, I provide a personal narrative of my encounter with different contemporary media theorists and theories and of how I came to synthesize their work into my own approach to media, focusing on Herbert Marcuse and the Frankfurt School.

Herbert Marcuse, the Frankfurt School, and Media Critique

In the 1960s, as a graduate student in philosophy at Columbia University, I first became interested in the media and the work of Herbert Marcuse and the Frankfurt School. There was frequent talk at the time of how we were becoming a media society, and the ideas of Marshall McLuhan were in vogue. I devoured *Understanding Media* (1964), which gave me a broad overview of the many media of communication that were proliferating during the era, and I still periodically teach McLuhan's groundbreaking work.

One evening at Columbia in May 1969, I attended a lecture given by Marcuse. The next day, during a reception in the philosophy department where none of the philosophy professors showed up, Marcuse asked me and other graduate students to escort him to the West End Bar, where earlier Allen Ginsberg and the Beat poets had hung out, and where at the time my fellow graduate students and I ate, drank, and discussed philosophy, politics, and other issues of the day.

Shortly thereafter, I began a sustained study of Marcuse's work that led to publication of my book *Herbert Marcuse and the Crisis of Marxism* (1984). A philosopher, social theorist, and political activist, Marcuse gained world renown during the 1960s as the "father of the New Left." Author of many books and articles and a university professor, Marcuse gained notoriety when he was perceived as both an influence on and defender of the New Left in the United States and Europe. His theory of one-dimensional society provided critical perspectives on contemporary capitalist and state communist societies, and his notion of "the great refusal" won him renown as a theorist of revolutionary change and "liberation from the affluent society" (Kellner 1984, 322). Consequently, he became one of the most influential intellectuals in the United States during the 1960s and into the 1970s.

In 1933, Marcuse joined the Institut für Sozialforschung (Institute for Social Research) in Frankfurt and soon became deeply involved in its interdisciplinary projects, which included working out a model for radical social theory, developing a theory of the new stage of state and monopoly capitalism, providing a systematic analysis and critique of

German fascism, and developing a theory of the new roles of mass culture and communication in modern societies. Marcuse deeply identified with the critical theory of the Institute and throughout his life was close to Max Horkheimer, Theodor Adorno, and others in the Institute's inner circle.

The analyses by members of the Institute for Social Research of the functions of culture, ideology, and mass media in contemporary societies constitute one of its most valuable legacies. The critical theorists excelled as critics of both so-called "high culture" and "mass culture" while producing many important texts in these areas. Their work is distinguished by the close connection between social theory and cultural and media critique and by their ability to contextualize culture within social environments and struggles. In particular, their theory of culture was bound up with analysis of the dialectic of enlightenment (Horkheimer and Adorno 1972). Culture—once a refuge of beauty and truth—was falling prey, they believed, to tendencies toward rationalization, standardization, and conformity, which they saw as a consequence of the triumph of the instrumental rationality that was coming to pervade and structure ever more aspects of life. Thus, while culture once cultivated individuality, it was now promoting conformity and was a crucial part of "the totally administered society" that was producing "the end of the individual" (Horkheimer and Adorno 1972, 17, 38).

Marcuse and the critical theorists thus came to see what they called the Culture Industry as a central part of a new configuration of capitalist modernity, which used culture, advertising, mass communication, and new forms of social control to induce consent to and reproduce the new forms of capitalist society. The production and transmission of media spectacles that transmit ideology and consumerism through allegedly popular entertainment and information were, they believed, central mechanisms through which contemporary society came to dominate the individual.

Marcuse's *Eros and Civilization* (1955) deploys Freudian and Marxian categories to describe the process through which sexual and aggressive instincts are tamed and channeled into socially necessary but unpleasant labor. Following the Institute's analysis of changes in the nature of socialization, Marcuse notes the decline of the family as the dominant agent of socialization and the rise of the mass media:

"The repressive organization of the instincts seems to be *collective*, and the ego seems to be prematurely socialized by a whole system of extra-familial agents and agencies. As early as the pre-school level, gangs, radio, and television set the pattern for conformity and rebellion; deviations from the pattern are punished not so much in the family as outside and against the family. The experts of the mass media transmit the required values; they offer the perfect training in efficiency, toughness, personality, dream, and romance. With this education, the family can no longer compete" (Marcuse 1955, 97).

In Marcuse's view, the mass media were becoming dominant agents of socialization, displacing the primacy of the family and removing it from its role in both Freudian and many U.S. social-science theories. The result is the decline of individual autonomy and the manipulation of mind and instincts by mass culture and communications: "With the decline in consciousness, with the control of information, with the absorption of individuals into mass communication, knowledge is administered and confined. The individual does not really know what is going on; the overpowering machine of education and entertainment unites him with all the others in a state of anesthesia from which all detrimental ideas tend to be excluded" (Marcuse 1955, 104). Marcuse continued to stress the manipulative effects of the culture industries in his later works and contributed to the widespread adoption of the so-called "manipulation theory" of the media by the New Left and others in the 1960s.

In *One-Dimensional Man*, Marcuse claims that the inanities of commercial radio and television confirm his ideas about the decline of the individual and the demise of authentic culture and oppositional thought in "advanced industrial society." Throughout the book, he assigns an important role to the media as "new forms of social control" that engender the "false needs" and "one-dimensional" thought and behavior necessary for the smooth reproduction of advanced capitalism (1964, 1).

One-Dimensional Man also theorizes about the decline of revolutionary potential in capitalist societies and the development of new forms of social control. Marcuse argued that advanced industrial society created false needs that integrated individuals into the existing system of production and consumption. Mass media and culture, advertising, industrial management, and contemporary modes of thought all reproduced the existing system and attempted to eliminate negativity, critique, and opposition. The result was a one-dimensional universe of thought and behavior in which the very aptitude and ability for critical thinking and oppositional behavior was withering away.

From Marcuse's writings and lectures, I got the sense that the media were a powerful instrument of the dominant capitalist system and ideology and a great force of reproducing consumer capitalism; Marcuse was developing and concretizing a model of the media that Horkheimer and Adorno had earlier developed in their famous analysis of the culture industry in *Dialectic of Enlightenment* (1972).

Because he was primarily a philosopher, Marcuse's work lacks the sustained empirical analysis in some versions of Marxist theory and the emerging critical communication theory. Yet Marcuse constantly shows how science, technology, and the media have a political dimension, which helps produce consumers and citizens who conform to the dictates of existing capitalist societies and causes a decline of critical thinking. Marcuse does not, however, develop theories of media literacy, although he is vitally concerned with education (for more on Marcuse's contributions to education, see Cho et al. 2009; Kellner, Lewis, and Pierce 2009). In the next section, I accordingly document how I became involved in teaching and writing about critical media literacy and how Marcuse's work helps provide a critical dimension to this project.

Media Culture, the Public Sphere, and Media Critique

In the mid-1970s, I became involved in Marxist studies groups at the University of Texas at Austin. After going through key Marxian texts, including the *Grundrisse* and *Capital*, we decided to study the American political economy and, in particular, television. Our study group began with sustained study and discussion of Horkheimer and Adorno's model of the culture industry in *Dialectic of Enlightenment* and Marcuse's critique of the media within one-dimensional society. We also became involved in alternative media and were given a chance to do a weekly public-access TV show, *Alternative Views*. Accordingly, from 1978 to the mid-1990s, Frank Morrow, myself, and others taped hourlong interviews combined with documentary programs to produce one show per week for years on end; they were eventually syndicated around the United States and briefly made me a celebrity in New York City, where the program was shown several times per week on the New York public-access channels. This project helped me to become a Deweyan public intellectual and to apply philosophical notions and abilities to issues of public concern in a public forum.

At the time, I was also deeply involved in study of the media and ideology, and in the 1970s I published in the *Socialist Review* one article on the concept of ideology (Kellner 1979a) and another on television ideology and emancipatory popular culture (1979b). Although I was associated with Herbert Marcuse's wing of Frankfurt School critical theory after publishing my book *Herbert Marcuse and the Crisis of Marxism* (1984), I also liked Habermas's work on communicative action, theory, and practice and other works and did not posit siding with Marcuse or Habermas as an either-or choice. But Habermas's student Albrecht Wellmer, who came to New York to lecture on Habermas, felt differently. In a proselytizing mode, he presented Habermas's work as far superior to Marcuse's and Horkheimer and Adorno's. This was the beginning of the development of a Habermasian camp, which would become a global intellectual subdiscipline that continues to this day.

In the 1980s, I had a Big Idea that was to shape my work for the next decades: our culture was a media culture. It was media that were shaping the patterns of everyday life: in our economy (through advertising and promotion); our increasingly mediated politics (Ronald Reagan was president, which made it clear that part of politics was acting, image construction, and spectacle); and our culture, in which all cultural forms were directly constructed or mediated through the media (i.e., description, interpretation, and evaluation of all cultural forms, from opera to popular music or from theater to film and television, were mediated through mass media).

This concept comes part from Marshall McLuhan, who in *Understanding Media* (1964) argues that with new forms of media, we have new forms of culture, consciousness, and everyday life. This idea also reflected the Frankfurt School's culture-industry thesis: that capitalism and technology were creating new syntheses that were coming to dominate culture, the economy, politics, and all forms of everyday life. Later I would agree with Antonio Gramsci that culture is a contested terrain rather than an instrument of domination and manipulation, which was a view of the Frankfurt School but also of Louis Althusser and the structuralists and other Marxist theories of media at the time.

Hence, I set out to develop a critical theory of media and technology that would articulate the ways that, following Marcuse, media could be used as instruments of power, domination, and social control and yet how the media could be used as forms of resistance to hegemonic power and for alternative forms of pedagogy, politics, and communication. I also recognized that media were so powerful, so proliferating and omnipresent, that it was impossible to really grasp their complex, singular, and often weird effects (so I also was open to poststructuralist theories of the media).

Having studied during graduate school in both Germany and France, I have long tried to synthesize German and French traditions rather than to oppose them, and this goal animated a book coauthored with Michael Ryan, *Camera Politica: The Politics and Ideology of Contemporary Hollywood Film* (1988). The idea was to combine critical theory and poststructuralist methods to interrogate the politics and ideology of Hollywood film. Ryan and I saw film as emerging as an especially powerful form of culture at a time when videocassettes and video-rental stores made it possible to see a tremendous amount of films in one's home and to make one's own copies of films to build up a personal film library. I literally bought the first Betamax video recorder in Austin, as I had read about this product previously and knew that it was exactly what I needed to do cinema and media studies. At this time, cable and satellite television was also proliferating. I remember being one of the first to hook up to cable TV and HBO in Austin (and to take tapes into class and play and discuss scenes with students, making video recorders transformative teaching tools as well as instruments of research and pleasure), and I recall that *Taxi Driver* was the first film I saw on HBO and one of the first that I recorded and could carefully study. Of course, my Betamax was soon obsolete and replaced by VHS machines, but I followed this trajectory with resignation, changing video recorders yearly, just as I would do during my first years with personal computers.

Working on *Camera Politica*, Ryan and I saw film as a contested terrain in which political battles over gender, class, race, sexuality, and, more broadly, ideology were transcoded, hence the title of our book *Camera Politica*. We saw that dominant film genres, auteurs, and specific films transcoded the contemporary social reality such that their decoding and interpretation could provide insights into the social and political struggles and passions of the day, as well as into people's fantasies, fears, hopes, and dreams.

My two books on television during the era of the Reagan and George H. W. Bush presidencies, *Television and the Crisis of Democracy* (1990) and *The Persian Gulf TV War* (1992), draw on both German and French traditions but attempt to rethink the problematics of Marcuse and the Frankfurt School critique of the culture industries through a concrete study of American television. *Television and the Crisis of Democracy* (1990) argues that in the Reagan era, television was used as a powerful instrument of governing and power and that capital and the construction of images and spectacle played increasingly powerful roles in society and politics, creating a crisis of democracy. In writing this book, I employed a structuralist model of economy, state, and the media and argue that corporations were coming to control the state and media. Liberal theories of a democratic society had postulated separation and division of power between the executive, legislative, and judiciary, with the media serving as a "fourth estate," to provide part of a system of checks and balances that could criticize misuses of power and corruption and provide voices and venues of participation. Of course, by the 1980s in U.S. society, giant corporations controlled the media, especially television, and used media to promote their own corporate interests (through advertising and glamorizing the consumer society in entertainment), as well as to support whatever political party or candidate best served their corporate interests. In the 1980s and into the 1990s, it was the Reagan and Bush administrations that provided tax breaks for the rich, deregulation, and whatever policies their corporate overlords and bagmen would demand (Kellner 1990). To be sure, there might be conflicts between various economic interests, but the Reagan and Bush regimes relentlessly promoted corporate interests, overlooking the interests and needs of ordinary people, workers, and the middle class, which required the sort of critical theory developed by Marcuse to properly conceptualize and critique.

Philosophy, Critical Theory, and Media Literacy

In all my own writings on media and politics, I use philosophy and critical-social theory to provide weapons of critique and tools of analysis that can be applied to concrete issues and problems. I thus use philosophy not as abstract dogma to be religiously worshipped but as a body of living thought to apply to contemporary problems and issues. The best of continental philosophy is critical and dialogical (Hegel, Marx, Kierkegaard, Nietzsche, Sartre, Marcuse, and the like), and its major thinkers have often drawn on the most productive elements of their predecessors while overcoming those aspects that are no longer useful or relevant. Thus, with Marcuse, I see philosophy as dialectical, assimilating new theories and ideas into its arsenal of theory and critique; making connections between different spheres of social existence, culture, and ideas; laying out dominant conflicts in the worlds of society and ideas; negating certain ideas and critiquing what are discerned to be oppressive social, political, and cultural realities; and providing new syntheses of theory and politics—just like Hegel, Marx, Dewey, Gramsci, Marcuse, and the Frankfurt School in earlier eras. With poststructuralism, philosophy can articulate differences, ambiguities, and complexities of the present moment and would resist any notion of completeness, certitude, or closure to a specific analysis and interpretation, as history is always open, always subject to new interpretations and events, and the times, indeed, are always changing, just as Bob Dylan clearly saw.

I had long been an advocate of media literacy, once receiving a grant, during Jimmy Carter's presidency in the 1970s, to teach media literacy to teachers in low-income high schools in the Mississippi Delta area. For months, I taught workshops on helping teachers provide curricula that would educate their students to critically read and decode media messages—including representations of gender, class, sexuality, and race—to help students and educators discern racist, sexist, homophobic, classist, and other negative representations in the media while also looking for positive images, meanings, role models, and programming.

At the University of Texas in the late 1970s, I devised a Philosophy of Culture and Communication course, which introduced theories of media, cultural studies, and critical media literacy in order to promote knowledge of media ownership and programming, teach textual analysis, and develop theories of media power and alternative progressive uses of media for politics, pedagogy, and social transformation. At UCLA in the mid-1990s, I transformed this course into a seminar, Introduction to Cultural Studies, that uses my book *Media Culture* (Kellner 1995) and a Blackwell reader, *Media and Cultural Studies: KeyWorks* (Durham and Kellner 2011), which brings together key texts in contemporary approaches to media culture and communication, ranging from Roland Barthes and Horkheimer and Adorno to recent studies of YouTube, Facebook, and social networking.

These texts apply the insights and methods of philosophy, critical social theory, and cultural analysis and critique to a vast array of cultural phenomena, and *Media Culture* (Kellner 1995) concretely analyzes the dominant forms of U.S. media culture, ranging from film and television to popular music and the emerging cyberculture. The approach to media literacy in this work follows Marcuse and the Frankfurt School by contextualizing and criticizing media forms within the context of contemporary capitalist society and the ways that cultural texts reproduce the dominant forms of power and ideology. Critical media literacy, using this model, is the ability to read and critique media texts from the standpoint of how they reproduce, contest, or are contradictory and ambiguous in relation to the dominant institutions of forms of power.

My approach to critical media literacy also involves analyzing how media provide representations of class, race, gender, sexuality, and other forms of life, either reproducing oppression and domination or presenting representations that contest or provide alternatives to hegemonic forms. In doing textual analysis of specific media texts like *Rambo* and *Avatar*, I apply a range of theories, ranging from Marxism to feminism to critical race theory to queer theory to poststructuralism, to interpretation and critique of cultural and political phenomena and contribute to developing a critical, multicultural, and political media and cultural studies (Kellner 1995, 2010).

By the mid-1990s, it was clear that the media were becoming increasingly powerful instruments of socialization and political indoctrination, as sources of meanings and identities on cable and satellite television mushroomed and talk radio and channels of broadcasting expanded as the Internet absorbed video, audio, and the culture of image and spectacle, and as new media and new technologies continued to proliferate. While at UCLA in the 1990s, it became clear to me that the Internet and new digital technologies were dramatically transforming culture, consciousness, and everyday life, and I organized a seminar at UCLA to explore technology and new media and the new technoliteracies necessary to interpret and critique Internet culture and social networking. Hence, I would now argue that new technologies require new literacies and that being technoliterate does not just involve knowing how to use computers and new technologies, as in some academic forms of technoliteracy, but also involves understanding the multiple functions of new technologies and new media in everyday life, understanding how they transform communication, social interaction, research and scholarship, politics, culture, economics, and our social relations and identities.

This work brings me back to appreciate the work of Marcuse, who, more than any figure of his era, theorized that the conjunction of capital and technology and the ways that development of technology and emergence of new technologies construct new forms of economy, politics, culture, and everyday life, as well as new forms of domination and resistance. Thus, I see critical media literacy as involving understanding new media and technologies as forms of power that have multiple and evolving social effects and uses, and I maintain that critical media literacy includes understanding new media and their impact on all forms of contemporary life.

Whereas much of the dominant literature on new media and technologies tends to be either celebratory or derogatory, I intend to provide a balanced appraisal of the costs and benefits of deploying new technologies. In particular, in debates concerning whether books or computer databases and resources provide the basis for contemporary education, I mediate between these extremes, arguing that education today should be based on a balance between book material and new computer- and multimedia-based material. Likewise, I argue that traditional literacy in print culture and traditional skills of reading and writing are more important than ever today but that we need to teach new literacies to supplement the skills of the past. Consequently, critical media literacy enables us to appreciate how previous forms of book literacy—reading, analyzing, and criticizing texts—can be applied to new media, but it also helps us understand how the development of new media involves learning how they affect the economy, politics, and social and cultural life, as well as our very identities.

REFERENCES

Cho, D., T. Lewis, D. Kellner, and C. Pierce. 2009. *Marcuse's Challenge to Education*. Lanham, MD: Rowman and Littlefield.

Durham, M. G., and D. Kellner. 2011. *Media and Cultural Studies: KeyWorks*. Malden, MA: Blackwell.

Horkheimer, M., and T. W. Adorno. 1972. *Dialectic of Enlightenment*. New York: Herder and Herder.

Kellner, D. 1979a. "Ideology, Marxism, and Advanced Capitalism." *Socialist Review* 42:37–65.

———. 1979b. "TV, Ideology and Emancipatory Popular Culture." *Socialist Review* 45:13–53.

———. 1984. *Herbert Marcuse and the Crisis of Marxism*. Berkeley: University of California Press.

———. 1990. *Television and the Crisis of Democracy*. Boulder, CO: Westview.

———. 1992. *The Persian Gulf TV War*. Boulder, CO: Westview.

———. 1995. *Media Culture: Cultural Studies, Identity and Politics between the Modern and the Postmodern*. London: Routledge.

———. 2010. *Cinema Wars: Hollywood Film and Politics in the Bush/Cheney Era*. Malden, MA: Blackwell.

Kellner, D., T. Lewis, and C. Pierce. 2009. *On Marcuse: Critique, Liberation, and Reschooling in the Radical Pedagogy of Herbert Marcuse*. Rotterdam, Netherlands: Sense.

Marcuse, H. 1955. *Eros and Civilization*. Boston: Beacon Press.

———. 1964. *One-Dimensional Man*. Boston: Beacon Press.

McLuhan, M. 1964. *Understanding Media*. New York: McGraw-Hill.

Ryan, M., and D. Kellner. 1998. *Camera Politica: The Politics and Ideology of Contemporary Hollywood Film*. Bloomington: Indiana University Press.

10 /

Henry Jenkins on John Fiske

HENRY JENKINS

John Fiske can be described as the Johnny Appleseed of cultural studies, given the ways that his personal journey as an academic who worked in the United Kingdom, Australia, and finally, North America helped spread and reframe the cultural-studies approach to new generations of scholars. Fiske provides an important bridge between his mentor, the Welsh-born critic and novelist Raymond Williams, and the scholars of my generation, many of whom were Fiske's students, who helped to adopt a British-based approach to the particulars of U.S. culture. Read together, our story represents one trajectory in the relations between cultural studies and media literacy.

Starting with a strong belief in the critical agency of "ordinary" people, the multidisciplinary field of cultural studies documents the ways in which everyday people create meaning and pleasure through their everyday practices. Media literacy as a movement has sought to ensure that everyone has access to the critical literacies that allow them to meaningfully consume, critique, produce, and—today—participate in the creation and circulation of media. I might argue that cultural studies is the theory and media literacy is the practice. We need look no further than "The Core Principles of Media Literacy Education," published by the National Association for Media

Literacy Education (NAMLE 2007), which insist that the concept of literacy can be applied to a broad range of different forms of media and popular culture, that media content gets actively interpreted by individuals and groups based on local frames of reference, and that media literacy is fundamental to the promotion of active political and civic participation—all concepts that come, at least in part, from the British cultural-studies tradition.

Along with the historian E. P. Thompson, the literary critic Richard Hoggart, and the theorist Stuart Hall, Williams is widely acknowledged to be one of the founders of the cultural-studies approach. More than any other essay, Williams's "Culture Is Ordinary" (1958) set the tone for the British cultural-studies movement. Throughout his early works, Williams offers a more inclusive model of culture, a concept he would describe in *Keywords* as "one of the two or three most complicated words in the English language" (1976, 76). In his 1958 essay, Williams tells us, "culture is ordinary: that is the first fact. Every human society has its own shape, its own purposes, its own meanings. Every human society expresses these, in institutions and in arts and learning. The making of a society is the finding of common meanings and directions, and its growth is an active debate and amendment under the pressures of experience, contact, and discovery, writing itself into the land" (93). Williams's conception of culture contrasts with that of Matthew Arnold, whose 1869 essay "Sweetness and Light" had defined culture in terms of "the best knowledge, the best ideas of their times," seeing the promotion of high cultural values to the general population as the best defense against what he saw as "harsh [and] uncouth" about modern industrial culture (Arnold 1924, 38). Under Arnold, some aspects of human life—the most elevated or perfected aspects, those removed from immediate utilitarian value and from the harshness of a growing machine culture—were worth passing down to the next generation, while others were disposable. Those who embrace Arnold focus on the value they see as intrinsic to "great works," while those who criticize the tradition focus on what it excludes—including most of what has been written by women, minorities, and those in the developing world, as well as media and popular culture.

Williams's approach is expansive, embracing the arts and the sciences, the exceptional and the ordinary, the traditional and the emergent. For Williams, culture is at once the stuff of learning—an acquired set of skills and appreciations—and the stuff of experience. Perhaps the essay's most radical element is the way Williams pits his own lived experience, growing up working-class in the Welsh countryside, against what his own mentors were teaching him at Cambridge: "When the Marxists say that we live in a dying culture and that the masses are ignorant, I have to ask them, as I did ask them, where on Earth they have lived. A dying culture, and ignorant masses, are not what I have known and see" (1958, 96). The cultural-studies discipline is committed to better understanding the ongoing struggle over what counts as culture and who gets to decide what culture matters.

Williams is at his most moving when he describes what reading and writing meant for his family: "My grandfather, a big hard laborer, wept while he spoke, finely and excitedly, at the parish meeting" (1958, 92), he tells us, while his father, a labor organizer, read through the lines of news stories to identify entrenched economic interests. He talks about the value his people placed on library books and tells us that many more would have gone to college were it not for the financial responsibilities they bore to their families and communities. He describes a visit home after some time in college and discusses the tension he felt within himself as he looked at their culture through eyes shaped by formal education: "Very well, I read different things, watch different entertainments, and I am quite sure why they are better. . . . But talking to my family, to my friends, talking, as we were, about our own lives, about people, about feelings, could I in fact find this lack of quality we are discussing? I'll be honest—I looked; my training has done this for me. I can only say that I found as much natural fitness of feeling, as much quick discrimination, as much clear grasp of ideas within that range of experiences as I have found anywhere" (1958, 99). He contrasts this sense of a community eagerly engaged in conversation with the snootiness of the tea shop just outside his university, which taught him in the most painful way possible that some see culture as "the outward and emphatically visible sign of a special kind of people" (93). Williams suggests, "If this is culture, we don't want it" (93). Through such images, Williams conveys his discomfort with the policing of cultural boundaries, the ranking of cultural products, and the dismissal of other people's cultures. While

he is critical of the "cheapjack" quality of the new industrially produced culture, Williams articulates a great distrust of the "directive"
impulse in the Cambridge intellectuals who seek to "impose" their
cultural assumptions on the unlearned masses. "There are no masses,
but ways of seeing people as masses," Williams writes (96). He also
distrusts the anti-intellectual impulses in his own background, the
ways that working-class critics dismiss "culture vultures" and "do
gooders," even when doing so cuts them off from resources that
might improve the quality of their lives. Something vital is at stake
in these struggles over culture, and his goal as an educator was to
help people to better articulate their own cultural politics.

"Culture Is Ordinary" was published in 1958, the year I was born.
I never knew Williams, heard him speak, or got to talk with him,
but I first encountered "Culture Is Ordinary" when doing a directed
reading with Fiske at the University of Wisconsin at Madison. When
Williams writes about the experience of taking a bus through the
mountains to go off to college, I trace my own drive across the Blue
Ridge mountains to go to graduate school, although I see myself
as perhaps several generations further into the process of cultural,
economic, and technological change that Williams describes. I had
been raised in Georgia, the son of a construction company owner,
the grandson of a sheet-metal worker, and the great-grandson of a
dirt farmer. Across three generations, my family had left the farm,
moved to the city and then to suburbia, and our class status had
shifted along the way. As an upwardly mobile middle-class youth,
I had experienced with distaste the trappings of "redneck culture"
that still found their way into my home: I wanted nothing to do with
that "shit-kicking" bluegrass music my grandparents listened to, and
I cringed when they used earthy language to describe themselves and
their values. Yet I was also starting to make peace with my roots.
When I was heading off to graduate school, my dirt-poor grandfather
gave me some money—a small amount for most but a kingly fortune
for him—to take with me on my journey. As I stood in his workroom,
surrounded by rusty wire and scrap metal he had salvaged by the
roadside, not to mention wooden crosses he had carved by hand, he
told me about his own first steps away from the family farm when
he went away to France during World War I. Despite having only a
fourth-grade education, he had marked in the front of his King James

Bible the number of times he read it cover to cover. And alongside it, in his desk, could be found his union card, a book of the collected speeches of Franklin D. Roosevelt, and a postcard depicting Will Rogers—each a marker of a particular form of grassroots politics that had shaped his worldview. I've come to hear some of that progressive politics expressed through the bluegrass music I once held in disdain; now, the twangier, the more atonal, the better. I've come to appreciate that my grandmother, who made quilts, was a remix artist who took patches of leftover cloth from the local textile mills and, working with other women, made them into pieces of art that could be used to express their shared joy when a new couple got married or a new baby was brought into the world. I don't think I ever felt so Southern as I did when I left the South to pursue my education. And so when I first encountered Williams's account of his struggles to reconcile what he had learned at the family dinner table with what he was being taught at Cambridge, I recognized myself in his conflicts. Through his eyes, I came to a deeper appreciation of who I was and where I had come from.

As a graduate student, I also felt a strange disconnect between what I knew as a media fan about the ways that everyday people might critically and creatively engage with media texts and what I was being taught by my own professors at a time when prevailing forms of media theory stressed the power of media texts to suture their readers into a powerful ideological system that always worked against their own interests. And this is the moment when Fiske entered my life. The first time I saw him, I was struck by his broad, toothy grin, the crinkle of his leathery skin, the wicked sparkle in his squinting eyes, and the Akubra hat he was wearing in the frozen wastelands of Iowa City. He entered our lives as "the Man from Down Under"—someone exotic, wild, and untamed, yet it did not take long to discover his gentleness, his modesty, and, above all, his care for his students. When Fiske came to the University of Iowa, he sparked a degree of intellectual excitement I have not experienced since. Every week, more students were showing up at his seminar, eager to learn what for us was a new conceptual framework, drawn from the cultural studies that informed his work. Like Williams, Fiske offered us a way to see the world that was critical of inequalities of opportunity and the imposition of cultural hierarchies and yet was hopeful about the prospects for meaningful change and respectful of diverse forms of cultural experience (Jenkins 2011).

Williams had been Fiske's personal tutor when he was pursuing his B.A. and M.A. in English literature at Cambridge, so it would be hard to imagine a better guide to the British cultural-studies tradition. I was lucky to have studied under Fiske twice—first when he was a visiting scholar at the University of Iowa and second when he was a faculty member at the University of Wisconsin at Madison. Like any great mentor, he empowered me to find my own voice, to draw on my own knowledge and experience, and to make my own original contribution to the field. I soaked up everything I could learn from this man and, in the process, absorbed vocabulary, concepts, philosophies, and ideological commitments that have become so deeply enmeshed in my own worldview that I am still surprised to come across phrases in his writing that I had thought entirely my own. And my own commitment to media literacy is deeply bound up with the things I learned from him and, through him, from Williams.

When I wrote to Fiske, now long retired, and asked him about his relationship to the concept of media literacy, he stressed that the term was one that he never used directly, but that in retrospect, he now realized that he had been working through ideas about media literacy across his entire career:

> I learnt the close reading skills of New Criticism while studying English literature at Cambridge, and soon realized that I wanted to apply them to popular media, television in particular, rather than literature. I had two interlinked aims. One was to show that TV was as multi-layered as poetry and thus worthy of equally serious attention, and the other was to equip "literate" TV readers with the analytic skills to protect themselves against the hegemonic thrust of mass TV. My later work on the active audience grew from evidence that teaching this defensive literacy was less necessary than I had believed. Audiences were already literate in their viewing and had little need of academics like me. They were using their literacy not just defensively but actively in a way that turned a hegemonic text into a subordinate pleasure. They taught me what actual media literacy was all about. (Fiske, personal communication, 2013)

Another way to map these transitions in Fiske's thinking about what might make one an empowered reader of popular culture is to consider how his work addresses some of NAMLE's core premises.

Media literacy education expands the concept of literacy (i.e., reading and writing) to include all forms of media. Fiske's first book, which he wrote with John Hartley, *Reading Television* (1978) explores the relationship of contemporary mass media to historic notions of literacy and orality. Fiske and Hartley start with the assertion that "television's customary output may be just as good in its own terms as Elizabethan drama and the nineteenth-century novel were to theirs" (13). Fiske and Hartley apply close reading practices to texts that were radically different in theme, style, and origins from the materials valued by the literature departments where they had trained. At the same time, the two young authors argued for the importance of medium-specific ways of "reading" works in other traditions: "Every medium has its own unique set of characteristics, but the codes which structure the 'language' of television are much more like those of speech than of writing. Any attempt to decode a television 'text' as if it were a literary text is thus not only doomed to failure but is also likely to result in a negative evaluation of the medium based on its inability to do a job for which it is in fact fundamentally unsuited" (15).

We learn to read literary texts through formal education, while the processes by which we learn to read television are taken for granted because they emerge from everyday, informal interactions with the people around us. Orality was reentering media theory as a concept at this time, thanks to groundbreaking research by Albert B. Lord (1960) and John Goody and Ian Watt ([1962] 1972), among others. Fiske and Hartley built on these ideas to describe television as a "bardic medium" (85), one that seeks to express the consensus beliefs or "common sense" of a community, often involves highly conventional forms of expression that build on (but also creatively rework) existing cultural materials, actively constructs and reproduces core mythologies, and remains popular, in the sense that it is "of the people." Given this focus on orality, there is a good reason why Fiske and Hartley do not talk here about "media literacies," but they remain very interested in understanding the processes of interpretation and discrimination through which we make sense of popular programs.

Media literacy education affirms that people use their individual skills, beliefs, and experiences to construct their own meanings from media messages. By the time he wrote *Television Culture* (1987), Fiske's perspective had been informed by a growing body of work on media audiences, much of it inspired by Stuart Hall's "Encoding/ Decoding" (1980). Early on, Fiske tells us, "A text is the site of struggles for meaning that reproduce the conflict of interest between the producers and consumers of the cultural commodity. A program is produced by the industry; the text by its readers" (1987, 14). Whereas others saw popular media as appealing to the lowest common denominator, Fiske argues that television texts are valuable for their polysemy, their capacity to yield multiple meanings and pleasures as they get taken up by diverse audiences. While Fiske does not refer to media literacy per se, he does talk about "cultural competence": "Cultural competence involves a critical understanding of the text and the conventions by which it is constructed, it involves the bringing of both textual and social experience to bear upon the program at the moment of reading, and it involves a constant and subtle negotiation and renegotiation of the relationship between the textual and the social" (1987, 19).

Fiske's conception of popular readerships differs from the NAMLE principles in a core way: NAMLE emphasizes "individual skills, beliefs, and experiences," whereas Fiske is interested in the collective dimensions of meaning-making. Fiske writes, "A 'viewer' is somebody watching television, making meanings and pleasures from it, in a social situation. This social situation is compounded of both the social relations/experience of the viewer (class, gender, etc.) and of the material, usually domestic, situation (which is also a product of his/her social relations) within which television is watched. . . . Viewing television news will be quite different for the woman who is cooking the family meal than for the woman slumped in an armchair in front of the set" (1987, 17).

Fiske's interests in the ways different groups read led him and his students to embrace what he would describe as ethnographic approaches—that is, the qualitative documentation of the diverse contexts within which people engage with media. In this way, Fiske, for example, opened space for the study of fan communities as sites for popular interpretation, discrimination, and production, a path

I followed in my first book, *Textual Poachers: Television Fans and Participatory Culture* (1992), which Fiske edited. Fiske had challenged me to try to write an insider's account of how fans create their own sets of cultural norms and productive practices. Earlier accounts had often depicted fans as hyperconsumers who were more or less passive and inarticulate, lost in awe of commercial texts that had little value when read against traditional cultural hierarchies, such as those associated with Arnold. Inspired by Williams and Fiske, my work depicts fandom as a subculture whose participants not only produce alternative readings of shared texts but also use mass-media content as raw materials for constructing their own stories, songs, artworks, or videos. I describe fandom as born of a mixture of fascination and frustration: it is fascination that leads people to engage intensely with favored texts and frustration that leads them to actively appropriate and rework them to speak to their needs and pleasures. In the case of the fans in *Textual Poachers*, they were female fans of a male-driven action-adventure series who often needed to reclaim characters or themes that were marginalized in the original works. Fiske, in turn, drew on my early writing to help support his accounts of active audiences in *Reading the Popular* ([1989] 2011) and *Understanding Popular Culture* ([1989] 2010). Fiske saw writing as an extension of his role as a teacher, so you can find in his books many traces of the intense exchanges we used to have in his seminar room.

Media literacy education develops informed, reflexive, and engaged participants for a democratic society. In his later writings, Fiske becomes increasingly interested in the relationship between what he calls "Micropolitics" (perhaps best summed up as "the personal is political") and "Macropolitics" (which is sometimes described as institutionalized politics) (Fiske [1989] 2010, 153). Something of that emphasis is expressed in a passage in *Understanding Popular Culture*, in which Fiske draws a link between Madonna's music videos and her young fans' entry into what we today might call Third Wave Feminism: "The teenage girl fan of Madonna who fantasizes her own empowerment can translate this fantasy into behavior, and can act in a more empowered way socially, thus winning more social territory for herself. When she meets others who share her fantasies and freedom there is the beginning of a sense of solidarity, of a shared resistance, that can support and encourage progressive action on the micro-social level" ([1989] 2010, 104).

Fiske stops short of describing how this process might fuel political change or how fandom can become a form of activism, yet this passage anticipates today's growing academic interest in participatory politics. Linda Herrera (2012), for example, interviewed young Egyptian activists to map the trajectory of their involvement with digital media prior to becoming revolutionaries. For many, their point of entry was through recreational use, downloading popular music, trading Hollywood movies, gaming, or sharing ideas through online discussion forums and social-networking sites. As Herrera concludes, "Their exposure to, and interaction with, ideas, people, images, virtual spaces, and cultural products outside their everyday environments led to a substantial change in their mentality and worldview" (343). Such practices involved forms of transgression against government and religious authorities, and these shared experiences led them to understand themselves in collective terms—as a generation that has had developed distinctive cultural and political identities through their engagement with each other through an ever-evolving array of digital platforms. My current research explores these forms of participatory politics as they are taking shape among American youth. For example, the Harry Potter Alliance is a large-scale network of fan activists committed to fighting for human rights and social justice around the world as an extension of the shared love for the world depicted in J. K. Rowling's popular fantasy series. They have, for example, campaigned—with some success—to get Warner Brothers, the studio that produces the Harry Potter movies, to shift its chocolate contracts to companies that follow fair trade standards banning exploitative child labor. Undocumented youth fighting for educational and citizenship rights (sometimes referred to as DREAMers because they are potential beneficiaries of the Development, Relief, and Education for Alien Minors Act) have deployed metaphors drawn from the superhero genre to describe their own experiences of having to hide their "true identities" in order to avoid deportation. These groups and networks, along with many others, deploy metaphors drawn from popular culture, practices drawn from fan communities, and a range of media technologies to get their messages out and mobilize their supporters, with each representing spectacular examples of critical media literacies in practice (Jenkins et al. 2016).

Most of Fiske's writings were produced in response to television culture and only peripherally address the dawning of an era of networked computing. Fiske's final book, *Media Matters: Race and Gender in U.S. Politics*, expresses some optimism that shifts in access to the means of cultural production and circulation would allow more diverse voices to be heard and official truths to be challenged through the creation and spread of "counterknowledge" (1996, 192). His primary example was the use of pirate radio as an alternative communication system within the African American community. Fiske explains, "A hierarchical society will always attempt to control the documentation and distribution of knowledge; the need to contest these attempts become more urgent as the diversity of the society increases. We can make our society one that is rich in diverse knowledges, but only if people strive to produce and circulate them" (238). Skills in reading and creating media, thus, become core to political struggles, which, Fiske hopes, may make America a more equal and more diverse culture as it undergoes profound demographic shifts in the first decades of the twenty-first century.

Yet unlike many of his contemporaries, Fiske was skeptical that access to technology alone would achieve these goals: "Technology is proliferating, but not equally: its low-tech and high-tech forms still reproduce older hierarchies, and although it may extend the terrain of struggle and introduce new weapons into it, it changes neither the lineup of forces nor the imbalance in the resources they can command" (1996, 239). Greater access to technologies, Fiske suggests, will not achieve the desired results if people do not acquire the skills to use them in the service of their own interests. Fiske's approach in *Media Matters* paves the way for current discussions of the digital divide, which typically describes technological obstacles, especially those concerning access to networked computing, and the participation gap, which has to do with unequal access to the skills, literacies, competencies, and sense of empowerment necessary for full participation. As we've broadened access to the means of digital production and circulation, work on digital media and learning needs to focus more on social, cultural, and educational barriers that make it difficult for many to fully enjoy the potentials for active citizenship that some believed might emerge as a result of the digital revolution.

Fiske had difficulty documenting the tactics for audience resistance and transgression that he theorized in his work and had trouble showing the routes that might lead a young Madonna fan into participation in a public demonstration for, say, equal pay for equal work. Today, we do not have to look far to see the explosion of grassroots creative production that constitutes the dominant content of YouTube, that forms the basis of exchanges through social media, that generates millions of Wikipedia entries, or that yields the stories housed in the top fan-fiction archives. As we have tasted what it means to participate within our culture, we've seen more and more grassroots movements arguing for our collective right to participate, whether directed against the terms of service on social-networking sites, debates about network neutrality, or struggles over intellectual-property law. At the same time, we are discovering the many diverse forms that participatory culture may take, and we are seeing what happens when diverse communities are brought together through shared media platforms and, in the process, learn from each other.

My white paper "Confronting the Challenges of a Participatory Culture" (Jenkins et al. 2006) was written twelve years after Fiske published *Media Matters*. The Pew Research Center's Internet and American Life Project had found that more than half of American teens—and 57 percent of teens online—had produced some form of media content, and roughly a third had circulated that content beyond friends and family (Lenhart and Madden 2005). Yet my colleagues and I knew that technological access alone would not be sufficient to ensure that everyone would be able to meaningfully participate in the practices and processes that were shaping contemporary culture. We write, "Participatory culture is emerging as the culture absorbs and responds to the explosion of new media technologies that make it possible for average consumers to archive, annotate, appropriate, and recirculate media content in powerful new ways. A focus on expanding access to new technologies carries us only so far if we do not also foster the skills and cultural knowledge necessary to deploy those tools toward our own ends" (Jenkins et al. 2006, 8).

We did not directly reference Fiske anywhere in this white paper, and yet his spirit, his influence on my intellectual development, can be felt on every page. For example, you can see the legacy of the cul-tural-studies tradition in our insistence that literacies be understood as social skills and cultural competences rather than as individual capacities and that the end goal of literacy is to empower the public to meaningfully participate in the core institutions and practices of our culture. I had honestly forgotten, until I sat down to write this essay, that Fiske had written about "cultural competencies" ([1989] 2010, 118)—no wonder that phrase seemed so right to me as we were refining the white paper's language. Many accounts of twenty-first-century skills stress those required for the workplace. While we cer-tainly want to broaden economic opportunities for all, our white paper, again inspired by work in cultural studies, stresses the value of such skills as networking, collective intelligence, appropriation, and transmedia navigation in expanding the civic and expressive capaci-ties of grassroots communities, thereby presenting the new media literacies as a means for fostering social change rather than simply integrating students into existing social structures.

We argue that the key changes here are social and cultural, not technological, and that the skills we want to foster might be taught through low-tech as well as high-tech means, ideas informed by Fiske's sense that people will deploy whatever technologies were avail-able to them as they struggle to articulate their own interests. We can also see here a legacy of Fiske's contention in *Media Matters* (1996) that powerful institutions—including educational institutions—tend to promote high-tech standards that are difficult for people with low incomes and limited access to formal education to achieve. There is a wealth of cultural-studies writing behind the argument that while some young people may acquire these new media literacies outside of formal education, those skills that are most greatly valued inside the culture are those that conform to the language of the classroom. Fiske and Williams had both argued for the importance of being attentive to the forces within the culture that worked to value some forms of culture over others and stressed that opportunities for participation should be available to all.

Six years—and much research—later, we now have a much deeper sense of how many different forms of cultural divides exist that work against our efforts to ensure that all people have the opportunity to meaningfully participate in their cultures. These concerns with inequalities of access and participation have extended into subsequent documents in the digital media and learning movement. Consider, for example, a recent MacArthur Foundation–issued report, *Connected Learning: An Agenda for Research and Design* (Ito et al. 2013). Many of the authors, like myself, come from a cultural- or critical-studies background. The report acknowledges the many different sites where informal learning takes place yet also stresses that many youth are unable to meaningfully identify opportunities for productive engagement without some form of adult mentorship, that many have difficulty bridging what they learn on their own and what they are taught in schools, and that schools fail to effectively supplement and expand the competencies young people bring with them into the classroom. At the same time, the report resists an assimilationist agenda in favor of one that still values diverse forms of knowledge and cultural expression. Williams would have certainly recognized the report's recognition of the family as a location where informal learning takes place, having described his own home as one that was deeply invested in "the shaping of minds, the learning of new skills, the shifting of relationships, [and] the emergence of different languages and ideas" (1958, 93). Williams would have insisted that what young people learn in these other contexts needs to be respected within schools as a source of distinctive knowledge that carries deep personal and collective values. That sense of respect for the critical literacies of "ordinary people" may be ultimately the most valuable thing that media literacy could take from the cultural-studies tradition.

REFERENCES

Arnold, M. 1924. "Sweetness and Light." In *Culture and Anarchy: An Essay in Political and Social Criticism; and Friendship's Garland, Being the Conversations, Letters, and Opinions of the Late Arminius, Baron Von Thunder-Ten-Tronckh*, 5–39. New York: Macmillan.

Fiske, J. 1987. *Television Culture*. London: Methuen.

———. (1989) 2010. *Understanding Popular Culture*. New York: Routledge.

———. (1989) 2011. *Reading the Popular*. New York: Routledge.

———. 1996. *Media Matters: Race and Gender in U.S. Politics*. Minneapolis: University of Minnesota Press.

Fiske, J., and J. Hartley. 1978. *Reading Television*. London: Methuen.

Goody, J., and I. Watt. (1962) 1972. "The Consequences of Literacy." In *Language and Social Context*, edited by P. P. Giglioli, 311–357. Harmondsworth, UK: Penguin.

Hall, S. 1980. "Encoding/Decoding." In *Culture, Media, Language*, edited by S. Hall, D. Hobson, A. Lowe, and P. Willis, 128–139. London: Hutchinson.

Herrera, L. 2012. "Youth and Citizenship in the Digital Age: A View from Egypt." *Harvard Educational Review* 82 (3): 333–352.

Ito, M., K. Gutierrez, S. Livingstone, B. Penuel, J. Rhodes, K. Salen, J. Schor, J. Sefton-Green, and S. C. Watkins. 2013. *Connected Learning: An Agenda for Research and Design*. Irvine, CA: Digital Media and Learning Research Hub.

Jenkins, H. 1992. *Textual Poachers: Television Fans and Participatory Culture*. New York: Routledge.

———. 2011. "Why Fiske Still Matters." In *Reading the Popular*, 2nd ed., edited by J. Fiske, xii–xxxviii. New York: Routledge.

Jenkins, H., R. Purushotma, M. Weigel, K. Clinton, and A. Robison. 2006. *Confronting the Challenges of a Participatory Culture: Media Education for the 21st Century*. Cambridge, MA: MIT Press.

Jenkins, H., S. Shresthova, L. Gamber-Thompson, N. Kligler-Vilenchik, and A. M. Zimmerman. 2016. *By Any Media Necessary: The New Youth Activism*. New York: New York University Press.

Lenhart, A., and M. Madden. 2005. "Teen Content Creators and Consumers." Available at http://www.pewinternet.org/files/old-media/Files/Reports/2005/PIP_Teens_Content_Creation.pdf.pdf.

Lord, A. B. 1960. *The Singer of Tales*. Cambridge, MA: Harvard University Press.

NAMLE (National Association for Media Literacy Education). 2007. "The Core Principles of Media Literacy Education." Available at http://namle.net/publications/core-principles/.

Williams, R. 1958. "Culture Is Ordinary." In *The Everyday Life Reader*, edited by B. Highmore, 91–100). London: Routledge.

———. 1976. "Culture." In *Keywords: A Vocabulary of Culture and Society*, 87–93. London: Croom Held.

11 /

Amy Petersen Jensen
on Bertolt Brecht

AMY PETERSEN JENSEN

Arts education underpins my work in media literacy: I know this is generally an unusual entrée into the field. As a theatre artist and educator, I realize that many of my media literacy colleagues approach the topic from the traditions, theories, and contexts of the communications field. My own experiences have led me to value the notion that media literacy draws its foundational structures from a wide body of scholarship, including arts practice and early arts-education models. This essay focuses on one of the progenitors of arts and instruction, Bertolt Brecht.

Brecht (1898–1956) was a theatre and media practitioner and theorist who envisioned new forms of art for the twentieth century. He did this first by reimagining the role of the spectator. As a playwright and director, he intentionally created politically motivated theatre, in which his audiences were responsible for critically engaging with the ideas presented in his work. He altered the centuries-old positioning of the audience member, from passive spectator to active participant. Specifically, Brecht invited his audiences to be informed participants who intentionally considered social bias, cultural prejudice, and other pervasive forms of manipulation. He believed that it was not enough to solely reflect on new ideas within the theater space; he invited his audience and performers to act on the ideas they had generated in practical settings outside the theater.

Brecht's theories demanded a re-functioning of the traditional theatrical space, from a place of entertainment into an educational space, in order to meet the needs of the ideal spectator that he imagined. This new space, the "Epic Theatre," as he described it, "appeal[ed] less to the feelings than the spectator's reason" and required that "instead of sharing an experience the spectator must come to grips with things [in the world]" (Brecht 1968a, 23).

The restructuring of the theater space also required new techniques. To do this, Brecht rejected the melodramatic spectacle of the popular theatre and instead produced a theatrical space composed of fragmented scenes, pictures, text, and music—each contrasting, contradicting, and interrupting the traditional theatrical trajectory in order to remind spectators that they were no longer participating in artifice. Brecht held that the theatre should "arouse [the viewers'] capacity to action" (1968b, 37).

Brecht's reimagining of theatre audiences, spaces, and techniques demanded new and timely literacies. While he never directly addressed the concepts of media literacy as we understand them, Brecht's practical work and writings were precursors to critical literacy and subsequent media literacy projects that developed later in the twentieth century. I first came to embrace critical theory because of Brecht's theoretical work. Through this line of thought, I discovered the critical pedagogies that deeply influence my own work as an arts educator and media literacy scholar. I have had three specific encounters with Brecht's writing that have shaped the questions I have asked as a student, as a media literacy scholar, and as an arts educator.

Valuing Participatory Spectatorship

I first encountered Brecht's ideas as an undergraduate theatre major at Brigham Young University in Utah. It was 1987, and I was a nineteen-year-old Mormon girl whose primary exposure to the theatre had been the religious pageants and roadshows put on by my church. My limited experiences with professional theatre production were the highly polished interpretations of Shakespeare performed at a regional equity house, the Utah Shakespeare Festival. Of course, I was also immersed in the 1980s films of John Hughes and others, and I had had some experience with art-house movies, but I had certainly not formulated a personal aesthetic.

When I imagined the purposes of theatre, film, or any of the arts, I was most compelled by the notion of story. I welcomed the poetic artifice and theatrical means that connected me, as an audience member, to the narrative of a play or film. I had not yet considered the importance of viewing a work of art as a material production that potentially represented the multiple contexts in which it was created. In a directing class, I was assigned to read selections from Brecht's "A Short Organum for the Theatre." Brecht had written this work late in his life with the intent of drawing a "description of theatre in the scientific age" (Brecht 1968c, 205). The ideas therein were based on his practical work in theatre. In my reading, I fixed on a sentence in which Brecht writes, "The theatre as we know it shows the structure of society (represented on the stage) as incapable of being influenced by society (in the auditorium)" (189). Contemplating his words, I became aware, for the first time, of the potential dialectic between spectators and the art they observed.

I had always loved being entertained by art. In fact, Brecht describes what had been my desired interactions with theatre and film at the beginning of "Short Organum": "[Popular theatre] consists of this: in making live representations of reported or invented happenings between live human beings and doing so with a view to entertainment" (Brecht 1968c, 180). I took great pleasure in consuming good art—and to be perfectly honest, even very bad art—for pleasure only. Because of this, I was a devoted consumer of art objects, but I was not a participatory spectator.

What Brecht describes is a different theory of the theatre, one where artifice is replaced with educational structures. In his essay "Theatre for Pleasure or Theatre for Instruction," he describes an "instructive theatre" in which "oil, inflation, war, social struggles, the family, religion, wheat, the meat market, all became subjects for theatrical representation.... As the 'background' came to the front of the stage so people's activity was subject to criticism ... [t]he theater became an affair for philosophers, but only for such philosophers as wished not just to explain the world but also to change it" (Brecht 1968d, 71–72).

Brecht's notions of the active and influential audience in "A Short Organum" and in "Theatre for Pleasure or Theatre for Instruction" compelled me to consider my responsibility to form a different, more active engagement with art and the world at large. I didn't fully realize this at the time, but my engagement with Brecht's theories had set me on a course of study in which I would vigorously begin to consider the social, cultural, and political implications of audience engagement with a work of art.

Reshaping Conversations about Art

I was reintroduced to Brecht in 1998 while studying at the University of Illinois at Urbana–Champaign. I was enrolled in a theatre history Ph.D. program and had designed a course of study that would allow me to take media coursework available in the English Department to compliment my theatre studies. My intent was to think deeply about how the perception of contemporary live performance was informed by mass media. I wanted to explore how live performance and media intersected and informed each other in popular culture. The core of my project, as I eventually described it, was "to document the strong influence of media's form and content on the production and reception of contemporary theatre" (Jensen 2007, 6). This time, I encountered Brecht in the context of the cultural-studies movement. Brecht's ideas resurfaced as I studied the theories put forth by the Frankfurt School. Reading his work through the lens of the critical thought associated with Walter Benjamin, Theodor Adorno, and Max Horkheimer, I became interested in the ways that both Brecht and Benjamin theorized about defamiliarization. Both men believed that for individuals to become aware of significant cultural and political shifts, and then act on their awareness, there must be a space where they could be shocked out of complete self-oblivion and absorption (Ezcurra 2012).

Neither Brecht nor Benjamin believed that the dramatic art forms popular in the early part of the twentieth century prepared the consumer for the political and social realities of their day. Both men envisioned art spaces in which art making and viewing was instructive and powerful enough to wrest complacency from the modern man. Each wanted a radical revision of art to reflect this transition. For example, in his 1936 essay "The Work of Art in the Age of Mechanical Reproduction," Benjamin reasons that the pervasiveness of art forms like photographs, film, and radio—forms created and represented through mechanical reproduction—signaled a shift in culture that no longer allowed for traditional authenticities associated with ritual and bound by religious viewpoints. He argues that "the instant the criterion of authenticity ceases to be applicable to artistic production, the total function of art is reversed. Instead of being based on ritual, it begins to be based on another practice—politics" (Benjamin 1999, 220). In this way, he called for new means of viewing that would aid individuals in preparing for the politically charged environs of the day.

While Benjamin was theorizing about the need for a change in art making to meet the needs of the moment, Brecht was actually constructing the politicized arts space—the Epic Theatre—that Benjamin called for in his writing. By the time Brecht and Benjamin left Germany as expatriates in the mid-1930s, Brecht had written and directed twenty works for the theatre. Each play was a testing ground for his ideas about art as a mechanism for change. Each of these fully produced plays demonstrated an innovative reconstruction of the stage space and its components.

The repurposing of the stage was intentionally political. Brecht's most prominent dramaturgical work from that time period, "The Modern Theatre Is the Epic Theatre," outlines the tenets for this type of theatre, in which everything traditional is altered for the purpose of helping audiences see the world through a new lens. The Epic Theatre produced a performing body that was no more important to the play than the other components of the work. The actor's body in these plays was no longer a representation of the unalterable hero, as presented in the dramatic theatre styles popular at the time; rather, it was one part of a mechanism—a technological body. Plays consisted of a series of unattached sequences. This theatre was made up of a montage that included choruses and songs, placards and film—all formed and fabricated into a fractured work of art intended to disrupt and awaken the audience. Brecht described this Epic Theatre as "a construction that must be viewed rationally and in which things must be recognized" (Benjamin 1998, 11). He worked to accomplish this through a term he coined as *Verfremdungseffekte,* which he defined as a stripping away of the familiar qualities of an art object to make something strange (Brooker 2006, 216). This was done in order for the spectator to recognize their previous lack of awareness.

In a critique of this principle, Benjamin perfectly describes the consciousness-raising potential of Brecht's theatre. He says:

> The point at issue in the theater today can be more accurately defined in relation to the stage than to the play. It concerns the filling-in of the orchestra pit. The abyss which separates the actors from the audience like the dead from the living, the abyss whose silence heightens the sublime in drama, whose resonance heightens the intoxication of opera, this abyss which, of all the elements of the stage, most indelibly bears the traces of its sacral origins, has lost its function. The stage is still elevated, but it no longer rises from an immeasurable depth; it has become a public platform. (Benjamin 1998, 1)

As a young scholar grappling with how societal change is represented in the production and perception of art within a particular time and space, I valued Brecht's intense effort to prepare a learning space in which art was shared for the purpose of engaging the audience in purposeful and active reflection. This conspicuous invitation to access art through my own lens, analyze art in my own context, evaluate art through my own experience, and create my own meanings is something that I have stubbornly held onto in my intellectual life. It is the philosophy that would eventually point me to media literacy as a field of study.

A Critical Media Literacy for Arts Educators

As a young student and later as budding scholar, I spent a lot of time wrapping my head around what Brecht and his contemporaries had to say about the work of art and its relationship to the advent of media technologies. I loved thinking and studying in this way. You would probably agree with me that it is rewarding to wrestle with another's theories and to discover how they might be appropriately leveraged to further develop our own ideas.

Today I am not only a student and a scholar; I am also a teacher. In my everyday existence I am responsible for the preparation of pre-service theatre and media-arts teachers who will eventually work in secondary schools across the United States. In those schools, teachers will need practical tools to engage in questions about artistic processes and their accompanying literacies. I want them to be exposed to arts and media literacy theories, but, more importantly, I want them to feel confident that their pedagogical approaches provide space for young people to ask important questions about the world. I want these teachers to be brave enough to leave room for young people to form tentative (and sometimes sure) answers for themselves based on their own perceptions and their understanding of the perceptions of others. I do not imagine that I am alone in this wish. I believe that this is at the core of media literacy.

Each year I teach an advanced-level course in media literacy to arts and English educators. In this context, I link Brecht's theories of the theatre to the educational paradigms of Paulo Freire. I invite students to consider how the revolutionary theories of an artist (Brecht) and a pedagogue (Freire) might work together to help them form their own practical understandings of critical theory, media literacy, and their potential pedagogies.

In the course, we begin our discussion with the closing section from the book *Paulo Freire: A Critical Encounter* (McLaren and Leonard 1993). The authors contextualize Freire's critical literacy project within a simple statement attributed to Brecht. It reads, "Art is not a mirror held up to reality but a hammer with which to shape it" (quoted in McLaren and Leonard 1993, 79). In dramatic fashion, McLaren and Leonard follow this statement by reminding the reader that for Freire, educational revolutions do not occur "without love." They go on to remark that Freire's work invites us to take Brecht's hammer and "forge on liberation's anvil new reciprocal discourses of knowing and freer, more equitable spaces for living" (McLaren and Leonard 1993, 82).

Sometimes when I am presenting McLaren and Leonard's ideas, I almost laugh out loud, mostly because I know that the "love" described here does not meet the measurability standards these teachers will be held to. I know that the love described is not always sustainable in a classroom of forty-five middle-schoolers. I don't laugh, though, because I want to engage in the complex problems that a critical pedagogy, which begins with love, might present in the real world. I don't laugh, because I believe in the possibility of new discourses. I don't laugh, because I want to be brave enough to secure equitable spaces for learning and living for young people. I don't laugh, mostly because I believe in Brecht's persistent hammer.

Brecht reshaped the field of theatre because he believed that "the radical transformation of the theatre [couldn't] be the result of some artistic whim." He says, instead, "it simply had to correspond to the whole radical transformation of the mentality of our time" (Brecht 1968a, 23). It is this kind of transformational critical thinking that, for me, heralded the discourses we now refer to as media literacy.

REFERENCES

Benjamin, W. 1998. *Understanding Brecht*. Translated by Anna Bostock. London: Verso.

——. 1999. "The Work of Art in the Age of Mechanical Reproduction." In *Illuminations*, edited by H. Arendt, translated by Harry Zohn, 217–252. New York: Schocken Books.

Brecht, B. 1968a. "The Epic Theatre and Its Difficulties." In *Brecht on Theatre: The Development of an Aesthetic*, edited by J. Willet, 22–24. New York: Hill and Wang.

——. 1968b. "The Modern Theatre Is the Epic Theatre." In *Brecht on Theatre: The Development of an Aesthetic*, edited by J. Willet, 33–42. New York: Hill and Wang.

——. 1968c. "A Short Organum for the Theatre." In *Brecht on Theatre: The Development of an Aesthetic*, edited by J. Willet, 179–206. New York: Hill and Wang.

——. 1968d. "Theatre for Pleasure or Theatre for Instruction." In *Brecht on Theatre: The Development of an Aesthetic*, edited by J. Willet, 69–76. New York: Hill and Wang.

Brooker, P. 2006. "Key Words in Brecht's Theory and Practice of Theatre." In *The Cambridge Companion to Brecht*, edited by P. Thomson and G. Sacks, 185–200. Cambridge: Cambridge University Press.

Ezcurra, M. P. 2012. "On 'Shock': The Artistic Imagination of Benjamin and Brecht." *Contemporary Aesthetics* 10 (1). Available at http://www.contempaesthetics.org/newvolume/pages/article.php?articleID=659.

Jensen, A. P. 2007. *Theatre in a Media Culture: Production, Performance, and Perception since 1970*. Jefferson, NC: McFarland.

McLaren, P., and P. Leonard. 1993. *Paulo Freire: A Critical Encounter*. London: Routledge.

12 /

Donna E. Alvermann
on Simone de Beauvoir

Midway through a grant-funded study some twenty-five years ago, I found myself staring at a large clock on the wall in a high-school classroom that housed a group of students, mostly young men, who were destined to leave school before graduating if their school records were to be believed. They, too, looked anxiously from time to time at the clock's minute hand that moved ever so slowly toward the dismissal hour. Identified by their classroom teacher as difficult to motivate, these tenth-graders self-identified as being uninterested in any school subject that required them to read and write. On a pre-study survey, they had said they didn't read, period. Having been a classroom teacher previously, I knew better than to engage in the blame game.

In retrospect, that clock-watching day was a turning point in my trajectory as a language and literacy researcher whose instructional responsibilities focus on preparing content-area literacy teachers at the middle and secondary levels as well as doctoral students preparing for academic appointments in literacy-teacher education. I recall thinking, as I still do, that surely there are venues in which young people who elect to turn their backs on schooled literacy can still identify as literate beings capable of making a difference in their own lives, in their communities, and in the more distant lives of others. I decided I would find those spaces and places, study them, and look for ways to draw implications from informal learning for more formal teaching and learning environments.

Over the years, informal learning opportunities for adolescents have increasingly pointed in the direction of digital-media literacy, which I define as the ability (including access and disposition) to use multiple modes of communication to encode and decode original and remixed texts composed of language, still and moving images, podcasts, and artistic performances, among other things (Alvermann 2011). Influenced by Colin Lankshear and Michele Knobel (2011), I view digital-media literacy as one of several new literacies—not new as in replacing something else but new in the sense that social, economic, cultural, intellectual, political, technological, and institutional changes are continually at work in transforming how we communicate. I also acknowledge Paul Gilster (1997), who coined the term *digital literacy* and insisted that critical thinking rather than mere technical competence is key to becoming digitally literate—a point that my colleagues and I have made elsewhere in relation to Web 2.0 and social media (Alvermann, Hutchins, and McDevitt 2012).

Digital and media literacy took a significant step forward in achieving its rightful place in American education circles in with the publication of Renee Hobbs's white paper, *Digital and Media Literacy: A Plan of Action* (2010). Up to that point, those of us in digital and media literacy education in the United States had depended largely on the scholarship of others, though not always educators, in Australia, Canada, and the United Kingdom. With Hobbs's plan of action in hand, it became easier to convince educators, community leaders, research-granting agencies, and a sprinkling of policy makers at the local, state, and national levels to support the analytical and communications skills necessary for successful teaching and learning in the twenty-first century.

However, as I argue in this chapter, it is Simone de Beauvoir's twentieth-century ideas and writings about personal freedom coupled with responsibility that contribute most fundamentally to the development of adolescents' critical literacy skills vis-à-vis digitally produced multimodal texts. In claiming Simone de Beauvoir as my academic grandparent, I draw on some incidents in both our lives that eventually led me to link her work with mine as well as to the larger field of digital and media literacy education.

Discontinuities and Connections

When Simone de Beauvoir arrived in New York City from Paris to begin a four-month-long journey across the United States in 1947, which she chronicled in *America Day by Day* ([1948] 1999), I was seven years old and beginning my second attempt at first grade in a small town near the Finger Lakes of upstate New York. I hadn't failed my first try; rather, I had dropped out, with my parents' permission, of course. The larger story (Alvermann 1999) is too long and complicated to include here, though it did have reasons I'd later associate with being made to feel like the Other in a classroom where I was the only child sent to school wearing camphor bags, which reputedly had antiseptic properties and were attached to the elastic ribbing of my leggings. Although my mother no doubt meant well in her attempt to save me from the various childhood diseases going around, the odoriferous camphor bags were an embarrassment and the cause of much teasing. That, coupled with the fact I was the first to be picked up by a rural school bus (before dawn in late fall and winter) and the last to be dropped off at our farm lane each afternoon, created a situation that I avoided by playing too sick to go to school on numerous occasions or, once in school, heading for the nurse's office with a made-up ailment that provided sanctuary until the bus delivered me back home. Eventually, my parents let me stay at home after learning that the first-grade teacher punished girls who talked (yes, I was a talker, even then) by making us hoist the backside of our skirts up and over our pint-sized chairs so that the ribbing of our leggings and covered behinds were exposed to anyone who cared to look—and laugh, I might add.

Simone de Beauvoir, by contrast, grew up in a bourgeois Parisian family, in "a society where every child of three was expected to have a personal calling card . . . and to present it as adroitly as any adult when the silver salver was placed before her" (Bair 1990, 21). Cultivated pretensions that separated the bourgeoisie from other segments of society in early twentieth-century France prevented Simone from speaking to other children, "let alone play with them, unless they were of the proper social class and her mother had first paid a formal call on theirs" (21). Even as a young child attending an exclusive private school at a well-known Catholic convent, de Beauvoir was "not allowed to speak to the little girls who were enrolled with her unless this strict formal etiquette had first been followed" (21). In *Memoirs of a Dutiful Daughter*, de Beauvoir would recall that over the years, and especially after the end of World War I, when the family's fortune had fallen on bad economic times, "nothing went to waste at our house: not a crust of bread, or a bit of string, not a complimentary ticket or an opportunity for a free meal" (1959, 66). By the age of seventeen, she had rejected her parents' opinions and the moral code of Catholicism and was beginning to formulate *otherness* as an imposed cultural construct. These developments, along with her commitment to existentialist philosophy, would lead eventually to the famous assertion, in *The Second Sex*, that one is not born but rather becomes a woman (de Beauvoir 1953).

Considering that de Beauvoir and I were separated by two generations and two continents—to say nothing of the social, familial, disciplinary, and linguistic disconnects between us—it is little wonder that I marveled to myself when her name came instantly to mind as a result of reading Renee Hobbs's invitation to choose a metaphorical grandparent for my field of study. The next thought that crossed my mind was how could I have read, at length and deeply, de Beauvoir's literary novels, feminist and philosophical treatises, and multivolume autobiography, supplemented by numerous secondary sources—I even visited her grave in Montparnasse and later imagined myself writing at a table on the second floor of Café de Flore—and yet never once have cited her in any of my research on digital-media literacy? Was I off base in thinking that I could draw connections now between de Beauvoir's line of inquiry and my own interests as a teacher educator researching adolescents' digital-media literacies? More to the point, would Hobbs, as editor of this volume, politely reject my first choice of an academic grandparent? And so I waited, but not for long; Hobbs's reply came quickly: "Hi, Donna, I'm counting you in, and yes, I see the connection!"

Thus began a fascinating project that involved furnishing my tiny home office with memorabilia from a much earlier trip to Paris during which I had traced de Beauvoir's footsteps moving about that city during World War II—my interests in such stemming from the fact I had minored in history throughout my bachelor's and first master's degree programs. I also pulled books on and by de Beauvoir from my personal library, reread turned-down pages, puzzled over underlined words, scribbled new questions in the margins, and generally became reacquainted with a woman whose ideas and writings I had admired from afar. Potential connections, such as the Other and personal freedom coupled with social responsibility, both concepts that I had overlooked earlier, became readily apparent as I rethought some of my own work on how youth who self-identified as nonreaders in school exhibited complex literate practices while engaging autonomously with digital media in informal learning contexts.

Participating as literate beings in out-of-school venues during after-school hours arguably freed these students from being Othered by school curricula and well-meaning educators bent on liberating so-called nonreaders from what was perceived as a lifetime of narrowed opportunities. In looking back at my own work, I had published data from research studies funded by the Spencer Foundation (Alvermann 2006) and later by the Bowne Foundation (Alvermann et al. 2012) that challenged the legitimacy of schools' labeling practices that marked adolescent (and mostly male) struggling readers as likely to become high-school dropouts and thus candidates for whatever the then-in-vogue remedial program might offer. When the young men and women in those two studies were in less-formal learning spaces—in a community-supported After School Media Club at a local public library with free access to the web and in a Saturday academic-support program designed to teach critical media literacy skills using student-selected online resources—they were self-actualized literacy users. In retrospect, had I interpreted the findings from these two studies using de Beauvoir's existential lens, I would surely have credited her for reminding me that throughout history, attempts to liberate Others by means that ignore individual will and choice are likely to produce new tyrannies that are arguably worse than becoming so-called nonreaders.

Despite finding de Beauvoir's writing on existential liberation compelling, I am aware of its limitations, especially when applied in educational settings. Case in point: while writing *The Blood of Others*, which was published in 1948, de Beauvoir is said to have worked out "her intention to express the paradox of freedom experienced by an individual and the ways in which others, perceived by the individual as objects, were affected by [that individual's] actions and decisions" (Bair 1990, 305). *The Blood of Others*, a fictionalized account of de Beauvoir's personal experiences in Paris during World War II, explores her commitment to the existentialist concept of individual freedom. When the book appeared in the United States a year after her four-month sojourn in this country, it was lauded as being a fictional primer on essentialism, and de Beauvoir was considered an author who represented "the most Existential of all the Existentialists" (Bair 1990, 306). Yet a stateside critical reviewer, Richard McLaughlin, writing for the *Saturday Review of Literature*, claimed serious doubts about "the ultimate achievement of [a state of pure individual freedom], since if the existentialists insist on total responsibility they also urge total involvement" (1948, 13). Following this line of reasoning in regard to total involvement, McLaughlin argued, would make it virtually impossible to remain untouched by the resolve of others; in fact, attempting to do so would deny a basic existentialist tenet—namely, that other people possess the same desire for total responsibility for their decisions and actions. This paradox, of course, has implications for schools, communities, and society at large.

For instance, while writing an early review of the literature on critical media literacy in a digital-rich environment—one in which students' choices about interacting, learning, and communicating were but a mouse-click away—my coauthor and I touched on the irony of adolescents' personal freedoms rubbing up against responsible and ethical online involvement, at least as we perceived such ambiguities through our own online experiences and as lifetime educators in K–12 and postsecondary schools in the United States (Alvermann and Hagood 2000). Unaware at the time that we were Othering those not like us in a none-too-complimentary manner, it was easy to omit mention of de Beauvoir's work in a list of references that numbered close to a hundred and contained, among other metaphorical grandparents, Michel Foucault.

However, it is less easy to rationalize why a little more than a decade later, any references to de Beauvoir's work and its relation to my own were still absent—this time from a review of the literature on young people's literate identities, multimodal texts, and critical media literacy in digital times (Alvermann 2011). Perhaps in perceiving de Beauvoir as a predigital-era writer and intellectual whose work would seemingly have little, if any, bearing on education in a digitally saturated twenty-first century, I had missed one opportunity after another to use her concepts of the Other, personal freedom, and social responsibility in interpreting my own work. If so, that was a serious error and one made visible precisely as a result of having been invited to write this chapter.

Reflections on de Beauvoir's *Old Age*

Writing as a scholar of new materialisms, Sonia Kruks uses de Beauvoir's experiences of the infirmities and oppressions she encountered in advancing age (de Beauvoir 1972) to illustrate how they provide insight into "the cultural and discursive media we produce" (Kruks 2010, 262). Specifically, Kruks calls attention to how society in a for-profit economy is largely responsible for the degradations of old age that devalue people who are no longer economically productive. Citing de Beauvoir's allusion to the aged as "pure objects," Kruks goes on to explain how exterior forces (e.g., the media) that make fun of older people and their infirmities by materially objectifying them as "useless . . . [and] not worthy of respect" can cause them to interiorize those labels (2010, 271).

A case in point that links this situation to a potential instructional activity for developing adolescents' critical awareness of how digital media can be complicit in Othering is a YouTube video that went viral in September 2011 titled "Webcam 101 for Seniors" (Mindy 2011). The video was uploaded by the retired couple's granddaughter, who had tried to teach Bruce and Esther Huffman from McMinnville, Oregon, how to record themselves using Esther's new laptop. Within four days of their repeated fumblings and eventual success (though unbeknownst to them), their video had attracted over 2.2 million views, according to *OregonLive* ("'Webcam 101 for Seniors' YouTube Video" 2011). The couple's display of advancing age and their cheerful online acceptance of being "computer illiterate" is a prime example of how de Beauvoir's work can be made relevant by educators today. As alluded to previously, a critical literacy activity that asks young people to view "Webcam 101 for Seniors" (which had attracted almost 12 million views as of November 2015) for the purpose of exploring who was Othered by whom, for what reason, and with what possible gain might be a starting point. Further discussion could lead to exploring the tensions between personal freedom and social responsibility, taking into account at the start that such an activity could backfire and accidentally reinforce the very stereotypes a teacher might be trying to avoid.

Some Parting Thoughts

Although de Beauvoir's work as the first twentieth-century woman to advocate a liberal feminism is undeniably important, it is her insistence on freedom coupled with responsibility and her tolerance for ambiguities—all themes of existentialist philosophy—that have informed this chapter. That de Beauvoir remains a force in the pantheon of feminist academics writing across three waves of feminism is evident if one takes at its word *Doing Gender in Media, Art and Culture*, a text published in 2009 for humanities students focusing on gender and media studies. Yet as Iris van der Tuin, the author of a chapter in that text, cautions, it would be foolhardy to think that location and generation are stable concepts; thus, "early feminist works are neither mechanically rejected nor automatically accepted" (van der Tuin 2009, 22). This sober reminder suggests to me that the thinking and writings of de Beauvoir will remain forever open to intellectual debates, in keeping with her existentialist outlook on life. It also suggests that future scholars will have the same opportunity as I have had here: to discover or reconsider how de Beauvoir's legacy advances the interpretive power of contemporary research on adolescents' digital-media literacies and their application to both theory and practice.

REFERENCES

Alvermann, D. E. 1999. "Writing Gender into Reading Research." In *Multicultural Research: A Reflective Engagement with Race, Class, Gender, and Sexual Orientation*, edited by C. Grant, 68–76. New York: Falmer.

———. 2006. "Ned and Kevin: An Online Discussion That Challenges the 'Not-Yet-Adult' Cultural Model." In *Travel Notes from the New Literacy Studies*, edited by K. Pahl and J. Rowsell, 39–56. Clevedon, UK: Multilingual Matters.

———. 2011. "Moving On/Keeping Pace: Youth's Literate Identities and Multimodal Digital Texts." In *Rethinking Identity and Literacy Education in the 21st Century*, edited by S. Abrams and J. Rowsell, 109–128.. New York: Teachers College Press.

Alvermann, D. E., and M. C. Hagood. 2000. "Critical Media Literacy: Research, Theory, and Practice in 'New Times.'" *Journal of Educational Research* 93 (3): 193–205.

Alvermann, D. E., R. Hutchins, and R. McDevitt. 2012. "Adolescents' Engagement with Web 2.0 and Social Media: Research, Theory, and Practice." *Research in the Schools* 19 (1): 33–44.

Alvermann, D. E., J. Marshall, C. McLean, A. Huddleston, J. Joaquin, and J. Bishop. 2012. "Adolescents' Web-based Literacies, Identity Construction, and Skill Development." *Literacy Research and Instruction* 51 (3): 179–195.

Bair, D. 1990. *Simone de Beauvoir: A Biography*. New York: Simon and Schuster.

de Beauvoir, S. (1948) 1999. *America Day by Day*. Translated by C. Cosman. Berkeley: University of California Press.

———. 1948. *The Blood of Others*. Translated by R. Stenhouse and Y. Moyse. New York: Knopf.

———. 1953. *The Second Sex*. Translated by H. M. Parshley. New York: Knopf.

———. 1959. *Memoirs of a Dutiful Daughter*. Translated by J. Kirkup. Cleveland: World.

———. 1972. *Old Age*. Translated by P. O'Brian. London: Weidenfeld and Nicolson.

Gilster, P. 1997. *Digital Literacy*. New York: John Wiley.

Hobbs, R. 2010. *Digital and Media Literacy: A Plan of Action*. Washington, DC: Aspen Institute.

Kruks, S. 2010. "Simone de Beauvoir: Engaging Discrepant Materialisms." In *New Materialisms: Ontology, Agency, and Politics*, edited by D. Coole and S. Frost, 58–280. Durham, NC: Duke University Press.

Lankshear, C., and M. Knobel. 2011. *New Literacies: Everyday Practices and Social Learning*. 3rd ed. Berkshire, UK: Open University Press.

McLaughlin, R. 1948. "Mouthing Basic Existentialism." Review of *The Blood of Others*, by Simone de Beauvoir. *Saturday Review of Literature*, July 17, p. 13. Available at http://www.unz.org/Pub/SaturdayRev-1948jul17-00013.

Mindy. 2011. "Webcam 101 for Seniors." *YouTube*, August 21. Available at https://www.youtube.com/watch?v=FcN08Tg3PWw.

Van der Tuin, I. 2009. "The Arena of Feminism: Simone de Beauvoir and the History of Feminism." In *Doing Gender in Media, Art and Culture*, edited by R. Buikema and I. van der Tuin, 7–23). New York: Routledge.

"'Webcam 101 for Seniors' YouTube Video Makes 'Adorable' Oregon Couple This Week's Viral Stars." 2011. *OregonLive*, September 15. Available at http://goo.gl/foDc92.

13 /

Jeremiah Dyehouse
on John Dewey

JEREMIAH DYEHOUSE

"Of all affairs, communication is the most wonderful," wrote the American pragmatist philosopher John Dewey in 1925. "That things should be able to pass from the plane of external pushing and pulling to that of revealing themselves to man, and thereby to themselves; and that the fruit of communication should be participation, sharing, is a wonder by the side of which transubstantiation pales" (1981, 132). Notwithstanding statements such as these, Dewey's searching inquiries into communication and communications technology are not well-known today. Instead, Dewey is best known for his work in education: his Laboratory School at the University of Chicago was a prominent site for early twentieth-century educational experimentation, for instance, and Dewey wrote widely on schooling and school communities. However, for Dewey, education was only one part of his inquiry into democratic life. Dewey made influential contributions in academic fields including psychology, logic, politics, ethics, and aesthetics. He was also a frequent contributor to public discussions of public affairs.

In general, Dewey's ideas are familiar to academics in digital and media literacy. However, conversations with colleagues make me believe that few know the extent of Dewey's thinking about literacy and mediated communication. Unlike the philosophy of technology (Hickman 1990, 2001, 2007), literacy is not an explicit focus of Dewey's writings. Yet Dewey's life experiences impelled him to think about this topic in a deep, sustained, and enriching kind of way.

In recent decades, a new and more international generation of academic readers has brought Dewey's writings to renewed prominence, and scholars from Europe and Asia especially are now reading Dewey's pragmatism. Although I live and work in Dewey's own northeastern United States, I consider myself part of this new global generation. I am proud to claim Dewey as an intellectual grandparent, and I have come to believe that his work holds special importance for students of digital and media literacy. In this essay, I seek to illustrate what I take to be one of Dewey's most pertinent insights for the field's contemporary inquirers: that shared understanding is not the *cause of* but rather a *result of* successful cooperations in action.

My own life experience has colored my views on Dewey's media thinking. Intellectually, I came of age in the mid-1990s. I remember sitting down to use the world's first popular web browser, NCSA Mosaic, in the basement of my college's library building, a few paces from the couch where I read Walter Benjamin's (1969) "The Work of Art in The Age of Mechanical Reproduction." Mosaic was a revelation. After having contended with DOS and VAX command lines, this program seemed a qualitatively better way to access computer networks. Like the hypertext software on which it was built, Mosaic allowed its users to follow links between page-like "documents" stored on different computers. (Mosaic also added support for inline images, which was an important feature for many users.) As a child who grew up with console-based video games, I remember my fascination with the open-ended, exploratory, and emergent qualities of the early World Wide Web. Not only did my screen connect with others around the globe, but I could add to the collection of documents that others could browse. To me, Mosaic manifested how media literacy could be more than the watching, reading, and playing I had previously known.

Just over a century before, Dewey was coming to his own fin de siècle enthusiasm for communications technology. As a young professor at the University of Michigan, Dewey's interests ranged widely across psychology, ethics, and politics, and they also included attention to developments in mass writing and communication. In 1891, Dewey wrote his colleague William James about a scheme he was hatching with former journalist and newspaper editor Franklin Ford and a group of Ann Arbor academics. In an explanation of what conversations with Ford had meant to him, Dewey (1999) shared the following prediction: "I believe that a tremendous movement is impending when the intellectual forces which have been gathering since the Renascence & Reformation shall demand complete free movement, and, by getting their physical leverage in the telegraph & printing press shall through free inquiry in a centralized way, demand the authority of all other so-called authorities." Building on ideas about what writing technologies like the telegraph and the printing press could accomplish, Dewey, Ford, and the others proposed to publish a new, philosophical kind of newspaper. This newspaper, to be called *Thought News*, was meant to stimulate individuals' awareness of our interconnectedness in what the group called the "social organism." The group also hoped that it would stimulate a reorganization of the existing global news industry. As Dewey and Ford believed, this broad change in news gathering and news publication would begin a worldwide democratic transformation of economic, political, and social activity.

Like the 1890s, the 1990s saw more than its share of visionary technology projects. When I was a graduate student, the project that particularly caught my attention was one that built on the successes of programs like Mosaic. Proponents of the Virtual Reality Modeling Language (VRML) argued that although the establishment of web pages gave computer networks a user interface drawn in two dimensions, what humans really needed was an interface built in three dimensions. Through the Web3D Consortium, work continues today on standards for sharing three-dimensional graphics on the World Wide Web. VRML, first specified in 1994, was the first major attempt to network these data types. For their part, VRML's proponents proposed that we should experience the web not *on* pages but *in* virtual worlds. VRML's main public advocate, Mark Pesce, suggested potentially far-reaching benefits for a "world"-based web interface, including fundamental changes to the Internet and improvements to democratic participation (Dychouse 2009). As it happened, however, this virtual world-building technology came to little. The project suffered from problems related to the slow data-transfer rates characteristic of dial-up connections. In addition, VRML users struggled to know what to do with the technology. I remember feeling genuinely disappointed to realize that VRML would not catalyze the broad technical, social, and political changes for which I had hoped. In retrospect, of course, I see that my expectations for a virtual-reality-based World Wide Web were not just unrealistic but impossible. At the time, however, the world seemed precisely this one technology short of radical transformation.

Like the rest of us, great thinkers can be captivated by bad thinking. In the early 1890s, Dewey did not realize that a new kind of newspaper could never inaugurate the "tremendous movement" he described in his letter to James. He and the other members of the *Thought News* group energetically promoted their periodical, and they promised students and members of the public that great things would follow from its specially promising kind of writing (Dyehouse 2014). Even after the group failed to produce even one issue of *Thought News*, Dewey continued to idealize writing. In lectures delivered to undergraduates in 1893 and 1894, for instance, Dewey predicted great changes to follow from the "Systematic Distribution of truth through the circulation of books and papers and use of mail, telegraph and telephone" (2010, 133). At this early point in his career, Dewey believed change in writing technologies would be central in unleashing broadly democratic social transformations.

Around 1894, Dewey began to think differently about communication and communications technologies. In the context of what he later called his drift "away from Hegelianism," Dewey ceased to privilege writing technology as a critical lever for social change (1984, 154). Instead, Dewey began to focus his attention on education, which he conceived as an enrichment of individuals' and their communities' practical life activities. In widely read works like *The School and Society*, Dewey (1976) proposed embodied, multisensory, and collaborative ways of educating as particularly promising means for enriching community life. By means of community-oriented schooling, Dewey proposed at the turn of the century, "we shall have the deepest and best guarantee of a larger society which is worthy, lovely, and harmonious" (1976, 20). In Dewey's view, as Robert Westbrook has summarized it, schools offered a particularly important opportunity to "foster the social spirit in children and develop democratic character" (Westbrook 1991, 105). Notwithstanding caricatures of Dewey's ideas offered by conservatives, Dewey did not wish to eliminate school curricula or to prevent students from learning self-discipline in schools. Rather, Dewey advocated for the reconstruction of curricula and forms of school acculturation that he saw as badly mismatched with contemporary values. In this educational project, Dewey anticipated a key focus of work in media literacy, which positions schools as intermediaries between home and mass-media cultures.

In second and third decades of the twentieth century, Dewey's practical and philosophical inquiries brought him to a changed perspective on formal schooling. Contrary to Dewey's progressive critics' persistent misreadings, Dewey's writings combine a broadened emphasis on education with attention to political activity in democratic community formation (Eldridge 1998). In this time, Dewey also articulated his mature philosophy of pragmatism, in which communication figures prominently as the practice in which "language hooks onto the world" (Sleeper 1986, 120). In Dewey's view, it is inquiry that makes possible the enrichment of our transactions with the various environments in and by which we live, and it is communication that makes productive inquiry possible at all (Dewey 1981). More generally, as Larry Hickman observes, "Dewey regarded communication as one of the most wonderful of human activities, and he thought that wherever enhanced communication is held honestly as a goal and an ideal, then new areas of agreement can be constructed and community life rendered more satisfactory for all concerned" (2001, 53).

Even in his earliest works, Dewey wanted to develop an alternative to theories of meaning as the representation of individuals' perceptions or ideas. Later in his career, Dewey particularly scorned the "pipeline" theory of communication, in which language transfers meanings, as self-subsistent thoughts, from consciousness to consciousness (1979, 88–89). Instead, Dewey understood meaning as a property of shared behavior. Through practical forms of cooperation in which not just language but also our bodies, tools, objects, and other living creatures play important roles, we learn about the potential consequences of our shared actions. In such learning—which may take place on the street, in a studio, or in a scientific laboratory—we pay special attention to when and how such consequences repeat themselves. Over time, we take such consequences for granted as the meaning of things we are using (Dewey 1981, 143; Pratt 1997). As Dewey argues, "A meaning is a method of action, a way of using things as means to a shared consummation" (1981, 147).

As part of his pragmatism, Dewey invented a media-focused theory of expression, which he developed most obviously in his 1934 book on art, *Art as Experience* (Dewey 1987). Put quickly, for Dewey, the artist's main task is to transform ordinary, everyday materials so that they clarify meanings found in experience. Beyond art narrowly conceived, Dewey was also interested in the many other ways that groups share meanings. Dewey conceived language in "its widest sense, a sense wider than oral and written speech," including "not only gestures but rites, ceremonies, monuments and the products of the industrial and fine arts" (1986, 51–52). Thus, while Dewey paid careful attention to literacy as writing and reading activity, he explicitly included in his focus on language a broad and evolving range of sign-making practices.

Over the course of his long career, Dewey attended consistently to the complex forms of sign-making practice we have learned to call "mass media." Arguably, however, he did not make his greatest contributions to digital and media literacy in his observations on and suggestions for historical practice. Rather, it is Dewey's more basic ideas about communication and media that most distinguish him today. Particularly notable in this regard is an idea Dewey rejected: that symbolic practices enable cooperative action because they generate shared understandings. Dewey's own view was more or less the opposite: he believed that shared understandings are the consequence, not the cause, of cooperative action. This point comes through strongly in Dewey's writings on education, in which he repeatedly rejects schools' traditional emphasis on memorization and observation. For Dewey, education is more basically a matter of "those situations in which one really shares or participates in a common activity, in which one really has an interest in its accomplishment just as others have" (Biesta 2006, 30). In such situations, successful cooperation in common activity produces learning or understanding. In schools, teachers must guide learning experiences, but it is the fact of cooperative activity that makes learning possible. Correspondingly, in Dewey's view, sign-making practices like gesture, speech, and writing are important adjuncts to the management of cooperative activity and to the enrichment of the lessons learned thereby. Nevertheless, for Dewey, the real key to understanding is in doing things together.

With this last point in mind, Dewey's life transition from newspaperman to educator is an especially suggestive one. As we have seen, not long after the failure of his philosophical publishing project, Dewey proceeded to immerse himself in the messy and practical activity of elementary education. One of Dewey's biographers has suggested that in William Rainey Harper, the University of Chicago administrator who most helped Dewey to found the Laboratory School, Dewey found another Franklin Ford (Martin 2002, 177). In light of Dewey's changing views on literacy and communication, however, we can also see why Dewey found the school a promising site for his continued investigations into action and understanding. Dewey's proposed periodical had had little chance of leading readers to awareness of the social organism or to the consequences that his group assumed would follow. In contrast, in the Laboratory School, Dewey could directly observe how shared social occupations—including cooking, sewing, and woodworking—led to shared social learning. It oversimplifies Dewey's life and work to say that, in the school, Dewey found action that led to understanding. Nevertheless, it was much more Dewey's vision for the school than his vision for the newspaper that inspired his later philosophy.

Today, of course, it is increasingly difficult to distinguish precisely between educational institutions and media products. In other words, the objects and experiences that people of Dewey's generation clearly understood as belonging to schools on one hand and to newspapers on the other are not so separate anymore. In all schools, students regularly engage contemporary media products, and many schools support students as evaluators and producers of media, including news. This blurring of boundaries has occasioned pathbreaking work in the field of digital and media literacy, whose specialists have settled down to work on problems that Dewey could not have imagined. Yet Dewey's works can still challenge us to think carefully about contemporary literacy and its relationship to social cooperation. In Dewey's view, we make meaning when we cooperate successfully, enriching the life activities that we share. In such cooperations, sign-making practices play many critical roles, but they are never exclusively important. "Where written literature and literacy abound," Dewey explained in 1938, "the conception of language is likely to be framed upon their model. The intrinsic connection of language with community of action is then forgotten" (1986, 54). As experts in literacy, we are tasked with reconnecting contemporary literacy with community of action. In fact, this is one of the ways that we help make contemporary literacy more effective for those who practice it.

It was not so long ago that I mourned VRML's failure to make great changes in the web and society. Since then, however, countless other communication-technology projects have also failed to deliver on their promises. This is the world in which we live. Yet as Dewey's writings and his example suggest, there is plenty of work to do— and enjoy—once we realize that understanding and action are never easily achieved. In my discipline, writing and rhetoric, we focus on the composition of media products and especially on writing activity. By engaging with students as they produce communications, we are learning about the labor and play involved in making media and meanings. Rhetoric highlights the interplay between producers, purposes, and audiences, while writing study emphasizes the inevitably material and embodied qualities of all language activity. On screens, in classrooms, in writing centers, and with community members, my colleagues and I promulgate effective composing practices. Moreover, because we know that theory exists to make practice more intelligent, we also *think* about literacy. Based on my researches into Dewey's philosophy, my own work has recently come to focus on thinking about literacy as critical for the way we behave in symbol-rich environments. Yet, these varied emphases notwithstanding, my own and my colleagues' work can attest to the widely felt significance of those problems in action and understanding with which Dewey wrestled. Like specialists in digital and media literacy, we also wish to reconnect meanings with community of action.

"Of all affairs, communication is the most wonderful," Dewey wrote in *Experience and Nature*, his most widely ranging philosophical work (1981, 132). In this disarming pronouncement, Dewey strikes that balance between hard-won wisdom and homey commonplace that we expect from good grandparents. Yet, as in many such pronouncements, Dewey's meaning here cannot simply be comprehended. Dewey has encouraged us to discover for ourselves and with others what is genuinely wonderful in communication today. This is perhaps the most general challenge of Dewey's thinking for students of digital media and literacy, and it is one that strikes me as entirely appropriate for us to inherit.

REFERENCES

Benjamin, W. 1969. "The Work of Art in an Age of Mechanical Reproduction." In *Illuminations*, edited by H. Arendt, 217–251. New York: Harcourt Brace Jovanovich.

Biesta, G. 2006. "'Of All Affairs, Communication Is the Most Wonderful': The Communicative Turn in John Dewey's *Democracy and Education*." In *John Dewey and Our Educational Prospect*, edited by D. T. Hansen, 23–37. Albany: State University of New York Press.

Dewey, J. 1976. *The School and Society*. In *John Dewey: The Middle Works, 1899–1924*, vol. 1, edited by J. A. Boydston, 1–109. Carbondale: Southern Illinois University Press.

———. 1979. "The Existence of the World as a Logical Problem." In *John Dewey: The Middle Works, 1899–1924*, vol. 8, edited by J. A. Boydston, 83–97. Carbondale: Southern Illinois University Press.

———. 1981. "Experience and Nature." In *John Dewey: The Later Works, 1925–1953*, vol. 1, edited by J. A. Boydston, 3–326. Carbondale: Southern Illinois University Press.

———. 1984. "From Absolutism to Experimentalism." In *John Dewey: The Later Works, 1925–1953*, vol. 5, edited by J. A. Boydston, 147–160. Carbondale: Southern Illinois University Press.

———. 1986. *Logic: The Theory of Inquiry*. In *John Dewey: The Later Works, 1925–1953*, vol. 12, edited by J. A. Boydston, 1–527. Carbondale: Southern Illinois University Press.

———. 1987. *Art as Experience*. In *John Dewey: the Later Works, 1925–1953*, vol. 10, edited by J. A. Boydston, 1–352. Carbondale: Southern Illinois University Press.

———. 1999. "Letter to William James." In *The Correspondence of John Dewey, 1871–1952*, vol. 1, edited by L. Hickman. *InteLex Past Masters*. Available at http://nlx.com/collections/132.

———. 2010. *The Class Lectures of John Dewey*, vol. 1, *Political Philosophy, Logic, Ethics*, edited by D. F. Koch and the Center for Dewey Studies. *InteLex Past Masters*. Available at http://nlx.com/collections/147.

Dyehouse, J. 2009. "The Cyberspace *Incrementum*: Technology Development for Communicative Abundance." *Rhetoric Society Quarterly* 39 (3): 281–302.

———. 2014. "Theory in the Archives: Fred Newton Scott and John Dewey on Writing the Social Organism." *College English* 76 (3): 252–272.

Eldridge, M. 1998. *Transforming Experience: John Dewey's Cultural Instrumentalism.* Nashville: Vanderbilt University Press.

Hickman, L. 1990. *John Dewey's Pragmatic Technology.* Bloomington: Indiana University Press.

———. 2001. *Philosophical Tools for Technological Culture: Putting Pragmatism to Work.* Bloomington: Indiana University Press.

———. 2007. *Pragmatism as Post-postmodernism: Lessons from John Dewey.* New York: Fordham University Press.

Martin, J. 2002. *The Education of John Dewey: A Biography.* New York: Columbia University Press.

Pratt, S. 1997. "'A Sailor in a Storm': Dewey on the Meaning of Language." *Transactions of the Charles S. Peirce Society* 33 (4): 839–862.

Sleeper, R. 1986. *The Necessity of Pragmatism: John Dewey's Conception of Philosophy.* New Haven, CT: Yale University Press.

Westbrook, R. 1991. *John Dewey and American Democracy.* Ithaca, NY: Cornell University Press.

14 /

Renee Hobbs on
Jerome Bruner

RENEE HOBBS

I'm a child of the space race. In the late 1950s, the United States was in the middle of a cold war with the USSR, a political, economic, and technological conflict made even more intense by the successful launch of the *Sputnik* satellite. Americans were in a panic—perhaps our education system was to blame for the lack of mathematicians and physicists. In fact, the National Defense Education Act was signed into law just days before I was born. Among other things, it provided the financial support for an interdisciplinary gathering of distinguished scholars at Woods Hole on Cape Cod in 1959 to examine how to improve public education. Participants included experts in mathematics, physics, education, psychology, history, the classics, and educational media. Although the conference was ostensibly to address the teaching of math and science, it took a much broader focus. Indeed, it ended up addressing issues of communication in education—both how to communicate knowledge of the subject matter and how to use new technologies in education.

Leading this conference was Jerome Bruner, who at the time was an important cognitive psychologist in the United States and a scholar known for bridging the gap between the scientific and humanistic approaches of his discipline. *The Process of Education* (1960) was a slender book about five key ideas that emerged from the Woods Hole conference. Its publication caused a sensation in education, and it was reprinted in numerous editions. It included the then-revolutionary idea that systems and structures matter for learning: in particular, the scope and sequence of curriculum needs careful, systematic design. It offered the bold claim that anyone can learn anything when learning experiences are designed in a way that promotes intellectual curiosity. The book emphasized the importance of intuitive, creative thinking through discovery over rote memorization and drill. It offered a hopeful and optimistic perspective on the educational use of films as "devices for vicarious experience" (81) that could help dramatize a subject by "leading a student to identify more closely with a phenomenon of interest" (83) and empower children who are "learning how to learn" (6).

While technology in education can be powerful, the book concludes by acknowledging that the problems of education cannot be solved by buying 16-milimeter film projectors but instead by "discovering how to integrate the technique of the filmmaker or the program producer with the technique and wisdom of the skillful teacher" (Bruner 1960, 92). *The Process of Education* served (for a time) as a manifesto for all who wanted to improve schools because "its attention was on the knower and the knowing" (Evans 2011, 85). It presented the value of inquiry learning as something that enables learners to recognize that the world is not a given and is subject to change.

As I write this, Bruner is celebrating his one hundredth birthday. Born in 1915, Bruner's lifelong project explores connections between mind and culture and between the social science and the humanities, connecting human development and human experience. In a way, Bruner has been expanding the concept of literacy by exploring the relationship between language, learning, cognition, science, arts, and culture. My work—which also seeks to expand the concept of literacy—is far more limited, practical, and narrow in scope. I'm fascinated with how media both reflects and shapes individual identity, cultural norms, social values, and expectations, and our sense of possibility about the future. Thus, I aim to provide educators with learning resources and pedagogical strategies that enable learners of all ages to have a kind of heightened consciousness about symbols, culture, and the meaning-making process through the practice of media analysis and media production.

I'm proud to acknowledge that Bruner is one of my intellectual grandparents: his work has influenced the way I think about media literacy education and about my life as a community-engaged scholar bridging the fields of communication and education. But, truthfully, his influence on my life began beyond my conscious awareness: in my first encounter with his work, I was actually too young to recognize him. Fortunately, in my second and, especially, my third encounters, I was able to appreciate and acknowledge his contributions to my own work in media literacy education. In this essay, I use three personal memories to explore the theoretical roots of media literacy education as embodied in Bruner's work.

First Encounter: *Man: A Course of Study*

I was probably eight or nine years old when I first encountered *Man: A Course of Study*. Growing up with a mother who was an elementary-school teacher and librarian, I practically lived at the school I attended and where my mother taught. Everywhere I looked, there were resources designed for learning. Our house was full of children's books and educational resources—including all manner of early educational technologies, such as film strips, photo sets, audio reels, programmed learning materials, and teaching machines. As a child, I learned to read with a tachistoscope, a fancy device (like a microscope for reading books) that presented words, and then phrases, and then whole lines of text in the briefest of microseconds, followed by comprehension questions. Speed-reading was the coolest game ever, and I loved it.

Somewhere in our house or at school, there was a collection of resources bundled together as *Man: A Course of Study*, developed by Bruner and his colleagues. It was an elementary social-studies curriculum in which the topic was humanity, and the content explored the questions "What is human about human beings?," "How did they get that way?," and "How can they be made more so?" (Bruner 1965, 4). The program's aim was to introduce children to key concepts of anthropology to demonstrate that all cultures are created equal.

This was an important lesson for me, growing up, as I was, in 1960s cloistered and suburban Detroit, where racism and social-class tensions were normative. Like millions of other children, I watched *The Wonderful World of Disney*, a television variety show that presented a world where cultural difference, on the few occasions when it was depicted, was stereotypical and exoticized.

Man: A Course of Study used a novel pedagogy that consisted of films, photographs, games, activities, and writing designed to introduce children to basic concepts in the social studies through exploring tool making, language, social organization, the management of prolonged childhood, and the human urge to explicate the complexity of the world through artistic expression. Social life was presented as a diverse variety of forms of communication and expression necessary for survival. I remember poring over these unusual and intriguing resources, written in just the right type of language for a ten-year-old. Even though these materials didn't look anything like anything I had ever seen before (did I perhaps try reading the teachers' manual?), I distinctly remember a small picture book that contrasted how humans and animals use their senses to pick up informational clues from their environment. Then there was a game about how bees communicate: you got to pretend to be a bee and use signals to tell the other bees how to find sources of food. There were short films (did I see them at school?) to explore the life of the Inuit and their various cultural activities, including hunting, tool making, storytelling, and family life. One film showed an Inuit family on a seal hunt, which was most gruesome but powerfully emotional and impressive. It was all quite magical stuff to me.

I didn't understand it at the time, but Bruner's aim in developing this radical new approach to curriculum (in which the process of learning was based in showing and exploring and doing and discussing) was to promote metacognition in ten-year-olds—to encourage children to think about their own thinking in order to gain awareness of how culture shapes experience. The resources were invitational: as a child, I was the detective who got to figure out how things fit together. There were no right or wrong answers in *Man: A Course of Study*. In describing the curriculum, Bruner wrote, "As for stimulating self-consciousness about thinking, we feel that the best approach is through stimulating the art of getting and using information—what is involved in *going beyond the information given* and what makes it possible to take such leaps" (1965, 21; emphasis added).

Indeed, my childhood was replete with experiences that enabled me to respect the powers of my own mind to figure things out. Only as an adult did I come to understand how Bruner helped fertilize my youthful intellectual curiosity. But the issues he raised are at the heart of my scholarly work as I explore how mass media, including television shows, movies, advertising, popular music, and social media, can help activate metacognition, critical thinking, and reflection in learners of all ages. In 1994, I had the opportunity to create *Know TV*, the award-winning multimedia curriculum for exploring the documentary genre that I developed in collaboration with Discovery Communications. It was my first experience in thinking through the problems of how to scaffold the practice of critical analysis of many different types of nonfiction television programming (including the then-new genre of reality TV) for high-school students. Later, I worked with a team of filmmakers, curriculum specialists, and teachers to create *Assignment: Media Literacy*, a K–12 media literacy curriculum, in collaboration with the Maryland State Department of Education and the Discovery Channel. We offered a six-hour professional-development program and were able to distribute thousands of curriculum boxes (containing printed lesson plans, books for students, and a VHS tape with clips for critical viewing and analysis) to teachers in schools across the state of Maryland. Clearly, Bruner's deeply collaborative and creative approach to working with filmmakers, scholars, and K–12 educators on *Man: A Course of Study* had been an inspiration to me.

Second Encounter: Harvard University

Bruner was already an academic legend at Harvard by the time I arrived at Harvard Graduate School of Education in the fall of 1981 to study at Project Zero with Howard Gardner, who was, at the time, engaged in research on children's artistic and visual expression that later fueled his important theoretical work on multiple intelligences. Gardner was an inspiration to me because of his own affiliation with Nelson Goodman, whose book *Languages of Art* (1968) had captured my imagination as an undergraduate. While reading this book, I remember first wondering whether people needed to "learn" to "read" the "grammar" of film, which became a focus of interest later on in my career (Hobbs et al. 1988). Gardner himself worked with Bruner as a research assistant on *Man: A Course of Study*.

Hailed as one of the scholars who helped overturn the dominance of behaviorism in the field of psychology with "the cognitive turn," Bruner had received his Ph.D. in psychology at Harvard in 1941. His mentor, Gordon Allport, had conducted groundbreaking studies of personality. One of the leading social psychologists of the time, Allport had also explored the psychology of the new technology of radio (Cantril and Allport 1935). Bruner was interested in both experimental cognitive psychology and the field of cultural anthropology. But he hated the way both these fields seemed to decontextualize and devalue the role of place, setting, motives, and dispositions in the context of human cultural life (Mattingly, Lutkehaus, and Throop 2012).

In his research on child development, Bruner (1966) observed that perception is a creative process, not just a biological one, and that people respond differentially to various modes of representation for learning about the world: enactive representation (experience), iconic representation (images), and symbolic representation (language). Unlike Piaget, Bruner did not position these as a set of developmental stages; he recognized that symbolic thought does not replace the other modes as we engage with experience, images, and language throughout our lifetimes. But he emphasized that perception is also inextricably tied to particular cultural and social conditions of lived experience.

In a very real sense, Bruner believed that the way we see the world is shaped by our culture's symbols. Not surprisingly, when Bruner first encountered the groundbreaking work of Russian psychologist Lev Vygotsky, he was entranced (Bruner 1973). Vygotsky had explored the role of cultural context in human development in the 1920s and written his seminal work, *Thought and Language*, in 1932, working with A. R. Luria and others to create a new approach to psychology. But in Stalinist Russia, these works were immediately suppressed. For twenty years after his death in 1934, it was forbidden to discuss or reprint Vygotsky's writing, and his work could be read only in a single central library in Moscow by special permission of the secret police (Dolya and Palmer 2005). After Stalin's death, the works were circulated to the West, and Bruner wrote the introduction to the English translation of *Thought and Language* in 1962. This and another work of Vygotsky's, *Mind in Society* (1978), had a substantial influence in the fields of both psychology and education (Cole 2009).

Influenced by Vygotsky's research, Bruner and his graduate students collaborated on a wide variety of projects that explored the complex relationship among language, literacy, and culture. For example, Patricia Greenfield examined the development of schooled and unschooled children in Senegal; another student went to Alaska to observe Inuit family life, education, and culture. At the time, this work was completely against the grain of the dominant discourse in the field of psychology, which was firmly based in stimulus-response behaviorism. Bruner and his students' work was, in many respects, the beginning of a field that came to be understood as cultural psychology (Bruner, Oliver, and Greenfield 1966).

Roy Pea describes working at Bruner's lab in the 1970s at Oxford University, where he was creating and analyzing videotapes that showed young children's everyday at-home and in-classroom interactions with adults. Bruner demonstrated with empirical evidence that babies develop the ability to establish joint attention with caregivers and that children of parents whose use of language followed the children's attention, rather than directed it, had larger subsequent vocabularies. This is where the term *scaffolding* was first used to describe the informal behaviors of parents in interacting with their young children. Through peekaboo games, parents use language with their children in ways that introduce them to practices of turn taking and meaning-making. The parent enables "the performance of a more complicated act than would otherwise be possible" only until the child is able to accomplish the activity independently (Pea 2004, 425).

The concept of scaffolding has been applied to practices of media literacy teaching and learning, and I have used it in my own work as a teacher and researcher. I try to encourage media-production and media-analysis activities that activate complex and multilayered social interaction at home, in school, and in nonschool settings. In my work in elementary and secondary schools, however, I have seen scaffolding used both well and poorly. Media literacy pedagogy creates high levels of motivation and engagement as students make connections between the classroom and the culture (Hobbs 2007). But it also disrupts traditional school hierarchies that position the teacher as the sage on the stage. For example, media-production activities can be made into a real drag for all concerned when the teacher insists on overstructuring them, breaking down the complex creative activity into many discrete steps. It's vital to respect the messy engagement that comes from tapping into students' creativity with digital media, popular culture, and mass media (Hobbs and Moore 2013). Talking about mass media in school, for example, raises complicated issues about what's appropriate for children and young people of different ages. Should young children discuss a celebrity's divorce, arrest, or drug use in school? Dynamic media literacy learning may occur when teachers use inquiry methods grafted onto authentic, current issues that are occurring in the community and happening on the popular-culture radar screen right now (Hobbs 2011). This often creates unpredictable situations that require a teacher to be able to take risks and use improvisational teaching techniques, just as in jazz performance (Hobbs 2013b). I have found, in my own teaching, that talking with undergraduate students about contemporary propaganda can lead to a complex, multifaceted conversation that may be noisy, unruly, and hard to control at times (Hobbs 2013a). In such learning spaces, I serve as facilitator and guide, not expert. For some, this shift in identity can be profound, and it can open up important insight and awareness of one's own motivations and values for implementing media literacy. When systematic reflection is part of a professional-development learning experience, teachers are better able to play in harmony with student voices and use their perspectives to deepen knowledge and skills in a climate of mutual trust and respect (Hobbs and Moore 2013).

Coming to the Harvard School of Education in 1981 as a boundary crosser into the field of education, I was flummoxed a bit by the great debates between the behavioralists, the cognitivists, the psychoanalysts, and the culturalists. But Vygotsky's powerful idea that "our productive activities change the world, thereby changing the way the world can change us" (Pea 2004, 426) was simply thrilling to me. And Bruner's meaning-centered psychology resonated with my background in English literature and film/video studies, in which the goal "was to discover and to describe formally the meanings that human beings created out of their encounters with the world, and then to propose hypotheses about what meaning-making processes were implicated." Bruner was curious about the "symbolic activities that human beings employed in constructing and in making sense not only of the world, but of themselves" (Bruner 1990, 2). It was obvious that Bruner was putting the questions of human communication and meaning-making at the center of his inquiry in an effort to improve the practice of teaching and learning by making connections among psychology, education, anthropology, and "the interpretive disciplines in the humanities and in the social sciences" (2).

Bruner was also a pragmatist whose theoretical work was embodied in education reform. He didn't just live in his ivory tower; he was active in the fray of education policy, serving on the President's Science Advisory Committee during the presidencies of John F. Kennedy and Lyndon Johnson and working collaboratively with filmmakers, anthropologists, and classroom teachers in developing *Man: A Course of Study* (Laird 2004). Because this course was considered to be a breakthrough in both content and format, Bruner received an award from the American Educational Research Association in 1969.

Because of its suggestion that all cultures were equal and worthy of respect, this curriculum was popular with both teachers and students. But the curriculum was attacked by the religious right. By 1974, when hundreds of thousands of children were using the curriculum in forty-seven states, the program ran into controversy as the Moral Majority, along with a group of right-wing politicians, flexed their muscles, using newspaper editorials to loudly object to the program's inclusion of content related to what Linda Symcox has called "reproduction, aggression, killing, religion, and views of life and death" (2002, 22). Representative John Conlon of Arizona held a hearing on the curriculum, claiming that it challenged American values by introducing children to the customs of other cultures at an early age, making children vulnerable to "foreign values and beliefs" (quoted in Symcox 2002, 22). By 1975, "*Sputnik*-inspired academics were sent back to their ivory towers" because religious conservatives believed that a social-studies curriculum that encouraged an inquiring mind to learn about human behavior and culture was "dangerous because it did not deal in absolutes" (Symcox 2002, 23). Bruner's work had opened up national public debate about traditional versus progressive education. This was the kind of integrative and grounded scholarship-in-action that I truly admired. In my career, I have occasionally taken solace in Bruner's big curriculum controversy as I faced my own, much smaller tempest, caused when some colleagues were outraged that I worked with teachers in schools that had adopted *Channel One* (a then-controversial television news program for teens) and encouraged the media industry to provide financial support for the media literacy community's national conference. This became one of the most vociferous of the great debates in the media literacy movement (Hobbs 1998).

Bruner certainly validated the idea that one's creative self could be connected to one's identity as a researcher, teacher, and learner. Perhaps, however, I've known this forever: while I love to learn by reading, watching, and listening, I actually learn best by making and doing things. An important aspect of my personal and professional identity has always come through creative expression. As an undergraduate, I enjoyed serving as a reporter and editor for the *Michigan Daily*, the college newspaper. I love the forced concision of Twitter and appreciate how my creativity flourishes under constraints of time, resources, and format. I am at my happiest when designing websites and interactive media, making videos, writing curriculum, composing essays, making speeches, curating images for my PowerPoints, and using a combination of moving images, language, and sound to express my ideas. So much of my creativity is practiced through collaboration. Making media provides a structure for engaging with both people and ideas—it is through working with people to create media and learning experiences that I do my best thinking.

One fundamental value of media literacy education is expressed in the idea that *by making media, we learn*. Jerome Bruner identified the powerful interplay between working with people and materials ("hands-on") and working with ideas ("minds-on") as fundamental learning practices. In the 1960s, this approach was revolutionary and Bruner's ideas were fueling the revolution. In my own teaching, I have discovered that many abstract principles and ideas become more engaging and accessible to learners when approached in an activity-based experience. By the way, this is just as true for graduate students as it is for young children (Hobbs 2015). Creative authorship is fundamentally a learning process: as Bruner explained, artifact creation is an essential aspect of cognitive activity and cognitive growth. He appreciated that for many learners, it is vital to explain "in things, not words, understanding by doing something other than just talking" (Bruner 1996, 151). And not only do such creative works instantiate the learning process; they inspire those who participate in creating and sharing them and cultivate "pride, identity, and sense of continuity" (22). Today, most media literacy educators insist on emphasizing the intersections that connect critical analysis to creative-media production (in print, visual, sound, and digital formats) as a core element of pedagogical value, reflecting a Brunerian line of inquiry in which learning is understood as a socially, culturally, and materially embodied process.

Third Encounter: Story Structures across the Generations

Stories reflect and shape our experience of reality. In *Actual Minds, Possible Worlds* (1986), Bruner tackles the problem of how people develop a grasp of the world around them and how stories trigger diverse interpretations and meanings. Aware of the limitations of the Piagetian perspective on human development, Bruner positions human growth and development within a fundamentally social and cultural context. An individual's working intelligence is never "solo," says Bruner. We learn from the people who are around us. Learning is really a process of mastering the "culture's treasury of tool kits" (Bruner 1991, 3), and most of us only learn a few of the multiple ways of knowing available to us within our culture. Knowledge is never separate from a particular point of view; the cultural products of knowledge shape our understanding of reality.

The powerful integration of arts and social sciences is evident in Bruner's reading of literary theory, in which, as a psychologist, he offers explorations of narrative that give insight and simultaneously inspire new questions. Stories have special features: they constitute the world by carefully structuring a sequence of events in time, offering particularities of detail that stand for more universal themes. Stories are greater than the sum of their parts: the parts and the whole are hermeneutically interdependent. Great storytellers exploit this hermeneutic for "narrative seduction," creating stories so seamlessly coherent that even the most implausible of situations becomes blazingly real, and "brilliant exploitation of the devices of text, context and mis-en-scene" predispose people to "one and only one interpretation," sometimes even leading to a mindless automaticity of interpretation (Bruner 1991, 9). Narratives are "good" and "tellable" when they breach expectations, making the ordinary strange; that's why we celebrate innovations in genre, as novels with first-person narrators break the authority of the omniscient narrator and reality TV provides fresh ways to express and appreciate the wonder, drama, and conflict in ordinary people's lives. When we encounter stories, we take into account the teller's intentions and accept different stories of an event without complaint: "the very context dependence of narrative accounts permits cultural negotiation," as lots of different stories from many different tellers accrue into a coherence that becomes a cultural tradition or a worldview (Bruner 1991, 18). Through stories, we perpetually construct and reconstruct ourselves.

I have always used storytelling as part of my own scholarly rhetoric. It suits my particular approach to research, in which I work in partnership with teachers and school leaders to explore media literacy education practices and solve real-world problems related to curriculum and instruction. When in 2009, I had the chance to meet Jerry Bruner, I got the opportunity to reflect on the power of storytelling and personal narrative as a force for intellectual development and cognitive growth. At the time, I was invited to participate in a panel discussion with him at Fordham University, in a session sponsored by the Institute on General Semantics titled "Across the Generations: Legacies of Hope and Meaning." The specialists in general semantics are interdisciplinary scholars who explore what I have called the representation-reality issues concerning how symbolic forms shape meaning, thinking, feeling, and action (Hobbs 2006b). At the time, Jerry was celebrating his ninety-fourth birthday, and getting to talk with him over dinner was a remarkable opportunity.

It was Bruner indeed who gave me the idea for this book, in sharing with me the experience of writing about life narratives. At the time I met him in person, I was thinking more and more about the various motivations that teachers have for beginning to explore digital and media literacy. I would frequently ask teachers why they started doing this work, and it would inevitably turn into a fascinating personal story. It seemed like these stories were important to teachers and that they helped explain the various curriculum choices they made and the kinds of instructional practices they used in the classroom. I began to incorporate reflection on motivation whenever I taught teachers. My colleagues and I were able to develop and validate an online questionnaire to measure people's profiles to examine differences in teacher motivations for digital and media literacy (Hobbs and Tuzel 2015).

Using a constructivist approach to the autobiography, Bruner often explained that people's personal life stories do not happen in the real world but, rather, are constructed in their heads (1983, 1991). Bruner claims that "the culturally shaped cognitive and linguistic processes that guide the self-telling of life narratives achieve the power to structure perceptual experience, to organize memory, to segment and purpose—to build the very 'events' of a life. In the end, we *become* the autobiographical narratives by which we 'tell about' our lives" (Bruner 2004, 694). Simply put, our own lives are variations on the culture's canonical forms and stories. This big idea echoes the work of Martin Heidegger, who invites us to recognize the "always already" state of being, enabling us to confront the paradox of living in relationship with other humans while being ultimately alone with oneself.

As I see it, that's why the stories of mass-media culture matter so much to understanding an individual's personal and social identity. This issue should be of vital importance to educators. Well before the advent of YouTube, critics noted how much of American popular culture is built on people seeking to become the mediated representations they consume in "a society in which individuals have learned to prize social skills that permit them, like actors, to assume whatever role the occasion demands and 'perform' their lives rather than just live them" (Gabler 1998, 10). Rather than see this as exceptional, worrisome, or absurd, we might concede that it's natural to conflate our own lives with the lives and stories we encounter through media. Bruner notes that "We seem to have no other way to represent 'lived time' save in the form of a narrative" because "'life' in this sense is the same kind of construction as a narrative is" (2004, 692).

Reflecting on the power of symbols not only offers the potential to rewrite one's own life narrative, but it holds the promise of building new shared narratives that enable and inspire social action. First, we have to internalize the process of asking critical questions about what we watch, see, and read. Only a few years before meeting Bruner, when the Institute for General Semantics invited me to give the fifty-fourth annual Alfred Korzybski invitational lecture in Fort Worth, Texas, I was honored and a little intimidated as I shared with this group the reasoning behind my development of the media literacy remote control, the visual metaphor I developed for articulating the abstract reasoning, deconstruction, and critical-analysis skills at the heart of media literacy (Hobbs 2006a). In particular, the media literacy remote control includes a question on the importance of recognizing omission as a way to recognize bias and point of view. The general semantics discourse community included Neil Postman, who played a leadership role as journal editor of the community's publication, *ETC*. I had first learned about this group when using S. I. Hayakawa's classic book *Language in Thought and Action* ([1939] 1978) as a young assistant professor teaching courses in human communication. In fact, Hayakawa had offered unexpected insight on media literacy by writing about the relationship between poetry and advertising. When everyone else was demonizing advertising as forms of propaganda and indoctrination, he provided an alternative conceptualization, an elegant media literacy lesson about the authentic personal value that may come from reflecting on those ordinary symbolic artifacts in the world around us. Instead of vilifying advertising for its "half-truth, deception, and outright fraud," Hayakawa urged us to see the parallels between advertising and poetry, to recognize how advertising works as it strives to "give meaning to the data of everyday experience . . . to make the objects of experience symbolic." Like poetry, advertising matters because it works to enter into our imaginations. As a result, it shapes "those idealizations of ourselves that determine our conduct" (Hayakawa 1978, 269). It's the first step in the spiral of empowerment: media literacy educators design learning experiences that enable people to gain awareness of our culture's interpretive processes by recognizing the way symbols affect reality.

In attempting to offer a personal examination of how and why Bruner serves as one of my intellectual grandparents, readers may appreciate how media literacy builds on and extends early twentieth-century ideas about the relationship between symbols, culture, mind, and society. When implemented in the classroom with integrity and respect for learners, media literacy has the potential to support the kind of metaphysical change that "is required to alter the narratives that we have settled upon as 'being' our lives" (Bruner 2004, 709). These ideas inflect the practice of education, the nature of knowledge in a symbolically rich cultural world, and the relationships among culture, cognition, emotion, and action.

REFERENCES

Bruner, J. S. 1960. *The Process of Education*. Cambridge, MA: Harvard University Press.

———. 1965. "Man: A Course of Study." Occasional Paper No. 3, National Science Foundation, Washington, DC. Available at http://www.macosonline.org/research/Bruner_MACOS%20-Occasional%20Paper%203.pdf.

———. 1966. *Towards a Theory of Instruction*. Cambridge, MA: Harvard University Press.

———. 1973. Introduction to *Thought and Language*, by L. S. Vygotsky, v–x. Translated by Alex Kozulin. Cambridge, MA: MIT Press.

———. 1983. *In Search of Mind: Essays in Autobiography*. New York: Harper and Row.

———. 1986. *Actual Minds, Possible Worlds*. Cambridge, MA: Harvard University Press.

———. 1991. "The Narrative Construction of Reality." *Critical Inquiry* 18 (1): 1–21.

———. 1997. *The Culture of Education*. Cambridge, MA: Harvard University Press.

———. 2004. "Life as Narrative." *Social Research* 71 (3): 691–710.

Bruner, J. S., R. Oliver, and P. Greenfield. 1966. *Studies in Cognitive Growth: A Collaboration at the Center for Cognitive Studies*. New York: Wiley.

Cantril, H., and G. Allport. 1935. *The Psychology of Radio*. New York: Harper and Brothers.

Cole, M. 2009. "The Perils of Translation: A First Step in Reconsidering Vygotsky's Theory of Development in Relation to Formal Education." *Mind, Culture, and Activity* 16 (4): 291–295.

Dolya, G., and S. Palmer. 2005. "Lev Vygotsky." *SuePalmer.co.uk*. Available at http://www.suepalmer.co.uk/education_articles_lev_vygotsky.php.

Evans, R. 2011. *The Hope for American School Reform: The Cold War Pursuit of Inquiry Learning in the Social Studies.* New York: Palgrave Macmillan.

Gabler, N. 1998. *Life the Movie: How Entertainment Conquered Reality.* New York: Knopf.

Goodman, N. 1968. *Languages of Art: An Approach to a Theory of Symbols.* Indianapolis, IN: Bobbs Merrill.

Hayakawa, S. I. (1939) 1978. *Language in Thought and Action.* San Diego: Harcourt Brace Jovanovich.

Hobbs, R. 1998. "The Seven Great Debates in the Media Literacy Movement." *Journal of Communication* 48 (2): 9–29.

———. 2006a. "54th Annual Alfred Korzybski Memorial Lecture: Literacy in the 21st Century." *General Semantics Bulletin* 73:40–44. Available at http://www.generalsemantics.org/wp-content/uploads/2011/04/gsb-73-hobbs.pdf.

———. 2006b. "Multiple Visions of Multimedia Literacy: Emerging Areas of Synthesis." In *Handbook of Literacy and Technology,* vol. 2, edited by M. McKenna, L. Labbo, R. Kieffer, and D. Reinking, 15–28. Mahwah, NJ: Lawrence Erlbaum.

———. 2007. *Reading the Media: Media Literacy in High School English.* New York: Teachers College Press.

———. 2011. "The State of Media Literacy: A Response to Potter." *Journal of Broadcasting and Electronic Media* 55 (3): 419–430.

———. 2013a. "The Blurring of Art, Journalism, and Advocacy: Confronting 21st Century Propaganda in a World of Online Journalism." *I/S: A Journal of Law and Policy for the Information Society* 8 (3): 625–638.

———. 2013b. "Improvisation and Strategic Risk Taking in Informal Learning with Digital Media Literacy." *Learning, Media and Technology* 38 (2): 182–197.

———. 2015. "Twitter as a Pedagogical Tool in Higher Education." In *Produsing Theory in a Digital World 2.0,* vol. 2, edited by R. A. Lind, 211–228. New York: Peter Lang.

Hobbs, R., and D. C. Moore. 2013. *Discovering Media Literacy: Digital Media and Popular Culture in Elementary School.* Thousand Oaks, CA: Corwin/Sage.

Hobbs, R., J. Stauffer, R. Frost, and A. Davis. 1988. "How First Time Viewers Comprehend Editing." *Journal of Communication* 38 (4): 50–60.

Hobbs, R., and S. Tuzel. 2015. "Teacher Motivations for Digital and Media Literacy: An Examination of Turkish Educators." *British Journal of Educational Technology.* doi:10.1111/bjet.12326.

Laird, C. 2004. *Through These Eyes.* Directed by C. Laird. National Film Board of Canada. Available at http://www.nfb.ca/film/through_these_eyes.

Mattingly, C., N. Lutkehaus, and C. J. Throop. 2012. "Bruner's Search for Meaning: A Conversation between Psychology and Anthropology." *Ethos* 36 (1): 1–28.

Pea, R. 2004. "The Social and Technological Dimensions of Scaffolding and Related Theoretical Concepts for Learning, Education and Human Activity." *Journal of the Learning Sciences* 13 (3): 423–451.

Symcox, L. 2002. *Whose History? The Struggle for National Standards in American Classrooms.* New York: Teachers College Press.

Vygotsky, L. 1978. *Mind and Society.* Translated by Michael Cole. Cambridge, MA: Harvard University Press.

15 /

Vanessa Domine
on Neil Postman

VANESSA DOMINE

There are many words circulating in the intellectual universe to describe Neil Postman. Among them are educator, social critic, media theorist, author, and distinguished professor. Some have even labeled him a neo-Luddite. Yet those who knew Postman personally understand the inadequacies of language to capture his essence. As one of his doctoral students, I engaged in many conversations with him about the possibilities and perils of technology. While he and I disagreed on a multitude of topics, I came to discover that underneath Postman's sardonic social criticism was a cautious optimist who perceived his role as hoping for the best by pointing out the worst. While Postman is most known for his critique of popular media (particularly television), his work is foundational to the growth of digital and media literacy as both a field of study and a movement. An educator-turned-communication scholar, Neil underscored the grammatical side of media, and he magnified for English language-arts teachers everywhere Marshall McLuhan's postulate that the form or language of media shapes message content, user experience, and societal systems. In this essay, I offer three key ideas that I fondly refer to as *Neilogisms*. They are (in no particular order): privileging humanism in a technologized world, valuing education more than schooling, and the importance of inquiry and discourse. These ideas have become foundational to my own work in educational technology, in which I consider digital and media literacy to be the keystone of teaching and learning (Domine 2011a).

Postman was born in 1931 in New York City and grew up during the Great Depression. He lived through numerous wars and other atrocities that plagued the twentieth century. Postman was a New York City English teacher in the 1950s and, later, a distinguished professor at New York University. He applied his linguistic wisdom and wit to critique the emergence of the electronic age and the proliferation of television. In the 1970s, Postman extended McLuhan's theory that media and technology profoundly influence human society. Postman introduced the term *media ecology* as the study of media environments (1970, 161). Invoking a biological metaphor, he later explained, "A medium is a technology within which a culture grows; that is to say, it gives form to a culture's politics, social organization, and habitual ways of thinking" (2000, 1). To say that Postman problematized technology is an understatement. He was deeply influenced by Harold Innis (among other harbingers, mostly male), who warned in *The Bias of Communication* (1951) that Western civilization faced a great crisis associated with mass communication, including an obsession with the present that disregarded the past and future. Among Postman's many trademark questions were "What is the problem to which this technology is the solution?" "Whose problem is it actually?" "If there is a legitimate problem, then what other problems will be created as a result of using this technology?" "Am I using this technology? Or is this technology using me?" (1999, 42). For Postman, technology presented not only a social, economic, and political problem but a moral one as well. To know Postman was to verbally joust with him about these very issues.

On the spectrum of technological determinism and social determinism, Postman and I were polar opposites. I was born in 1969 in California and raised in Silicon Valley, the technological capital of the world. In the 1970s, my father worked for IBM as an electrophysicist and assisted in the development of the first VCRs and personal computers. I experienced firsthand the emergence of the information age. Among my favorite childhood memories of my father were the custom-built radios and other electronic devices that he would bequeath as birthday gifts. My family was one of the first in our sprawling suburban neighborhood to own a personal computer, and I distinctly remember the joy when we replaced our TRS-80 computer (that operated via cassette tapes) with a new Apple IIe computer. My childhood experiences with media and technology were seemingly utopian, as they coincided with growth and progress in my family. I grew up watching *Sesame Street*, yet I was also highly print literate and loved to read books. I watched MTV and played hours of Atari video games, yet I was highly social with many friends. I spent at least four hours a day, if not more, using television and computers, yet I also loved to learn in school and I earned good grades. But when my father died suddenly when I was just twelve years old, it emotionally and financially devastated my family. From that point forward, using media and technology became symbolic of many things for me. Not only did it eventually become a means of earning a living (survival), but it was also a symbolic way for me to honor my father.

It wasn't until I was an undergraduate communications major in college and read Postman's *The Disappearance of Childhood* (1982) that I seriously reflected on my media-saturated childhood and its possible impact on my social, emotional, and intellectual development. Postman's argument about the obsolescence of childhood through the introduction of broadcast media did not resonate with my lived experience. I did not readily perceive any disadvantages until I read the widely popular *Amusing Ourselves to Death* (1984) that essentially rebuked television entertainment for overextending into the realm of serious and sacred spaces in our personal lives. Postman drew on the work of Walter Ong (1958) who theorized the loss of reason and logic as a result of the transition away from orality and print into the visual culture characteristic of the modern electronic age. The dissonance between Postman's ideas and the reality of my own childhood propelled me further into deeper (graduate-level) study of media, technology, and human communication. I encountered Herbert Blumer's (1969) work on how humans navigate symbolic environments to shape the world. I decided to tap the creative possibilities of educational technology while conscientiously minimizing the perils and pitfalls to learning. This was a long shot, since the disparity between the rapid pace of technological innovation and the stagnancy of educational change during the early 1990s was both obvious and disturbing.

When it came time to conduct my master's thesis research, I was less concerned with looking inward and more interested in looking outward at the influence of media on children and adolescents, particularly in the context of the school classroom. In *Amusing Ourselves to Death*, Postman (1984) expresses skepticism of the uses of television in schools. He believed the way television was used in schools did not teach students to love learning but to love television viewing. Drawing on McLuhan and others, Postman argues that since the codes and conventions of television are highly emotive and demand the opposite of rational deliberation, its presence in schools promotes individualism, isolationism, and authoritarianism—values that contradict the community-centered, democratic ideal of schooling. For me, this was a powerful and important distinction between the possibility of education and the reality of schooling. These ideas also resonated powerfully during the mid-1990s, when broadcast media were still criticized for perpetuating a linear, one-way mode of communication in schools. In the process of reviewing the literature, I discovered a history of instructional technology littered with attempts to use television as a replacement for a teacher and rife with lost opportunities for conversation, dialogue, and debate (Greenwood 1994).

As a neophyte scholar of communication, I was mystified and intrigued by the relationship between education and schooling more than the study of technology itself. I was particularly interested in language or, more broadly, communication as the medium of education. Like Postman, I was deeply influenced by Jerome Bruner's (1986) narrative construction of reality and the view that language is not just the vehicle for expression; it is also the driver. Postman felt strongly that language instruction should not be confined to an English or language-arts classroom. At the same time, it is not the words, symbols, or technologies themselves that are important per se; it is the *process* of using them to engage and inquire. Along this vein, I chose a critical-interpretive research framework to study the *Channel One* controversy that came to a head in one California school district in 1993. Through my research, I learned about the constructive power of language and that a community's views of schooling are inextricably connected to their assumptions about media, technology, and learning. I posed the possibility of changing education by changing the ways in which we talk about media, technology, and schooling.

I did not realize how much Postman's work would ultimately influence my intellectual development until I researched doctoral programs. Out of numerous communication programs across the country, I discovered the media ecologists at New York University to be asking the most interesting questions: What does human communication reveal about the purpose of technology? About the purposes of schools? About the nature of learning? About the role of the teacher? About knowledge and how curriculum is established? About the function of language and symbols in education? So in 1995, I moved across the country to a tiny apartment in Greenwich Village to study media ecology and linger within these questions. Many, including Postman himself, wondered why a Gen-Xer would leave sunny California to study in gritty New York City with an alleged neo-Luddite. The answer was simple: I realized that I was more interested in asking smart questions about education than finding the correct answers about media and technology. Media ecology allowed me to do both.

I learned that more than three decades earlier, Postman had already foreshadowed a pedagogical solution to the perils of instructional television in his first book, *Television and the Teaching of English* (1961). Postman wrote about the promising potential of using television to teach English language arts (and vice versa) and alluded to the need for inquiry-based media literacy education:

> Facts will always be the raw material of education. But "fact-saturated" television channels may force schools to re-evaluate their traditional preoccupation with providing answers and undertake, as never before, the task of developing in students the capacity to make disciplined inquiries, sensible evaluations, and especially, to ask meaningful questions. The examination of the future may be one in which students will be asked to formulate questions rather than supply answers. (1961, 36)

In 1969, Postman and Charles Weingartner waved the progressive banner of schooling as a mechanism for social critique and change. Together they asserted that schools should be the institutional mechanism in providing young people with a critical perspective on society through, among other things, "crap detecting" and asking, "What's worth knowing?" (xv). Given that teachers have sustained access to children, it made sense that the classroom teacher should be responsible for media literacy education. Through Postman's earlier writings, I became convinced of digital and media literacy as a primary responsibility of *all* schoolteachers, regardless of subject area. Postman's liberal view of schooling and curriculum resonated loudly within the constraining bureaucracy of American education.

In the more liberal, social, and political climate of the 1970s and 1980s, however, Postman developed a much more critical and conservative approach to media, in which he reclaimed the traditional values of print-based literacy as opposed to the image-oriented culture that had emerged. In his solo counterpoint, *Teaching as a Conserving Activity* (1979), Postman promoted a more conservative role of education, arguing that the purpose of the school classroom was to counterbalance social disconnection and the morally bereft media messages promoted outside of schooling. I came to understand how Postman's cautious, conservative, and even caustic approaches to technology earned him the title "neo-Luddite." His conservative shift from progressive educator to conservative critic was magnified by his frequent admission that he intentionally avoided using a computer, voice mail, or a fax machine whenever possible. For Postman, these technologies constrained inquiry and human conversation and, therefore, served little, if any, purpose. Few communication technologies of the twentieth century (e.g., radio, TV, film, computers) facilitated the depth of communication and understanding that Postman perceived to be at the heart of academic inquiry and democracy (1999, 55). While I debated with Postman on multiple occasions the virtues of e-mail, I came to understand, empathize with, and ultimately respect his refusal to use it as a symbolic rejection of technological progress *as synonymous with* moral or social progress. He was rewriting the technocentric story of education in the 1980s and 1990s in a way that was highly critical yet deeply humanistic. Postman's inclusive rejection of technology on moral ground paralleled my inclusive acceptance of technology in remembrance of my father. Neither of our approaches was logical, but together they generated lively conversation. And, for Postman, that was entirely the point.

I recall one particularly heated debate with Postman over the subject of using computers in the classroom. During my doctoral study, I worked as a media educator and technology consultant for Media Workshop New York, a nonprofit organization that employed me to work closely with teachers and principals in New York City schools throughout the five boroughs. While a surface glance of my work might suggest that I was simply herding teachers and principals toward the recent windfall of computers and the Internet in their schools, the work of curriculum development at the classroom level (when successful on occasion) was both creative and critical. Postman (1995b) found my employment to be paradoxical and somewhat amusing as he publicly criticized the use of computers in school classrooms and the emphasis on individualized learning at the expense of group learning. He characterized students as desocialized and isolated information junkies sitting in front of screens. While I understood Postman to be the much-needed moral conscience during a time of blind acceptance of computers in schools, I witnessed collaboration, shared discovery, and transformative understanding *when* teachers conscientiously and systematically used computers to support student learning. To be fair, the teachers who lacked a solid understanding of their subject area or their students' learning needs could not effectively integrate technology into their teaching. I also yielded to Postman that the few success stories were not nearly a high-enough return on the financial investment of equipping schools with computers and Internet access. Nevertheless, Postman's skepticism became my moral compass for conscientiously exploring and experimenting with computers in schools rather than dismissing them entirely. I remembered from my master's research that much can be learned about an educator's worldview by listening carefully about how they talk about computers in schools. I realized by the end of my doctoral study that problematizing technology wasn't necessarily the end (or purpose) of media literacy. Rather, the importance lies in the discursive means (or medium) for teaching critical thinking. Postman taught me that the communication biases of technology necessitate an intentionality and thoughtfulness about pedagogical choices. As a result, I learned to privilege the agency of the learner, not just that of the teacher. I can't help but wonder what Postman would think about the current trend of "flipping" the classroom: asking students to access content (usually video-based) outside the classroom (as homework) for the purpose of using classroom time for focused inquiry, debate, and discussion. While I can't image Postman entirely embracing video-based instruction, I am fairly certain that he would embrace the emphasis on communal discussion in the classroom, as I like to believe that he was far more pro-discourse than he was antitechnology.

One of my favorite books is Postman's *The End of Education* (1995a), in which he argues that the purpose of schools should be to teach students how to think, not what to think. Too often, well-intentioned teachers will simply transmit the ideological message that they want their students to internalize, in a misguided attempt at cultivating critical thinking. Even media literacy educators, under the guise of "inquiry," fall into the trap of teaching students what to think ("What ideology is presented here?") rather than how to think ("How do you know what you know?"). I learned from my service on the board of directors for the National Association for Media Literacy Education (NAMLE) that building capacity for both the critical and creative uses of media and technology is much easier said than done in a climate of competing curriculum standards, high-stakes testing, and evaluation of teacher performance. Compounding the challenge are the diverse constituencies that compose the digital and media literacy movement (Domine 2011b). My brief tenure as coeditor of the *Journal of Media Literacy Education* also taught me that field-based research on the efficacy of digital and media literacy education in schools and communities is both crucial and in short supply. Such research is more likely to occur if individual states mandate digital and media literacy as part of the formal school curriculum—a call not too far removed from Postman's own plug for television education more than fifty years ago.

Ultimately, Postman's polemics propelled me to ask smarter questions about media, technology, and, most importantly, education. My greatest challenge thus far as a teacher educator is to elevate the conversation about technology as instructional technique to a place where digital and media literacy informs an essential pedagogical framework (Domine 2011a). Instead of merely critiquing media and technology, teacher education must require digital and media literacy across all subject areas in intentional and systematic ways that are grounded in questions of morality and ethics. This is crucial in a world where technological evolution and curriculum standards are highly politicized and continuously moving targets that detract from engaging in deep inquiry in the classroom. Yet I find myself continuously leaning on a foundational Neilogism—the importance of asking the right questions. Like Postman, I believe the primary purpose of schooling in a democracy should be to learn reason, logic, dissent, and deliberation. An authentic understanding of inquiry is essential to these democratic practices. The single most important lesson I hope to enact among my preservice teacher candidates is the ability to discern between what they observe in an urban school setting (data) and what they infer to be true (interpretation) (Domine and Bello 2010). The work of teacher educators should therefore be to leverage media and technology to help students ask incisive questions and, conversely, to ask incisive questions about media and technology. Such discernment requires instruction in both media literacy and technological proficiency (Domine 2011a).

It wasn't until a decade after studying with Postman that I arrived at my own narrative for technology and learning. In 2009, I coined the neologism *communification* to denote the integration of communication, education, and technological processes and products to convene diverse groups of people who achieve interdependence through a shared vision and a common goal. Communification implies that technology (in all its forms) serves schooling in ways that are communicative, unifying, and communal. I am fairly certain that the ultimate value of technology in schools will be measured according to its capacity to satisfy human need to communicate, commune, and connect with others in order to (re)construct the world around us (Domine 2009). I only wish Postman were around to debate this theory with me.

More than three decades have passed since my father's death, and it has been a little more than a decade since Neil's passing. Neither of them witnessed the invention of the smartphone, iPad, Twitter, or Facebook. I long to share these technologies with them, each for entirely different reasons and affect. As much as I desire to see my father's jubilation at experiencing an iPad, I equally desire to discuss with Postman his thoughts on the reduction of his legacy to a 2,500-word Wikipedia entry (excluding references and footnotes). I envision myself offering consolation in the form of "Neil, it's not the word-count but the hyperlinks that matter." In contrasting Postman's twentieth-century view of critical restraint with my twenty-first-century pursuit of creative possibility, I arrive at the conclusion that both approaches are requisite to achieving the full potential of education and schooling in the United States. This critical yet creative approach is crucial for continual growth of digital and media literacy as both a field and a movement. I am proud to share my father's biological DNA of technological adeptness combined with Postman's intellectual DNA of cautious optimism. Because of them both, I can appreciate the tremendous educational opportunities afforded in the current networking age while simultaneously navigating the undercurrent of technological change.

REFERENCES

Blumer, H. 1969. *Symbolic Interactionism: Perspective and Method.* Englewood Cliffs, NJ: Prentice-Hall.

Bruner, J. 1986. *Actual Minds, Possible Worlds.* Cambridge, MA: Harvard University Press.

Domine, V. 2011a. "Building 21st Century Teachers: An Intentional Pedagogy of Media Literacy Education." *Action in Teacher Education* 33 (1): 194–205.

———. 2011b. "Think Global, Act Local: Expanding the Agenda for Media Literacy Education in the United States." *Library Trends* 60 (2): 440–453.

Domine, V., and J. Bello. 2010. "Stewarding Urban Teacher Education in Newark: In Search of Reflection, Responsibility, and Renewal." *Education and Democracy: A Journal of the National Network for Educational Renewal* 2:155–168.

Greenwood, V. 1994. "Instructional Communication: Bridging the Gap between Education and Technology." Paper presented at the Western Speech Communication Association Annual Convention, San Jose, CA, February 23–27.

Innis, H. 1951. *The Bias of Communication.* Toronto: University of Toronto Press.

McLuhan, M. 1964. *Understanding Media: The Extensions of Man.* New York: McGraw-Hill.

Ong, W. 1958. *Ramus, Method, and the Decay of Dialogue: From the Art of Discourse to the Art of Reason.* Cambridge, MA: Harvard University Press.

Postman, N. 1961. *Television and the Teaching of English*. New York: Appleton-Century-Crofts.

———. 1970. "The Reformed English Curriculum." In *High School 1980: The Shape of the Future in American Secondary Education*, edited by A. C. Eurich, 160–168. New York: Pitman.

———. 1979. *Teaching as a Conserving Activity*. New York: Delacorte Press.

———. 1982. *The Disappearance of Childhood*. New York: Delacorte Press.

———. 1984. *Amusing Ourselves to Death: Public Discourse in the Age of Show Business*. New York: Viking Press.

———. 1993. *Technopoly: The Surrender of Culture to Technology*. New York: Vintage.

———. 1995a. *The End of Education*. New York: Alfred A. Knopf.

———. 1995b. Interview by Charlene Hunter Gault. *The MacNeil/Lehrer NewsHour*, July 25. Available at http://www.youtube.com/watch?v=49rcVQ1vFAY.

———. 1998. "Technology and Society." *C-SPAN*, February 7. Available at http://www.youtube.com/watch?feature=endscreen&NR=1&v=13bXaYsn33U.

———. 1999. *Building a Bridge to the Eighteenth Century: How the Past Can Improve Our Future*. New York: Alfred A. Knopf.

———. 2000. "The Humanism of Media Ecology." *Proceedings of the Media Ecology Association* 1:1–16.

Postman, N., and C. Weingartner. 1969. *Teaching as a Subversive Activity*. New York: Dell.

16 /

Peter Gutierrez
on Scott McCloud

PETER GUTIERREZ

"You—you're the comic book guy, right?"
At first heard as flattering, then mildly annoying, and finally self-affirming in the quietest and most powerful of ways, it's a phrase that, usually with the beginnings of a grin, those who half-recognize me have used countless times in greeting me over the years. Even when the grin isn't present physically, it is there, in intonation or a certain brightening of the eyes. But what is behind it? Simply the brief pleasure of connecting my face or name to some stray bit of prior knowledge? Or is it reflective of what it means to be associated with comic books generally? Often I have suspected that a coded reference was at work, one predicated on how endearingly quirky or nerdy comics were, thus making the entire interaction mildly patronizing before it has really started.

Of course if all this sounds more than a tad neurotic, mea culpa and then some. Please know, however, that it's a neurosis with something of a cultural bent, a sore spot both intensely personal and grandly impersonal. Being identified as a comics guy would, if only for an instant, prompt me to regress to that practically friendless twelve-year old who, upon discovering copies of *The Uncanny*

X-Men in the local five-and-dime, felt that the universe had shifted and revealed some private corner of wonder. Yet at the same time, the nonprivate nature of such an exchange, typically at a cocktail party, triggers dread (wonder's secret sibling) at the prospective burden of explaining it all, of answering the unstated question that looms behind the curiosity—namely, why *comics* of all things?

So let us first be clear about context. Until recently it has been hard to be a comics fan in the United States—let alone a comics-friendly educator or comics scholar. With the cultural witch hunts of the 1950s, and the subsequent dominance of a lone genre (superhero adventures) for the next several decades, the bias against the medium became so entrenched and pervasive that even its supporters seemed resigned to it. As someone who fell in love with comics in the 1970s, looked for ways to bring them into my K–12 classroom teaching when I entered the field in the late 1980s, and became a creative professional in the industry in the 1990s, I can recall that this outsider status occasionally served as a perverse badge of honor. In the long run, though, it became exhausting for me and (at the risk of making an outrageous presumption) everyone else who took comics seriously. Into this sad state of affairs came Scott McCloud's *Understanding Comics: The Invisible Art* (1993), and suddenly everything began to change. It crystallized many things that longtime comics readers instinctively knew while simultaneously legitimizing the object of our love to those with whom we had longed to connect—tastemakers, academics, librarians, and that most elusive demographic of all, thinking adults.

Confession time: that "suddenly" a couple of sentences back is wrong, but since I'm now openly acknowledging its wrongness, perhaps it can be spared being called a flat-out lie. While *Understanding Comics* landed hard and sent crater dust far into the stratosphere, it seemed to take more than a decade before McCloud's wisdom consistently entered the realm of praxis. My evidence for this claim is both anecdotal, based on the vanguard maneuvers I've been witness to, and exceedingly personal, perhaps myopically so. Indeed, as you continue reading the rest of this odd ode, keep in mind that whatever its faults, the experience is without question preferable to reading *two* of my résumés, which is what you would have been subjected to a decade ago if for some reason you were at all interested in my career. And the fact that that particular type of bifurcation is no longer necessary is a testament to the impact of McCloud's work.

To be clear, those two résumés weren't just alternate versions of each other—they were dueling documents, with my personal contact information being the only real area of overlap. One listed my career in pop culture, with my writing and editing of comics given prominent placement. The other represented a serious-minded account of my K–12 experience, both in the classroom and in the publishing houses that market into it. After all, as a freelance developer of curriculum and the instructional materials that support it, it simply wouldn't do to spotlight much in the way of what *had* to be a frivolous hobby of some sort. This two-faced approach to my own career chafed, to put it mildly—especially since the area that I gradually seemed to be staking out for myself concerned high-interest media and how to leverage the associated outside-of-school literacies.

Eventually this came to look like examining pop-culture fandoms across media, and I was grateful to publish my work on the topic in esteemed journals. As a blogger for *School Library Journal*, I explored the intersection of fandom and critical literacy, a natural-enough fit as librarians always seem to be a bit ahead of the game in terms of embracing both the teaching-and-learning potential of student-selected media and the independent, fiercely nonacademic habits and discourse that young people bring to their favorite texts.

Yet even when the concept of fandom literacies (i.e., the cognitive and communicative skill sets that fans consistently bring to the fan object) wasn't my focus, I was concerned with the intimately related notion that the pre–"media literate" know more about media than anyone, including themselves, might reasonably expect. The idea was that not only is there more behind pop culture than many suppose—that itself isn't original at all (see Steven Johnson's *Everything Bad Is Good for You* [2005])—but also fans, even casual ones outside of organized fandoms, already instinctively "get" certain things. In fact, it is this evolving but largely hidden understanding that often deepens their appreciation of pop culture. With students, however, a "let's save analysis of pop culture media for college" rationale seemed to be the unwritten law that most of us working in, or serving, K–12 populations seemed to obey.

Indeed, the goal of gently overthrowing this assumption was the impetus behind the first-ever media course I taught, back in 1991, when I realized that there was no reason fifth- and sixth-graders couldn't learn the language of moving-image media. They already knew about different kinds of shots: they just didn't know what they were called, so they noticed them less, questioned them less, and reflected on them less. And this is the same approach, of activating what might be called latent knowledge, that I used more than fifteen years later, when I taught even younger students how comics were made, a process that culminated in their working together as a team; they "kind of" knew this stuff already. That is, it was half-buried in their schema and just needed to be brought out into full relief. And the same thing, dare I say it, is largely true in terms of digital literacy, too.

The fundamental belief that there's more to it—which in a K–12 context means more than certain gatekeepers give credit for, more than students themselves are aware of—was at the heart of McCloud's motivation to pen *Understanding Comics* in the first place. It also shows why his book grabbed that wide-eyed, twelve-year-old me and introduced him to the thirty-year-old version, the one who ended up loving the medium all the more for having what he already sort of knew explained back at him in all its glory. Because I guess that has always been my approach as well—not just to comics, but to pop music, sports, television, the digital expressions that fandom takes, and other neglected, often denigrated forms of culture: there's more to it.

Here's McCloud on his own middle-school self, the one who became "totally obsessed with comics," both reading and then drawing them: "I felt that there was something lurking in comics . . . something that had never been done. Some kind of hidden power! But whenever I tried to explain my feelings, I failed miserably." Hence the impetus, much later, for the grown-up McCloud to take up the challenge of explaining what had previously seemed frustratingly inexplicable, to tackle a project that would be no less than "an examination of the art-form of comics, what it's capable of, how it works" (McCloud 1993, 2). Clearly the phrase *hidden power* is a key one, or at least it has been to me, for it speaks simultaneously to the faith of the fan, to the practitioner, and to teachers and students of media literacy.

So sure, I'd been familiar, experientially, with the art of comics, but I wasn't quite sure *how* it operated; thus the brilliant simplicity of McCloud's subtitle: *The Invisible Art*. In fact, that credo of "there's more to it"—isn't that the start of all inquiry? Namely, what exactly is that "more"? Where and how can it be found? And what are its implications—how does that "more" affect how media work on us and through us? To me, this is media literacy, and media literacy education, in its purest and most potent state.

On the Indivisibility of Art and Media

In fact, it always shocked me that *Understanding Comics* wasn't immediately considered a core text of the media literacy education movement in the United States. As proof of its merit in this respect, one need only revisit how the author outlines his central questions in terms that could not be more recognizable to the media literacy crowd: "How do we *define* comics, what are the *basic elements* of comics, how does the mind *process* the basic language of comics— that sort of thing" (McCloud 1993, vi; emphasis in original).

Already, by declaring such straightforward objectives, it begins— that all-important process of focusing on how a given medium actually works regardless of what it ostensibly says. McCloud describes this as the "aesthetic surgery" that is necessary to "separate form from content" (McCloud 1993, 5). Moreover, and of special cultural import in the context of comics, the notion of value-free analysis was subtly introduced: marginalized content and highbrow aspirations alike were effectively rendered beside the point. Yet that didn't mean readers were in for an arid exercise in pure theory. No, there was fun on every page, usually multiply so.

Oh, did I not mention that McCloud's seminal work was itself a comic?

I guess not. Moreover, because of this, it served as a prime piece of evidence in its own argument—the medium's unique strengths to speak engagingly and lucidly to its audience. And make no mistake: "medium" was McCloud's word, not mine, although it speaks to a distinction that I and countless others have had to make between the defining traits of all comics and their varied manifestations, both in genre and format (i.e., graphic novel, "floppy" comic book, newspaper comic strip, etc.).

The end result, however, of all this playful metacreativity was not a simple piece of procomics chauvinism. On the contrary, McCloud constantly invoked the confluence of other media, either in comics themselves or in his thoughts about them. This was never done ostentatiously, to buttress comics' reputation with the accepted. Rather, his facility with making authentic connections to everything from fine art to advertising was not only internally logical but liberating. Incidentally, this informed my own turnabout from hesitancy in introducing comics into literacy education to leaping between the affinity shared by comics and *anything*—literature, myth, games—in pretty much all of my media literacy work. Eventually this led to my looking for, and building on, pedagogically, shared connections in terms of composition; the result was a book I wrote on scriptwriting that attempted to show educators how students who wrote comics could transfer their skills to writing for other media, such as film and video (Gutierrez 2013b).

Ultimately, I think that what I and, I imagine, others responded to so deeply in McCloud's analysis was the way it moved effortlessly between media and art. All too often, concepts seem to be culturally compartmentalized, almost as if somehow reflecting the hemispheric division of the brain itself. For McCloud, though, one can't be separated from the other. Indeed, his book culminates in a grand yet exceedingly straightforward presentation of what he calls the six-step creative process that applies to "*any* work in *any* medium" (McCloud 1993, 169; emphasis in original). After first positing that much of human activity, including "language, science, and philosophy," is, in fact, art (McCloud 1993, 167), he clarifies each of these half-dozen stages: idea/purpose, form, idiom, structure, craft, and surface.

While there is much that could be said, and, yes, refuted about McCloud's ideas in this area and much that is inspiring about them, the most striking thing is that such a far-ranging thesis was conducted from within the realm of comics; again, yes, other media are cited, but the entire argument not only flows from McCloud's own understanding of comics but also—let's not forget—is put forth via comics. The lesson here was not lost on me, and in the new century

I began advocating the use of comics as an underused springboard to media literacy (Gutierrez 2007). What this looked like in practice was an elementary-level course I taught called What Makes a Superhero Super? It lured students with the promise of the familiar and the fun, but as we explored superheroes over time and across media, the curriculum was undeniably one of media literacy: the idea was to lead with comics content and then introduce media forms as a natural follow-up, and it worked. To be clear, one doesn't need to be a fan of a specific art form to teach the analysis of its messages and mechanisms. But if we want to reach young people, why not start with what they already like? And this doesn't mean employing a mere bait-and-switch tactic: we'll hook you on content and then move onto analysis. Instead, the intellectual elegance of *Understanding Comics* lies in how it shows comics-readers that underlying what they love are signs and systems, the learning of which can actually deepen their appreciation of the art.

The notion that art emerges from the constraints and the strengths of any given medium is also hardly news. But McCloud's contribution was to argue successfully—and this success was due largely to the fact that his argument took a form that offered a demonstration of its own validity—that the art of comics is sufficiently complex and profound to merit inclusion in all those wider and more legitimized cultural conversations. In this regard it's important to remember that McCloud was not an academic with a side talent of drawing didactic comics. No, McCloud understood the art of comics as a practitioner first and foremost, from the inside out, if I may be permitted to invoke a cliché.

When he undertook *Understanding Comics*, then, it wasn't as an illustrator or designer who just happened to dabble in the medium but as a master cartoonist whose best known work, the science-fiction epic *Zot!* (2008), was (and is still) widely admired in its own right. The richness of its storytelling should come as no surprise to anyone who encounters it after his nonfiction work on comics; nor should the fact that the later, online version of *Zot!* reflects McCloud's restlessness as an experimenter, as an artist who wanted to test and refine the precepts of both *Understanding Comics* and its follow-up for the digital era, *Reinventing Comics* (McCloud 2000a). Perhaps most famous and startling in this regard is the third part of *Zot!*

Online, wherein a 6,000-pixel-tall panel depicting free-fall requires the reader to keep scrolling in a way that, obviously, would be impossible in the print medium (McCloud 2000b). Yet the form follows the narrative function: to convey the vertical vastness of such a fall, not just to tire out the fingers of his readers or to show off the possibilities of new technology (an idea worth bearing in mind when, it a different context, it becomes necessary to distinguish between the use of "ed tech" and authentic digital literacy).

In short, this is thinking-informed-by-doing, and vice versa, which just so happens to align nicely with a central tenet of mainstream media literacy pedagogy: the importance of actual media production to the learning process. To separate considerations of art too severely from those of media is not just messy and perhaps dishonest intellectually but also hampers the ability to learn, understand, and, ultimately, teach. More about this later; first let's take a quick look at what McCloud discovered when he explored comics from within.

Constructedness and Creation

Though its economy, aesthetic pleasures, and scholarship are to be applauded, the first chapter of *Understanding Comics* offers what might seem like a predictable and even rather standard historical apologia for comics: they've always been around, from ancient Egypt to popular woodcut narratives. It's in that second chapter, though, that things get intensely interesting because that's where, though with a tone that's far from polemical, McCloud tackles the chief gripe about comics head-on: their supposed simplicity, even primitiveness, in terms of visual representation.

Thus begins his book's focus on those middle steps of the creative process, after comics are selected as the medium of choice and yet before the final stages of what might be called practical technique. The central question of this territory might then be phrased as "How is meaning itself relayed via comics' formal elements?" To this end, McCloud begins with a somewhat counterintuitive claim that, paradoxically, seems completely intuitive once he's done explaining it. That apparent reduction of physical specifics into the caricature-like tendencies of comics? It doesn't mean that comics become generic in the sense of eschewing the detailed and the realistic in favor of a lazy, lowest-common-denominator artistic strategy.

On the contrary, the abstracted form that, say, human faces take on—and this is just but one example from a more profound analysis of what McCloud terms "icons" (1993, 26)—helps evoke the most specific thing of all: the reader's recognition of self. After all, the more finely rendered the image, the more loudly it announces itself as a distinct, external entity, while when it's stripped artfully back to its essence, it becomes a serviceable mirror for the audience. Thematic and narrative engagement thus flows more freely, as we insert ourselves into a comic in ways that are medium-specific. Figure 16.1 shows a panel from McCloud's work on this topic.

Figure 16.1 A panel from *Understanding Comics* by Scott McCloud (1993, 36)

Such considerations lead seamlessly into an equally eye-opening examination of seamlessness itself. That is, *Understanding Comics* then moves on to the compelling topic of *closure*, a term that refers to the audience's participation in a text via extrapolating the whole from its parts, essentially coauthoring the text from fragments of representation. McCloud convincingly shows how closure lies at the heart of many diverse art forms, how it conjures a solid and accessible reality from all those carefully arranged slices of content. Though he doesn't use the term "suture" in his discussion of movies, film-studies folks will be quick to recognize it as a variant on the same conceptual theme; we get woven into the work of art, embedded as it were, and usually by covert means. And of course this is, in part, what makes the work of comics so invisible.

Perhaps most significant in McCloud's quest to make the invisibility slightly more visible is his groundbreaking examination of the role of the gutter in comics. If you're not familiar with the term, know that the neat thing about it is how it reflects the unseen or invisible in a literal way, as it refers to the (understandably) overlooked space that exists between panels. Borrowing from McCloud and citing his work explicitly, I conducted "comics and literacy" workshops for teachers and librarians in which I'd connect the instinct for closure that readers exercise via the gutter to commonly recognized reading and comprehension skills such as making inferences. The point was obvious: with comics, readers are constantly filling in the gaps of the text, and the best comics, interestingly, often hide this process most adeptly. We see Spider-Man look out a window and then, in the next panel, we see him swinging from skyscraper to skyscraper—we never need to see him leap out the window, as we can assume this action transpired in the gutter. This part of my presentation would work for the purposes of getting educators to think about comics in new ways, but it would also model for them the same interaction that they could have with their students: What's not shown? How can you imagine that not-shown? And would you, if you were the creator, have chosen something else not to show? This same approach eventually showed up in my work on digital literacy in terms of the way that fans draw conclusions and make predictions based on incomplete or ambiguous pieces of online information (Gutierrez 2011). This may seem like a stretch, to connect comprehension strategies across media and student reading levels, but it's precisely that high level of transference that builds habits, if not in the student then certainly in the teacher. In short, the goal is always be looking at not just what you bring to the text, but what, in some way, you're *expected* to bring. And that's not merely an interesting tangential observation to literacy of all types—it's intrinsic to it.

In his analysis of the gutter, McCloud goes much further than my generalities here would imply, establishing a taxonomy of different transitions, such as moment-to-moment and subject-to-subject. My favorite, by the way, is aspect-to-aspect, in which one might witness isolated parts of an event and subconsciously infer that larger, unifying whole from the facets of it that are presented (e.g., otherwise unconnected panels depicting fallen leaves, a scary mask, and a pumpkin signal a Halloween setting). Arguably, one sees this device more in artier comics, but the point, thanks to McCloud, is that suddenly one has a name for this type of storytelling. Again, ask comics fans and they'd know instantly what's being discussed here, but when a name is given to the phenomenon, thus differentiating it from other options available to creators, the concept takes on a new kind of utility. It becomes something to note, to evaluate, to value—which, in turn, serves to link readers with creators in yet deeper ways. No longer simply identifying with characters in a narrative, readers who practice critical thinking gradually come to identify with the authors themselves, experiencing text as a series of extrinsic choices as well as intrinsic dramatic incidents.

The Death and Life of Comics

The fact that McCloud's *Understanding Comics* sold surprisingly well and seemed to be universally acclaimed makes it easy to overstate the changes it wrought. After all, it didn't single-handedly save comics, especially after the disastrous early 1990s implosion of the speculator market and the subsequent collapse of so much of the retailer base. The steady rise of the graphic novel and manga, both in sales and stature, as well as other factors (e.g., the new online connectedness of fandom) surely had much to do with rescuing an industry that had already fallen off the cliff and was now hanging on to a few strands of dry grass. Nonetheless, McCloud's book served as an accelerant splashed upon still-glowing embers. It allowed both the intelligentsia and the general public not simply to give comics another look but to make that look far more thoughtful and extended than ever before. In short, the terrific graphic novels that surfaced in the late 1990s and early 2000s directly benefitted from the newfound esteem that comics enjoyed as a result of McCloud's efforts. At once a "Comics for Dummies" and a "Comics for Smart People," *Understanding Comics* set off ripples in multiple ponds. And every time a new stone landed in the water and splashed the cultural status quo in the face, I applauded wildly. Never before, at least to my knowledge, had a media literacy text served to catalyze such newfound interest in the medium that it sought to explicate.

If you wanted to work in the field of media literacy, what could be more inspiring? Eventually all those ripples expanded, as ripples are wont to do. In both K–12 and media literacy circles (which, of course, are not mutually exclusive), I sensed McCloud's work setting the stage. For what exactly, I wasn't sure. But after being present to innumerable conference presentations and journal citations, there could be no doubt that *not* to act on his insights was becoming akin to cowardice.

So, yes, I ended up contributing to all those ripples myself. I was fortunate enough to get platforms that ranged from major comic conventions to annual teacher gatherings. The strategy was simple: be that specific someone who married many of the major themes in what might be termed conventional media literacy education (conventions that were themselves not sufficiently old to be called "traditional") to what we could teach about the art and business of comics, such as target audience, representation, branding, the production process, the commercial impulse, and the concept of creative ownership.

But I wasn't the only one. While I and James Bucky Carter and Katie Monnin and many others sought to marry the incredible artistry of comics to the lofty goals of K–12 curricula, several others followed more directly in McCloud's footsteps: master cartoonists and even creative geniuses saw that their role of educator—both to the general public and to schoolkids—was integral to their professional identity and perhaps even their artistic identity. I'm talking about people like Gene Luen Yang and Eric Shanower, who freely made educational resources available on their websites. Acclaimed graphic novelist Kevin C. Pyle started teaching courses to kids of the same age that I'd been working with, except he brought a more thorough firsthand knowledge of the medium as a result of being both writer and artist (full disclosure: both my own boys have studied with him). Meanwhile, the team of Matt Madden and Jessica Abel took a break from their own amazing work to produce *Drawing Words and Writing Pictures* (Abel and Madden 2009), a how-to book for young creators that became so much more as they supported it with outreach into schools and online. Most spectacularly of all, James Sturm, the director of the Center for Cartoon Studies and a hugely gifted cartoonist in his own right, teamed up with some former students to create *Adventures in Cartooning* (Sturm, Arnold, and Frederick-Frost 2009), a meta-didactic guide to the power of comics that is a direct descendent of McCloud's work, although it is aimed at kids.

What does all this have to do with media and digital literacy, though? Only everything. In recent years a variety of digital tools, both online and local, have made the process of creating comics much more user-friendly for students (Gutierrez 2013b), and schools have been surprisingly quick to embrace these innovations. The quiet breakthrough in this regard hasn't passed unnoticed by some of the strongest advocates of media and digital literacy (Gutierrez 2013a)—no longer does one have to possess specific training and skills in draftsmanship or design or have access to specialized materials. Rather, the art of composing comics can be done in purely McCloudian terms, as students can use prefab figures or upload their own photographs and other digital images: this frees them up to consider the building blocks of storytelling itself such as sequence, time, structure, and so on. In short, they learn the medium by doing, and, again, the art is inseparable from the media literacy.

And let's not forget, not for an instant, that school *is* culture; indeed, it is what shapes and informs the culture that we'll be stuck with, for better or worse, in years to come. Of course, on many other levels besides formal education, the convergence of comics culture and culture as a whole is still occurring, but the good news is that for several years now I've had a single résumé. Over time, the very deficiency I'd detected in myself became a strength—media literacy education, and K–12 education in general, came to embrace comics, and without warning I found myself in the right place at the right time. I'd been invisible beforehand, to be sure, but I'd never been absent, and now my own outside-of-school literacies turned out to be more valuable than I could ever have imagined. For proof of this, one need only consider the inclusion of this chapter in a book such as this.

Comics, like any art form, survive and thrive when the walls between audience and creator, between practitioner and teacher, and between student and neophyte artist are dissolved in a grand love of the medium *and* an understanding of it. Heart and mind, working together, and inspiring more of the same. That's McCloud's legacy to me and so, so many others.

REFERENCES

Abel, J., and M. Madden. 2009. *Drawing Words and Writing Pictures.* New York: Macmillan.

Gutierrez, P. 2007. "Sparking Media Literacy with Comics." *Diamond Book-Shelf.* Available at http://www.diamondbookshelf.com/Home/1/1/20/182? articleID=71056.

———. 2011. "Blockbuster Central." *Screen Education* 62:34–39.

———. 2013a. "4 Questions for Richard Beach about Literacy and Digital Comics Creation." *Connect the Pop,* January 18. Available at http://blogs .slj.com/connect-the-pop/2013/01/comics/4-questions-for-richard-beach -about-literacy-and-digital-comics-creation/.

———. 2013b. *The Power of Scriptwriting: Teaching Essential Writing Skills through Podcasts, Graphic Novels, Movies, and More.* New York: Teachers College Press.

Johnson, S. 2005. *Everything Bad Is Good for You.* New York: Penguin.

McCloud, S. 1993. *Understanding Comics: The Invisible Art.* New York: Kitchen Sink Press.

———. 2000a. *Reinventing Comics: How Imagination and Technology Are Revolutionizing an Art Form.* New York: Paradox Press.

———. 2000b. *Zot! Online.* Available at http://www.scottmccloud.com/1-web comics/zot.

———. 2008. *Zot!* New York: Harper Collins.

Sturm, J., A. Arnold, and A. Frederick-Frost. 2009. *Adventures in Cartooning.* New York: Macmillan.

17 /

Susan Moeller
on Roland Barthes

SUSAN MOELLER

How do we make sense of our world? For me, always, images have been central. I'm a visual learner and a visual processor of both intellectual and sensory information. My memory is entirely tied to visual representations. Situations that I should process in words, numbers, sounds, or touch are recalled in my brain through images. I remember history through a progression of illustrations—even if I myself have to conjure the illustrations. I recall data by way of charts and graphics—or failing those, of the simple recollection of the shape of the numbers on a page. Music is called up as color for me, and I remember the softness of my dog's fur or my daughter's cheek via the visual reminiscence of the curly coat or the flushed skin.

That kind of processing results in an overflowing file cabinet of images in my brain, a virtual repository of personal scenes and faces alongside visual notations from the public sphere. In that cluttered cabinet, certain images, especially photographic ones, stand out as aesthetic, political, and even moral markers. When I reference my "file cabinet," there are certain pictures that surface first, that surface repeatedly, that are always accessible. I always wondered why.

Philosopher, semiotician, and literary theorist Roland Barthes taught me why. He taught me to be consciously, photographically, and visually literate.

"The Most Quoted Book in the Photographic Canon"

Roland Barthes's *Camera Lucida: Reflections on Photography* (1981) is arguably the most influential book yet written about individuals' encounters with photographs. I read it in the midst of my doctoral program in the history of American civilization at Harvard, during my immersion in historiography and literary theory. I have since read and assigned it countless times.

According to Geoffrey Batchen, a professor of photography and editor of a collection of essays on *Camera Lucida*, Barthes's last work is likely "the most quoted book in the photographic canon" (2009, x). By the look of it, the book's canonical role in the field is surprising. A slight book of only 119 pages, with no footnotes to add additional heft, *Camera Lucida* (or, in the original French edition, *La chambre claire*) is deceptively simple. The book has broad margins, few words on a page, and multiple black-and-white photographs scattered throughout (with one color frontispiece). The whole is divided into forty-eight fragments—a function perhaps of the fact that Barthes wrote the book in just forty-nine days.

Camera Lucida is not a work on the semiotics of photography—the kind of examination that followers of Barthes might have expected. As a review in the *Guardian* notes, it is "neither a work of theoretical strictness nor avant-garde polemic, still less a history or sociology of photography." Barthes "has no interest in the techniques of photography, in arguments over its status as art, nor really in its role in contemporary media or culture, which he leaves to sociologists such as Pierre Bourdieu" (Dillon 2011). The *New York Times*, in its review, said that *Camera Lucida* "does not reveal the long-sought 'grammar' of photographs, nor does it provide much in the way of clues to their 'reading.' It is more intimate than theoretical. . . . 'Camera Lucida' forsakes the analytic methods on which the author built his reputation in favor of a more personal discourse. . . . [H]is reflections on photography merely confirm his growing disaffection with semiotics and his decision to use his own emotions as a prime source of insight" (Grundberg 1981).

Indeed, the book begins with Barthes's telling of his fraught encounter with a photograph taken over a century earlier, at the dawn of photography in 1852—a photograph of Napoleon's youngest brother. Barthes's haunted recollection would not be amiss as the opening to a tale of mystery: "One day, quite some time ago, I happened on a photograph of Napoleon's youngest brother, Jerome, taken in 1852. And I realized then, with an amazement I have not been able to lessen since: 'I am looking at eyes that looked at the Emperor.' Sometimes I would mention this amazement, but since no one seemed to share it, nor even to understand it (life consists of these little touches of solitude), I forgot about it" (Barthes 1981, 3). Starting with that reminiscence, Barthes continued to use the pronoun "I" throughout the book—together with "we" and other inclusive language. It is, as the *Guardian* observed, a book "frankly personal, even sentimental" (Dillon 2011). It has, said art critic Martin Herbert, "a certain kind of vulnerability" (quoted in Dillon 2011).

So if the book is not a work of theory, if it doesn't offer academics a grammar or "ways of seeing" or "reading" photography, as John Berger's BBC series (1972) and book (1990) did for art, why, then, has *Camera Lucida* been so influential? Why does the book matter?

Philosopher Martha Nussbaum might have the answer. In 1988, she appeared as a guest on Bill Moyers's PBS series *A World of Ideas*. "The common perception of a philosopher is of a thinker of abstract thoughts," observed Moyers in the course of their conversation. "I think that the language of philosophy has to come back from the abstract heights on which it so often lives to the richness of everyday discourse and humanity," responded Nussbaum (Moyers 1988).

Camera Lucida matters because it grounded photography in the everyday concerns and emotions of those who engage with photography—everyday individuals who look at photographs and respond to them.

It's true that the book feels at times like a regurgitation of the stream of consciousness of a polymath. Barthes muses on the ideas of Zen Buddhism and psychoanalyst Jacques Lacan on the same page. The book is dedicated to Jean-Paul Sartre's *L'imaginaire* and includes photos by Robert Mapplethorpe. But Barthes is not just showing off his erudition. His point is that insights are found at the intersection of disciplines; the weighing of truths does not occur solely in philosophy but also in religion, neuroscience, literature, and art. His point is that photography connects to everyone, every day.

For me, the book is the ultimate example of how being media literate can inform one's understanding of the world. Media literacies—all kinds of literacy, actually—are crucial to critical thinking. Barthes demonstrated his media literacy across *Camera Lucida's* chapters, as he brought disparate fields to bear on core questions: Why do certain images seize our attention? What power is present in certain photographs so that we keep looking? Why are we troubled by those images—troubled as water is troubled when a stone is thrown in?

The Way Photos Work

When I teach media literacy, my favorite lecture is always the one I give about photography. I know my students have been looking at pictures their entire lives, and I know they have been taking and sharing photos at least since they first received a camera-equipped mobile phone. But even those students who think of themselves as photographers rarely ponder the quantity and quality of information, messages, perspectives, and emotions they both imbibe and disseminate through photography. And rarely do students stop to think about why a web editor selected a certain photo for her news site's home page rather than one of the hundreds of others possible. Indeed, why *do* editors at different news outlets choose different photos—or occasionally the same photo—when they cover the same event? Do their choices have to do with differences in audiences? With their own biases? With who took the photo? With their understanding of the meaning of the story? With their assessment of what they ran two hours ago and what they might run two hours from now? Yes. Yes. Yes. Yes. Yes.

These are important questions—media literacy questions, life questions. And these questions are just a few of those that I raise in the first fifteen minutes of my class on photography.

This is why I believe that *Camera Lucida* is such a valuable text. Barthes gives explanations for what the world observes in images but rarely thinks about. Barthes explains the banality of so much photography and why few images hit their viewers with gut-wrenching force.

In *Camera Lucida*, Barthes argues that inherent in every photograph is what he calls the *studium*: the subject of the photo, the part that signals to an observer the geographical, historical, cultural, or other context of that image. "The studium is a kind of education," Barthes explains. All photos have a studium, and while they may be "indexical"—they reference a given reality—this specificity does not prevent the mass of images from being boring, pedestrian, not worth a second glance, forgotten as soon as the viewer looks away (1981, 26).

But then there are other photos, the ones that are bothersome. Barthes says these have a detail, a *punctum*—"a Latin word derived from the Greek word for trauma" (1981, 26–27)—that holds our gaze and "pierces" our souls (80). The punctum creates a direct relationship with a particular observer. The detail may be central to the aesthetic form and narrative content, or it may be ancillary to them; either way, the detail personally connects the viewer to the image and is perceived differently by different viewers.

Photos to Remember

Stop and think. What images hold you in their grip? What photos have a punctum that pierces you?

In my life, I have been seized—even literally changed—by several historically iconic images: the photo of a young boy, really just a toddler, staring straight at me, straight into the camera, as he sat starving during the famine in Ethiopia; the photo of a naked girl screaming down the road after having been struck with napalm during the Vietnam War; the photo of a mother with hands outstretched, perhaps pleading to God, as she roamed a Crimean battlefield of death looking for her son's body in the midst of World War II. Yet I have also found myself emotionally bound by quotidian photos of family members: a photo of my brother on a tennis court, stretched nearly horizontal to reach a ball that can be seen as a whitish blur, and a photo of my parents, married for over forty years, walking hand-in-hand down a beach in midwinter, leaning into each other for shelter.

Why is it that the photos of global events that I have found most troubling are those in which I can see faces, yet in the photos of my family members that I have found to best capture their essences, their eyes are not visible? I'm not sure.

Barthes explains that when one is pierced by a punctum's arrow, the photo fascinates, even if we do not know why we are caught. If we take the time to ponder the answer, however, we may learn more, both about the image and about ourselves. A pas de deux of sorts can result in that investigation of meaning. As I have thought about the photos in my life, and as I have considered Barthes's reasoning, I have noted that as I advance toward understanding why a particular photo may have a power over me, the photo itself retreats. Like two parties in a waltz, the image retreats in sync with my consideration of it. I may never be able to articulate all there is to know about a photo (even a personal one)—the photograph "escapes" language—but in my dance with the image, I can gain a sense of how I have been moved.

When I read *Camera Lucida* in grad school just a few years after it was translated into English in 1981, I felt as if I had found a fellow traveler, someone else who used images to signpost his world. Here in print was confirmation that there are others who not only care about photographs, who not only file photographs away in their minds, but who are moved by photographs, who find in photographs a distilled essence of their lives. Barthes's work confirmed for me that photographs matter not just because a photograph reproduces the subject in front of the camera but because photographs do more than document their subjects, or at least *can* do more than document them. "The photograph is literally an emanation of the referent," writes Barthes. "From a real body, which was there, proceed radiations which ultimately touch me, who am here" (1981, 80).

Photographs, observes Barthes, those that "prick" their observers, are in essence memorials to what has happened and never will happen again. As political activist and fellow photography theorist Susan Sontag wrote in her seminal book *On Photography*, "All photographs are memento mori. To take a photograph is to participate in another person's (or thing's) mortality, vulnerability, mutability. Precisely by slicing out this moment and freezing it, all photographs testify to time's relentless melt" (1977, 15).

To Barthes, because still images are a constant, tangible presence, they not only reproduce what is seen through the camera lens but also conjure the present moment of the viewing and the indefinite future in which the images can be viewed. Images denote what's *here* in ways beyond what is possible through language. They also articulate what's gone. Photography stops time and allows a lingering gaze—a gaze arrested by beauty or asymmetry, by joy or trauma.

In Barthes's consideration of an 1865 photograph of Lincoln conspirator Lewis Payne in custody on board the monitor USS *Saugus*, he writes, "He is dead and he is going to die" (1981, 95). During his contemplation of the image, Barthes was aware that Payne had been hanged for his attempted assassination of U.S. Secretary of State William Seward—an attack made on the same night as the assassination of President Lincoln. Barthes knew that Payne, John Wilkes Booth, and others had also planned to murder Vice President Andrew Johnson and General Ulysses S. Grant that night. Barthes, in other words, knew the ending of the story—the story not just of Payne and his fellow conspirators but of Seward, Lincoln, and the Union itself. Yet Barthes's knowledge of the future of the photo (events in the historical past) collided with Barthes's experience of his viewing moment, when he saw, via the image, Payne's sprawl in his seat against the iron cladding of the monitor and his steady gaze into the camera—Payne's steady gaze, in effect, into the eyes of everyone ever who has looked at that photo over the last century and more.

In Barthes's understanding, therefore, photographs are equally time machines into the past, mirrors of the present and crystal balls into what may matter in the future. Is there an object more potent—or one that more needs to be understood?

Media Literacy Is, in Essence, a Philosophy of Caring

When I started reading *Camera Lucida*, I believed I was reading a work entirely dedicated to deciphering the artistic impact and temporal authority of photography. But it gradually dawned on me that not only was Barthes writing about photography but photos were his means to explore life, loss, and memory. It became clear that Barthes's emotional responses to the death of his mother, Henriette, in 1977, underlay and gave force to his intellectual perceptions about photography: "It is said that mourning, by its gradual labour, slowly erases pain; I could not, I cannot believe this; because for me, Time eliminates the emotion of loss (I do not weep), that is all. For the rest, everything has remained motionless. For what I have lost is not a Figure (the Mother), but a being; and not a being, but a quality (a soul): not the indispensable, but the irreplaceable" (1981, 75).

Almost exactly halfway through *Camera Lucida*, Barthes begins part 2 of the book, which details his search to "find" his mother in photographs of her—photographs that not just capture her likeness but hold her soul. He doesn't find her spirit embodied in recent images of her or, indeed, in any of those that pictured her as an adult. But he does find one photograph, he writes, that expresses what he considers to be her true likeness. It is a photo of her taken in 1898, in a garden in winter. She is five. Describing his discovery of the photograph, Barthes simply wrote in his journal, "I cried" (quoted in Dillon 2011).

When I read that page, I recognized Barthes's keen anguish. I understood his turn to acknowledging the intimations of death inherent in all photography because not only do I, too, process the world visually, but I, too, had turned to old photographs to try and find the essence of someone whom I had lost. I, too, had suffered a cataclysmic death in 1977, when my brother was killed.

What is compelling and important about *Camera Lucida* is that Barthes is unashamedly writing about his own pain. It is a raw book. Barthes pretends no distance from his subject—which purports to be photography; he does not pretend to be dispassionate. He demands that his readers similarly bare themselves. *Camera Lucida* uses photography as a simulacrum for its readers to consider their own vulnerability to love and their own consequent encounters with loss, grief, and mortality. The book helped me negotiate my own tragedy.

Perhaps as a consequence, it was Barthes's humanistic approach to understanding photography that made the greatest impact on me. I wasn't alone in my response. Others also remarked that the book was "so moving" because of its duality (Dillon 2011). Barthes used his mother's death and his search for her in images to propel forward his idea that photography is more than a referent. When he found the photograph of his mother that held the most meaning for him, the one he called the Winter Garden photograph, he recognized both the indexical nature of photography and photography's embedded humanity—its seizure and its pinning down of the ephemeral so that a viewer has the opportunity to grasp and hold onto the ephemeral in a manner otherwise impossible:

> The Winter Photograph was my Ariadne, not because it would help me discover a secret thing (monster or treasure), but because it would tell me what constituted that thread which drew me toward Photography. I had understood that henceforth I must interrogate the evidence of Photography, not from the viewpoint of pleasure, but in relation to what we romantically call love and death. (Barthes 1981, 73)

Is that, then, the reason why the photos of my brother playing tennis and my parents walking on the beach away from the camera resonate for me above all others? It is no coincidence, I believe, that those photos that for me best capture the "true likeness" of my family members who have died are the photos that capture them literally moving in time and space. Understanding the punctum in those photos makes it certain: it is less my brother's and my parents' faces that I miss than their active presence in my life.

From the Personal to the Professional

What did I learn from this, Barthes's final book?

Camera Lucida taught me to embrace "the subjective"—an approach that was "in academic terms quite scandalous" (Dillon 2011). I also learned to be media literate, even if, at the time of my first reading, that phrase was not yet in my vocabulary. From Barthes I learned that media literacy is not a cold set of skills to be taken out of an academic toolbox in order to unpack meaning in texts, to decipher intentionally or unintentionally coded signs and symbols. Media literacy teaches critical thinking. As Barthes writes, "Ultimately, Photography is subversive not when it frightens, repels, or even stigmatizes, but when it is 'pensive,' when it thinks" (1981, 38).

That is what I teach. I try to teach students to think critically, about photography and all the media and messages coming into their lives.

Barthes taught me—and I now teach others—to be alert for the studium and punctum not just in photography but in all media. Be alert to what gives you context about news and the world. Be aware of what kinds of media, what kinds of stories you fasten onto, and what kinds fasten onto you. Be conscious of why. If you do all those things, you will be media literate. And if you do all those things, you will learn important things about who you are.

I now have taught Media Literacy as a general education course to thousands of students at the University of Maryland at College Park. Every semester, I tear the course apart and teach it anew: the changing tools and technology of media insist that I do so. And as media have become ever more visual, having students learn about images, why they matter, and why they are powerful has become more and more central to the course. But even as I remake the syllabus and update the assignments, I'm aware that what matters most to me is that the course nurture in students a deep concern for how the world is represented and for how they themselves represent the world.

It is for that reason that I cofounded the Salzburg Academy on Media and Global Change in 2007. The program annually brings together students from five continents to work in cross-border teams to brainstorm and develop solutions to global challenges posed by international organizations and foundations such as the United Nations Educational, Scientific, and Cultural Organization (UNESCO), the United Nations Development Programme UNDP, and the Open Society Foundation. The students, mentored by more than a dozen faculty members representing universities from such nations as China, Lebanon, Uganda, Argentina, and the United Kingdom, focus on the roles that media and media literacy education can play in addressing global concerns, including environment and sustainability, poverty reduction, and human rights. In every instance, visual media are integral to real-world problem solving.

Barthes taught me (and I now teach others) that ideas don't have to be—and *should* not remain—theoretical preoccupations; ideas should be applied, in ways central to the well-being of others. What I learned from Barthes is that media literacy is, in essence, a philosophy of life, a philosophy of caring: "I am interested in so many photographs, whether I receive them as political testimony or enjoy them as good historical scenes: for it is culturally (this connotation is present in studium) that I participate in the figures, the faces, the gestures, the settings, the actions" (1981, 26).

I believe it is Barthes's modesty and admission of his own frailties, together with his heartbreaking efforts to hold onto that which ultimately must be lost, that makes *Camera Lucida* his greatest book. I recognize my own frailties in his description of his own, but I continue to be inspired by the passionate humanity that informs his intellectualized analysis of what photography is and what photography can do.

REFERENCES

Barthes, R. 1981. *Camera Lucida: Reflections on Photography.* Translated by Richard Howard. New York: Farrar, Straus and Giroux.

Batchen, G. 2009. *Photography Degree Zero: Reflections on Roland Barthes's Camera Lucida.* Cambridge, MA: MIT Press.

Berger, J. 1972. *Ways of Seeing.* Television series. London: British Broadcasting Corporation.

———. 1990. *Ways of Seeing.* London: Penguin.

Dillon, B. 2011. "Rereading *Camera Lucida* by Roland Barthes." *The Guardian,* March 25. Available at http://www.theguardian.com/books/2011/mar/26/roland-barthes-camera-lucida-rereading.

Grundberg, A. 1981. "Death in the Photograph." *New York Times,* August 23. Available at http://www.nytimes.com/1981/08/23/books/death-in-the-photograph.html.

Moyers, B. 1988. "Martha Nussbaum." *A World of Ideas,* November 16. Available at http://www.pbs.org/moyers/journal/archives/nussbaumwoi_flash.html.

Sontag, S. 1977. *On Photography.* London: Penguin.

Epilogue

RENEE HOBBS

It's humbling to write about the past. Whatever you think you do know, you are always aware that there is so much more that you don't know. More than three hundred years ago, in *Discourse on Method*, René Descartes described these same feelings of hesitation regarding his writings about scientific and philosophical inquiry: "I am quite willing it be known that the little I have hitherto learned is almost nothing in comparison with that of which I am ignorant" ([1637] 2004, 85).

If you're like me, every once in a while, you enjoy flipping through old picture albums and remembering days gone by. Such nostalgic activities have the potential to remind you of who you really are. This book offers a counternarrative of sorts to the ways in which media literacy education's intellectual roots have been typically described in relation to media arts, critical and cultural theory, educational technology, and media-effects scholarship. There is no one "right" way to tell the stories of the past. Indeed, "any story one may tell about anything is better understood by considering other possible ways in which it can be told" (Bruner 2004, 709).

To understand the present and improve the future, we need to look at the roots, origins, assumptions, and values of those who have come before. And as each generation recognizes the need for "emancipation from alienation," as Charles Reitz (2009, 230) has described it, we must recognize and resist the many forces that contribute to dehumanization within our contemporary culture and the global political economy.

Looking backward in time only intensifies the feeling that there is so much more to know. This book reminds me of how much I fear staying "within the safe bounds of expertise," where teachers "maintain the delusion of mastery" (Palmer 1983, 114). Certainly my own (sometimes perverse) antipathy toward expertise and authority is bundled up with my personal identity as a lifelong learner. It has made me wonder: Why is media literacy such an unfinished project that must be reinvented anew each generation?

All our understandings of media, literacy, technology, and culture are inevitably situated in the particularities of a certain time and place: our understandings of the people, objects, and practices of the world are bound to simple circumstance. As we live in the current context of the Internet's cultural dominance, this book helps us appreciate our continuity with the recent past. It has been seventy years—nearly three generations—since television's expanding empire in the aftermath of World War II led scholars to chronicle the seismic shifts in culture that were occurring as commercial media systems grew to dominate American political and social life. The scholars in this book, who have grown up since then, experienced cultural and educational change, as revealed in these pages, that affected their personal identity and relationships with their parents, teachers, and peers. They've helped us see digital and media literacy as a process of heightening awareness of form, content, and context and probing the deeply social nature of representation and interpretation as we experience as users, consumers, and creators of media and technology.

They've also reminded us of the need to keep our eyes open and our minds alert to the dark side of contemporary culture in the context of the period we now call the twenty-first century. Despite all the hype of technology's saving power, we face a world with a seemingly endless array of challenges: the quality of our air and water, extreme weather, our industrialized food system, broken political and judicial systems, the greediness of global capitalism, the global scourge of terrorism, the school-to-prison pipeline, and the distorted values of a test-obsessed education system. The vast inequalities of wealth and poverty, the glorification of violence, and the rise of anti-immigration bigots, propaganda, and political extremism all push us to focus on *what can be done now*. As we see in this volume, digital and media literacy is tied up with ideas that arts and social activism are intertwined with an examination of language and literacies in helping people reengage the head, heart, hands, and spirit as we seek to address the challenges we face and live with integrity in a rapidly changing global world.

In analyzing the autobiographies in this volume, which weave together bits of the authors' life stories with the ideas of their intellectual grandparents, I am aware of the indeterminacy and incompleteness of the process of reconstructing a history of digital and media literacy education in the United States and around the world. So much more needs to be said.

Two people in particular have enabled this book to come into being. I am especially grateful to Elizabeth Thoman, founder of the Center for Media Literacy in Los Angeles, for inspiring my interest in media literacy history by sharing her archive, a treasure trove of resources for future historians. I am also grateful to Michael RobbGrieco for helping envision all the value that a historical perspective can offer the future of the field. And of course, the distinguished authors of the essays in this volume intensified my curiosity and desire to learn more. They have generously shared their own particular journeys of intellectual discovery while introducing us to key ideas from some of the most important thinkers, scholars, and voices of the twentieth century.

Although this book offers insights on the ways in which media literacy developed in relation to key philosophical and theoretical ideas advanced by scholars and researchers in the twentieth century, there are limitations to using personal narrative to examine the historical roots of media literacy. Autobiographical narrative is reflexive: its author and its subject are the same. As Bruner (2004) explains, this creates some problems: we may rationalize our experiences and actions in light of our current perspective on the world; our telling of our experiences cannot be easily verified; and the very act of telling the story distorts our memories. In stories, because the protagonists are the agents, stuff happens to them and they cause things to happen. In life, it's more far complicated than that.

The essays in this book invite us to enter the interior worlds of the authors as they "wonder about appearance and reality" (Bruner 2004, 699). In some ways, the characteristics of these essays, with their transparent, self-centered articulation of how people have engaged with symbols, meanings, representations, forms, and ideologies across lifetimes, are the book's real assets. This book may invite you, as the reader, to consider your own past, current, and future contributions to digital and media literacy as it is embedded in the fabric of your everyday relationships, learning, and life experiences.

We are not alone in thinking that digital and media literacy education represents one way for the humanities to thrive in a digital age. There are so many allies for whom this work matters. In the late 1990s, I corresponded via e-mail with Boston-based journalist and writer Ken Sanes, who shared his insights on living in a media-saturated culture on a media literacy website called *Transparency*. Sanes (1997) wanted to explore the soul of contemporary culture "to discover what it reveals about the human condition," recognizing that "many of the stories that are told in the media contain an ethical vision that expresses our desire to create a new society, a new identity, and a new order of nature that embodies our highest values." Through connecting media literacy's past to the present and future, we imagine how to move toward this important goal.

REFERENCES

Bruner, J. S. 2004. "Life as Narrative." *Social Research* 71 (3): 691–710.

Descartes, R. (1637) 2004. *Discourse on Method*. London: Collector's Library of Essential Thinkers.

Palmer, P. 1983. *To Know as We Are Known: A Spirituality of Education*. San Francisco: Harper and Row.

Reitz, C. 2009. "Herbert Marcuse and the Humanities: Emancipatory Educations versus Predatory Capitalism." In *Marcuse's Challenge to Education*, edited by D. Kellner, 229–258. New York: Rowman and Littlefield.

Sanes, K. 1997. "A Message to Teachers and Students." *Transparency*. Available at http://www.transparencynow.com/teach2.htm.

Contributors

Donna E. Alvermann is Appointed Distinguished Research Professor of Language and Literacy Education at the University of Georgia, where she also holds the endowed Omer Clyde and Elizabeth Parr Aderhold Professorship in Education. Formerly a classroom teacher in Texas and New York, she now teaches doctoral and master-level students. Her research focuses on young people's digital literacies and their use of popular media, and she has authored numerous articles published in *American Educational Research Journal*, *Reading Research Quarterly*, *Journal of Literacy Research*, and the *Journal of Adolescent and Adult Literacy*. Alvermann's books include *Adolescents and Literacies in a Digital World*; *Reconceptualizing the Literacies in Adolescents' Lives*; *Adolescents' Online Literacies: Connecting Classrooms, Digital Media, and Popular Culture*; and *Bring It to Class: Unpacking Pop Culture in Literacy Learning*. Her current research project involves designing an interactive website (http://www.becoming3lectric.com) to learn how an online research community pushes boundaries while creating and disseminating original and remixed work under a Creative Commons license.

Gianna Cappello is an associate professor in digital-media sociology and education sociology, with a specialization in media literacy education, at the University of Palermo. She has been a visiting professor at the Instituto de Investigaciones de la Comunicación (ININCO-FHE); Universidad Central de Caracas, Venezuela; and the College of Education, Zhejiang University, Hangzhou, China. She cofounded MED, the Italian Association for Media Literacy Education, and currently serves as its president. Cappello's research interests include critical theory, cultural and media studies, and studying the relationships among media, children, and education within an action-research-ethnographic methodological framework. Among her latest publications (with F. M. Lo Verde and I. Modi) is *Mapping Leisure across Borders.*

Vanessa Domine is a professor, thought leader, and researcher at the intersection of communication, education, technology, and media literacy. She holds bachelor's and master's degrees in communication studies and a doctorate in media ecology from New York University. For the past thirteen years, she has engaged in urban teacher preparation in New Jersey public schools as part of her professorship at Montclair State University. Domine has served on the board of directors for the National Association for Media Literacy Education (NAMLE) and on the editorial boards of various journals, including the *Journal of Media Literacy Education* and the *Journal of Digital and Media Literacy.* She is the author of *Rethinking Technology in Schools* and *Healthy Teens, Healthy Schools: How Media Literacy Education Can Renew Education in the United States.* She is the mother of four and the wife of one.

Jeremiah Dyehouse is associate professor of writing and rhetoric at the University of Rhode Island's Harrington School of Communication and Media. His research focuses on theories of rhetoric and public writing, with a special emphasis on the contemporary implications of twentieth-century American pragmatist philosophy. His in-progress book, *John Dewey and Public Writing (1886–1927)*, recovers the significance to public writing theory of Dewey's experiments in public writing inquiry in the first half of his career. Dyehouse's articles on rhetoric and composition have appeared in *College English, Technical Communication Quarterly, Rhetoric Society Quarterly, College Composition and Communication, Written Communication*, and *JAC: A Journal of Rhetoric, Culture, and Politics.*

Peter Gutierrez is a writer and former middle-school teacher with expertise in pop culture, education, and media literacy. He has been nominated for a Will Eisner Comics Industry Award and an Edublog Award. His work has been published by the *ALAN Review, Booklist, Diamond BookShelf*, the *Financial Times, ForeWord Reviews, Graphic Classroom, Graphic Novel Reporter, Language Arts, Library Journal*, the *Montclair Times*, the *New York Times*, Pearson Education, ReadWriteThink, *Rue Morgue*, Scholastic, *School Library Journal, Screen Education*, TribecaFilm.com, and Teachers College Press. His teaching guides for graphic fiction and nonfiction have been published by Abrams, Bloomsbury USA, TOON Books, Top Shelf Comics, and the Rise Above Social Issues Foundation.

Renee Hobbs is professor of communication studies and director of the Media Education Lab (http://mediaeducationlab.com) at the University of Rhode

Island's Harrington School of Communication and Media, where she codirects the Graduate Certificate in Digital Literacy program. Her research focuses on digital and media literacy, copyright and fair use for digital learning, and teaching and learning about contemporary propaganda. She has published more than 150 scholarly and professional articles and authored five books, including *Reading the Media: Media Literacy in High School English*, *Copyright Clarity: How Fair Use Supports Digital Literacy*, and *Digital and Media Literacy: Connecting Classroom and Culture*. She has developed award-winning educational curriculum resources, including documentary videos and educational games, and is the founding coeditor of the *Journal of Media Literacy Education*.

Henry Jenkins is Provost Professor for Communication, Journalism, Cinematic Art and Education at the University of Southern California and the founder and former codirector of the Comparative Media Studies Program at MIT. He has authored or edited seventeen books on various aspects of media and popular culture. Among those most relevant to media literacy educators are *The Children's Culture Reader*, *Confronting the Challenges of a Participatory Culture*, *Reading in a Participatory Culture*, *Participatory Culture in a Networked Era*, and *By Any Media Necessary: The New Youth Activism*. Visit his website at henry jenkins.org.

Amy Petersen Jensen is professor and associate dean for research and creative work in the College of Fine Arts and Communications at Brigham Young University. Her current research focuses on arts literacies in school settings. She serves on the leadership team for the National Coalition for Core Arts Standards, which published national standards for dance, music, theater, visual arts, and media arts in 2014. Amy has served as the coeditor of the *Journal of Media Literacy Education* and as the general editor of the *Youth Theatre Journal*. She is a member of the board of directors of the American Alliance for Theatre and Education and has previously served on the board of directors of the National Association for Media Literacy Education. Her most recent book publication is the coedited (with Roni Jo Draper) volume *Arts Education and Literacies*.

Douglas Kellner is George F. Kneller Philosophy of Education Chair at UCLA and is author of many books on social theory, politics, history, and culture, including (with Michael Ryan) *Camera Politica: The Politics and Ideology of Contemporary Hollywood Film*; *Critical Theory, Marxism, and Modernity*; *Jean Baudrillard: From Marxism to Postmodernism and Beyond*; *Media Culture*; *Media Spectacle*; a trilogy of books on postmodern theory with Steve Best; and a trilogy of books on the media and the Bush administration, *Grand Theft 2000*, *From 9/11 to Terror War*, and *Media Spectacle and the Crisis of Democracy*. Author of *Herbert Marcuse and the Crisis of Marxism*, Kellner has edited the collected papers of Herbert Marcuse, six volumes of which have been published by Routledge. Kellner coedited (with Meenakshi Gigi Durham) *Media and Cultural Studies: KeyWorks* and (with Rhonda Hammer) *Media/Cultural Studies: Critical Approaches*. He is also author of *Cinema Wars: Hollywood Film and Politics in the Bush/Cheney Era* and *Media Spectacle and Insurrection, 2011: From the Arab Uprisings to Occupy Everywhere!*.

Cynthia Lewis is professor and chair of curriculum and instruction at the University of Minnesota, where she holds the Emma M. Birkmaier Professorship in Educational Leadership. Her current research examines the role of emotion in urban classrooms focused on critical media analysis and production. She has published widely on the intersection of social identities and literacy practices in and out of school, including two books that were awarded the Edward B. Fry Book Award from the Literacy Research Association: *Literary Practices as Social Acts: Power, Status, and Cultural Norms in the Classroom* and the coedited (with Patricia E. Enciso and Elizabeth Birr Moje) volume *Reframing Sociocultural Research on Literacy: Identity, Agency, and Power*. She is a member of the board of directors of the Literacy Research Association and is coeditor (with Jennifer Rowsell) of the book series Expanding Literacies in Education.

Susan Moeller is director of the International Center for Media and the Public Agenda (ICMPA) and full professor of media and international affairs at the University of Maryland. She is cofounder of the Salzburg Academy on Media and Global Change in Austria and author of *Packaging Terrorism: Co-opting the News for Politics and Profit*; *Compassion Fatigue: How the Media Sell Disease, Famine, War and Death*; and *Shooting War: Photography and the American Experience of Combat*. Moeller was formerly the director of the journalism program at Brandeis University, a senior fellow at the Kennedy School of Government at Harvard University, and a Fulbright professor in Pakistan and in Thailand. In 2008, she was named a Carnegie Scholar for her work on Islam and named a Teacher of the Year by the State of Maryland. Moeller received her doctorate and master's degree from Harvard and her bachelor's degree from Yale.

Dana Polan is professor of cinema studies at New York University. He is the author of eight books in film and media study, including *Scenes of Instruction: The Beginnings of the U.S. Study of Film*, which uses extensive archival research to examine early twentieth-century classes held at Columbia University, Harvard University, and the University of Southern California, among other institutions. Polan works on theories of popular and mass culture and has published on such cultural critics as Roland Barthes, Raymond Williams, and Edmund Wilson.

Srividya "Srivi" Ramasubramanian is associate professor of communication and associate dean for climate and inclusion at the College of Liberal Arts at Texas A&M University. Within digital-media literacy, she is interested in the sociopsychological effects of race, ethnicity, gender, and sexuality. She is cofounder and executive director of Media Rise (http://mediarisenow.org), a volunteer-driven nonprofit global alliance that brings together media educators, socially conscious creatives, media-industry professionals, activists, and policy makers for promoting meaningful media. Her work has been featured in many of the leading communication journals as well as media outlets such as the *Huffington Post*, National Public Radio, the *Dallas Morning News*, and *India Today*. She received her doctorate from Penn State University in 2004.

Michael RobbGrieco is a media literacy historian and an educational technology leader in Vermont, where he is the director of curriculum and technology integration for K–12 schools in the Windham Southwest Supervisory Union. He is an affiliated faculty member of the Media Education Lab at the University of Rhode Island and an associate editor of the *Journal of Media Literacy Education*. His research interests include media literacy history, educational affordances of remix practice, new theories of agency in media education, and using humorous media to teach savvy media use.

Lance Strate is professor of communication and media studies at Fordham University and the 2015 Harron Family Endowed Chair in Communication at Villanova University. He is the author of *Echoes and Reflections: On Media Ecology as a Field of Study*, *On the Binding Biases of Time and Other Essays on General Semantics and Media Ecology*, *Amazing Ourselves to Death: Neil Postman's Brave New World Revisited*, and *Thunder at Darwin Station*. The coeditor of *Communication and Cyberspace: Social Interaction in an Electronic Environment* (with Ronald L. Jacobson and Stephanie B. Gibson); *Critical Studies in Media Commercialism* (with Robin Andersen); *The Legacy of McLuhan* (with Edward Wachtel); *Korzybski and . . .* (with Corey Anton); and *The Medium Is the Muse: Channeling Marshall McLuhan* (with Adeena Karasick), he is also founder and past president of the Media Ecology Association, past president of the New York State Communication Association, and a trustee and former executive director of the Institute of General Semantics.

David Weinberger writes about the effect of technology on ideas. He is the author of *Small Pieces Loosely Joined* and *Everything Is Miscellaneous* and is the coauthor (with Rick Levine, Christopher Locke, and Doc Searles) of *The Cluetrain Manifesto*. His most recent book is *Too Big to Know*, about the Internet's effect on how and what we know. Weinberger is a senior researcher at the Berkman Center. He has been a philosophy professor, a journalist, a strategic-marketing consultant to high-tech companies, an Internet entrepreneur, an advisor to several presidential campaigns, and a Franklin Fellow at the U.S. State Department. He was for four years the codirector of the Harvard Library Innovation Lab, focusing on the future of libraries. He blogs at http://www.hyperorg.com/blogger.

Index